Engaging with Fathers

of related interest

Child Development for Child Care and Protection Workers
Brigid Daniel, Sally Wassell and Robbie Gilligan
Foreword by Jim Ennis
ISBN 1 85302 633 6

The Child's World
Assessing Children in Need
Edited by Jan Horwath
ISBN 1 85302 957 2

Imprisoned Fathers and their Children
Gwyneth Boswell and Peter Wedge
ISBN 1 85302 972 6

Birth Fathers and their Adoption Experiences
Gary Clapton
ISBN 1 84310 012 6

Helping Families in Family Centres
Working at Therapeutic Practice
Edited by Linnet McMahon and Adrian Ward
ISBN 1 85302 835 5

Effective Ways of Working with Children and their Families
Edited by Malcolm Hill
ISBN 1 85302 619 0

Child Welfare Services
Developments in Law, Policy, Practice and Research
Edited by Malcolm Hill and Jane Aldgate
ISBN 1 85302 316 7

Social Work with Children and Families
Getting into Practice
Ian Butler and Gwenda Roberts
ISBN 1 85302 365 5

Preventing Violence in Relationships
**A Programme for Men Who Feel They Have a Problem
with their Use of Controlling and Violent Behaviour**
Gerry Heery
ISBN 1 85302 816 9

Engaging with Fathers

Practice Issues for Health and Social Care

Brigid Daniel and Julie Taylor

Jessica Kingsley Publishers
London and Philadelphia

First published in the United Kingdom in 2001 by
Jessica Kingsley Publishers Ltd,
116 Pentonville Road, London
N1 9JB, England
and
325 Chestnut Street,
Philadelphia PA 19106, USA.

www.jkp.com

Library of Congress Cataloging in Publication Data
A CIP catalog record for this book is available from the Library of Congress

British Library Cataloguing in Publication Data
A CIP catalogue record for this book is available from the British Library

ISBN 1 85302 794 4

Printed and Bound in Great Britain by
Athenaeum Press, Gateshead, Tyne and Wear

Contents

Acknowledgements

Many organisations and individuals gave their time and expertise to help us compile practice examples for this book. They are acknowledged within the text as their contributions are presented. We are extremely grateful to them and admire their commitment to developing positive approaches to work with fathers.

We thank John McFaddyen, James Cox, Anne Aberdein and Fiona Kemp for reading and commenting upon drafts. Members of the Department of Social Work, University of Dundee also helped with discussion of the issues, reading of drafts and exploring the ideas with practitioners. We are grateful to the groups of social work and health practitioners who helped us shape the ideas. Stacey Farmer provided a tremendous amount of patient administrative support and back-up.

Thank you to Christine Henderson and Shirley Keyworth for support and encouragement throughout the process of writing the book.

We would like to thank the Society for Research in Child Development for permission to reproduce the table in Figure 3.1 from M. Main and D.R. Weston, 'The quality of the toddler's relationship to mother and father: related to conflict behavior and the readiness to establish new relationships', *Child Development* 52 (1981), 932–940. Blackwell Science Ltd gave permission to reproduce the diagrams shown in Figures 3.2 and 3.2 from C. Goulet, L. Bell, D. St-Cyr Tribble, D. Paul and A. Lang, 'A concept analysis of parent-infant attachment', *Journal of Advanced Nursing* 28, 5 (1998), 1071–1081, and to reproduce concepts, ideas and some of the wording in B. Daniel and J. Taylor, 'The rhetoric versus the reality: a critical perspective on practice with fathers in child care and protection work', *Child and Family Social Work* 4, 3 (1999), 209–220. The Office for National Statistics gave permission to reproduce the graphs shown in Figures 4.1 and 4.2 from J. Pullinger and C. Summerfield, *Social Focus on Men and Women* (Office for National Statistics, © Crown copyright 1998). Appendix III has been reproduced with permission of Martin Herbert and was originally published in M. Herbert, *Child Care and the Family Resource Pack* (NFER-Nelson, 1980). The table in Figure 6.1 was originally published in the Scottish Office, *Statistical Bulletin Child Protection Management Information 1994–95* ISBN 07480 5672 6 (October 1996).

Introduction

The aim of this book is to provide social workers and health visitors with theoretical and practical information in order to guide their practice with fathers and father-figures. Unless otherwise stated, the term 'father' will be used to refer to biological fathers and other father-figures.

The main focus of the book is on practice with families where children are considered to be vulnerable to, or have experienced, abuse and neglect. This is not because the issue is not important for all children. However, with families where children are vulnerable, social workers and health visitors are attempting to intervene for the benefit of children and with the aim of improving their welfare. Our view is that such practice could potentially be more effective if both mothers and fathers were engaged with purposefully.

There has been a dearth of research about fatherhood, both from the perspective of the father and from that of the child, despite the long-standing recognition that there is no intrinsic necessity for the main carer to be the mother (Rutter 1981). More recently, however, a body of research is emerging which describes the multiplicity of potential roles for the father, the attitudes of fathers and the kind of relationships that men can have with their children (Burghes, Clarke and Cronin 1997). There are policy and legislative developments, and a number of pressure groups are coming into existence.

Within the realm of child care and protection practice there has been a severe lack of research-based information with the attendant consequence of a lack of a clear framework for practice with fathers and father-figures (Daniel and Taylor 1999; Greif and Bailey 1990). What little information there is tends to focus on male perpetrators of sexual abuse or upon the impact of domestic violence. There is literature that criticises health visitors and social workers for concentrating all their child protection efforts on the mother; however, given the complexity of the findings about fatherhood in general and the lack of policy guidance it is perhaps not surprising that practitioners are struggling to formulate a coherent approach to men. What has become apparent to us is that much of the theoretical rhetoric about fathers and fatherhood does not match the reality that practitioners face in their everyday contact with families. One of the main underlying problems is the lack of a coherent theoretical framework to guide practice.

The book aims to move from the recognition that current practice focuses on women, to explore practical and realistic suggestions for broadening practice to include fathers. The overall aim, therefore, is to provide a practical guide, but one that is based on theoretical analysis. We believe that all child care practice should be underpinned by a sound theoretical base and therefore each chapter is solidly grounded in theory.

We completely support the notion of evidence-based practice; nonetheless we recognise that there is much evidence still to be gathered about child care and protection practice, and in particular about the place of fathers. As yet, practice lacks definitive answers. There are, however, many strongly held opinions and feelings. Writing this book, we have at times felt caught between a rock and a hard place. The majority of individuals and organisations that have contacted us have been very constructive and their experience has largely shaped our arguments. We are enormously grateful to them. However, we are also aware of views that represent the two extreme ends of a dimension of opinion. So, for example, at one extreme there is a position that all men are (or potentially are) dangerous, that they use their power inappropriately and that the priority of intervention should be upon empowering women: engaging fathers would only augment their powerful position. At the other extreme, there is a position that asserts that by far the greater risks to children are posed by women, that men are excluded by an alliance of mothers and female professionals and that the balance of power must be redressed. We acknowledge that there are occasional nuggets of truth to be found even in the extremes and by taking a pragmatic approach we try to find a middle path through these extremes. The guiding principle which can help with finding this path is the imperative that we make the welfare of the child the central focus.

Engaging with men is not *always* useful or desirable and although we want to be fair to the positions of both men and women in this debate, our bottom line is always the welfare and protection of the child. Achieving what is best for children, rather than what is best for mothers or fathers (although this will sometimes amount to the same thing) is our overall intention. We also recognise that engaging with men in child protection can endanger mothers and it can endanger health and social care professionals. Their safety is another paramount concern and if there is any likelihood of harm to individuals then protective measures are essential.

We therefore have two guiding principles in writing this book:

Principle 1

Although we assert that men, even perpetrators of harm to children, can be engaged with purposefully, the central focus must be upon what is in the best interests of the child.

Principle 2

Practitioners should not be expected to place themselves at risk and they should always be mindful of the safety of themselves and of the women and children (and occasionally men), they work with.

Each chapter in the book (except for the final one) is in two parts; the first part sets out theoretical and research information. The second part unpacks what this means for practice. Issues are highlighted with case studies and examples in boxes. Each chapter presents a list of ten main points emerging from the theory and ten related messages for practice. The chapters are grouped into three sections. The first section explores fatherhood today. In Chapter 1 we set out the contemporary demographic and legislative situation with regard to fathering. Practitioners should always keep this large picture in mind because it provides the context of their work with all children who, whatever their circumstances, should have the same opportunities for a rich and fulfilling family life. In Chapter 2 we look for answers to the question: 'What does being a father mean?' Without having an understanding of the array of complex roles that men can play in the lives of their children, practitioners are in danger of using simple stereotypes as their templates.

The second section looks at theoretical approaches currently drawn on in social work and health visiting and examines what they offer with regard to practice with fathers. Attachment theory (Chapter 3) is probably the most influential and enduring theory for both social work and health visiting practice, although it has traditionally focused upon attachment to the mother. We suggest that it can be a rich theory to guide practice with fathers, as long as it is augmented by an appreciation of the different social pressures upon men and women. The messages can be applied throughout the range of work with children, as well as with specific situations of abuse and neglect. Social work, in particular, has embraced the concept of anti-discriminatory practice, based upon theories of oppression. Feminist theory is, clearly, the most relevant for consideration of gender issues and in Chapter 4 we look at the extents and limits of its application to fathers. One of the main concepts that underpins health visiting, and to an extent, social work is that of caring. In Chapter 5 we look at the ways in which nursing theory has elaborated the theme of caring into a guiding principle for practice and consider how far it can be extended to work with fathers.

The final section draws out more specific practice themes. In what is perhaps the most challenging chapter (6) we confront the risks that men can pose to women and children. It is in this chapter that the attention is most closely focused on the child protection aspects of practice. Conversely, in Chapter 7 we set out the ways in which men are, or potentially could be, assets to their children. The final chapter brings the main themes together to set out a broad framework for practice by setting out a series of questions that practitioners can ask themselves when carrying out an assessment.

Finally, what about the gender of the researchers, writers and practitioners in child care and protection practice? It appears to us that much of the innovative practice with fathers is being carried out by men, whilst much of the writing and research is being carried out by women, often women who have previously applied their interest in gender issues to the role of women in society. We are no exception to this trend. The people who are, perhaps, least engaged with men are the female practitioners, and in social work and health visiting this means the majority of the workforce. As authors of this book, we do not claim to be able to see things from the father's perspective. But then, a male practitioner cannot automatically assume that he has special access to that perspective either. What we urge throughout is that such an assumption can be made by no one, and that in practice we should *ask* the father about his viewpoint, needs, wants and hopes. Of course, asking someone for his views means noticing him in the first place!

Chapter 1

Contemporary Context

Introduction

In this chapter we set out the contemporary sociological and legislative context of fatherhood, mainly from a British perspective. It is essential that practitioners have such information, as it provides the backcloth to their work with all children. Practice suggestions based upon this contemporary context are provided and are not necessarily considered to be specific to work with vulnerable children. We shall also consider the context with regard to children about whom there are specific child care and protection concerns, and the way the child protection system responds to mothers and fathers. In some ways the circumstances of the fathers of these children may not always be typical of those of fathers in general; we highlight such differences and provide practice suggestions. However, the messages from the general context should also be applicable to the situations of many children about whom there are concerns.

As with all chapters, contextual information is given in the first part of the chapter and specific practice suggestions are developed in the second part. In this chapter we introduce many themes that are explored in more detail in subsequent chapters.

Contemporary Context

Demography

A comprehensive, recent review of current fatherhood in Britain revealed that:

> most fathering still takes place in intact two-parent first-families, and it is still the case that eight out of ten fathers live with all their biological

children (under 18) and three out of four children under 16 years old will not experience their parents' divorce. (Burghes *et al.* 1997, p.13)

The review by Burghes describes the current demography and economics of contemporary fatherhood in substantial detail and some points will be summarised here. One interesting statistic is that women are more likely to become mothers than men to become fathers. This means that men are more likely to have children by more than one woman, than are women to have children by more than one man. Women are also more likely to be teenage parents than men; in other words the fathers of children born to teenage mothers are usually older than the mother. Despite the public discourse of concern about the fragmentation of family life, only a minority of fathers have very complicated family histories; it is still the case that 93 per cent of children reported by men are born within marriage. Around 73 per cent of children live with both birth parents, 19 per cent with a lone mother, 8 per cent in reconstituted families (Ryan and Little 2000). Lone mothers outnumber lone fathers by more than eight to one (Burgess and Ruxton 1996). Of the fathers in Britain today:

- 85 per cent live with all their children (under 18 years old)
- 13 per cent do not live with any of their children
- 2.5 per cent live with some of their children.

A father is more likely not to be living with his children if he was not living with the mother at the time of birth. Burghes *et al.* (1997) report seven in ten non-resident fathers as having contact with their children. They also suggest that physical and psychological absence need to be distinguished. A father may live with his children but be psychologically absent, whereas a non-resident father may be psychologically available to his children. Contact is more likely between separated and divorced than never-married parents and the pre-divorce relationship affects the post-divorce contact, which may be mediated by the mother. Many factors affect ongoing contact, including resources, housing, geographical distance and emotional costs. Contact can be maintained in different ways, for example:

- helping with homework
- taking children to and from school

- offering an alternative home.

It is important that practitioners keep this national picture in mind: it provides the background context to work with more vulnerable children. The demographic picture is a little different for children referred to the social services.

In a re-analysis of the research studies summarised in the Department of Health's *Child Protection: Messages from Research* (1995), Ryan and Little (2000) draw out the demography of children involved in the child protection process, which contrasts with the national picture. At the time of initial enquiry only 38 per cent of referred children were living with both birth parents, 31 per cent lived with a lone mother, 28 per cent in reconstituted families and 2 per cent with a lone father. As the child protection proceedings continued, so the number of fathers still living within the household reduced. After the initial case conference 26 per cent of children were living with both parents but by ten years after registration only 17 per cent of children were living with the same two parents as at the time of registration. Of course, these figures include the full range of types of abuse and neglect and a range of perpetrators, both male and female. Of non-resident fathers, some had left at the time of enquiry, sometimes because they were implicated. Of those who had previously left, some were implicated as perpetrators of abuse and some not.

Contemporary views about fatherhood

Some insight into the public views of men about fatherhood is given in a MORI poll commissioned by the Readers Digest. Four hundred young men aged between 16 and 25 were asked a series of questions about fatherhood. The survey results (MORI 1999) present a complex picture. Of the men questioned, 85 per cent disagreed (to varying extents) with the statement that 'Bringing up a child is women's work' and 58 per cent agreed with 'Children need to be brought up by two parents in the same home'. Although challenging the stereotype of child care as women's work, these young men did express the value of the father's financial support role: 91 per cent disagreed that financial responsibility for children would end if the relationship with the mother broke down. There was far less consensus about whether they would marry their girlfriend if she were to become pregnant, with 33 per cent saying it would be likely, 26 per cent unlikely and 36 per cent uncertain. Only 25 per cent said they would stay for the sake of the children after a relationship broke down.

In a survey of 40 16–24-year-old, single, non-resident fathers, all respondents stated that they wanted to, or had managed to keep contact with their children, despite not being in a relationship with the mother. They wanted to be good fathers and did not see child care as 'sissy'. They described the main block to contact as being restrictions from the mother; but other issues were identified such as lack of professional support from social workers, problems with housing and lack of knowledge about legal rights.

Such studies suggest that for young men there may be a conceptual decoupling of the close link between marriage or long-term commitment to a partner and potential commitment to children, which appears to be separate. This separation of the couple relationship and the individual parent–child relationships is an important concept that can be helpful as a guide for practitioners. It is a theme that will be returned to as the book progresses.

Nearly half of parents describe child care as being shared, and when both parents work, domestic chores are more likely to be shared, but detailed figures suggest that mothers are still more likely to have prime responsibility for child care, even when they are also working full-time. Mothers, overall, also carry out about two-thirds of core domestic tasks. Even when the father is not in paid employment, he is unlikely to assume full responsibility for domestic chores.

The element of financial responsibility appears again and again in contemporary accounts of fathering. Breadwinning, both in fact and aspiration, still makes up the bedrock of fathering activity. Although mothers are increasingly likely to be in paid employment and to contribute significantly to household economics, fathers are the main breadwinners in six out of ten families with dependent children in Britain (Burghes et al. 1997). A recent study specifically addressed the issue of the interaction between work and family for men, explored family members' views on contemporary fathering (Warin et al. 1999) (see Box 1.1) and concluded:

> For many men, it may be almost impossible to separate their desire to be a loving, caring, 'involved' father from their desire to provide. Providing becomes an expression of paternal love which can be crucially

important to men themselves, even if they are not enthusiastic about what their youngsters expect them to provide (p.22).

Box 1.1 Fathers, work and family life

The overall aim of this study was 'to examine the impact of work patterns on family relationships, specifically fathers' relationships with their teenage children' (Warin et al. 1999, p.9).

The views of 95 parents, both fathers and mothers, from across a range of household compositions and material circumstances were surveyed. Parents and children in 74 households were also interviewed about the role of fathers and the impact of work.

What was found was that the importance of work does not relate to the amount of time that men have available for their families; rather, it lies in a belief that material provision is intrinsic to fathering (p.9):

> The most overwhelming finding was the frequency with which the father role was equated with providing. In 135 of the 140 interviews the word 'provider' was used spontaneously. It was used by men who were working and men who were not, and it was used by women, even when the father was absent or when they were the main provider themselves. Further, although many women were also in paid employment, their providing role was not emphasised, instead the caregiving role was. For men, many of whom expressed dislike for their work, providing was the most important aspect of work.

> Providing for them is absolutely critical because it justifies – it justifies to a certain extent my existence, that 'why am I doing this?' (p.17)

A very clear picture emerges of providing being the cornerstone of identity as a father. This was particularly evident in fathers who were unable to provide because of unemployment, disability or low wages. Here the impact upon self-esteem and self-respect was marked. Nor were these fathers more likely to take a more active part in caregiving; that only occurred in two out of the families in the study and 'there did not seem to be an ideological commitment to changes which would offset the 'breadwinner' imperative' (p.17).

Emotional availability and involvement were considered important, but these were not seen as taking the place of the provider role, rather as being overlaid upon it.

In fulfilling their breadwinning role, fathers in Britain have been found to work longer hours than all in Europe. Very few work part-time and many work unsociable hours. Where the man is unemployed, the woman is likely to be as well (Burghes *et al.* 1997).

It appears that the father role is expanding to incorporate other elements of caring and nurturing, without, at the same time, shedding the traditional element of financial responsibility. This perhaps reflects a broader shift in the values of parenting in which parents of either gender aspire to relationships with their children based upon 'quality time' together. A study in which 100 parents were interviewed showed that although both mothers and fathers described more positive emotions about their children than any other emotion, parents felt that parenting is harder now than it ever has been. Of the fathers, 45 per cent felt that they did not spend enough time with their children (NOP Family 1998). The actual amount of time spent on child care has increased for both men and women, but for men the increase is greater – showing a fourfold increase since 1961 (Burghes *et al.* 1997).

Very little is known about the views about parenting held by mothers and fathers of abused and neglected children. The studies that have been done focus on their views about the child protection process and do not usually report on fathers and mothers separately. The bulk of research has probably been carried out into the views of non-abusing mothers. This lack of information specifically about the views of fathers is a significant gap. Their views may be similar to those of the general population of fathers, but equally they may not.

This raises the more general question about whether the mothers and fathers of abused and neglected children are in some way different from the parents of children who are not abused and neglected. This is a complex area that is beyond the scope of this book. The conclusion drawn by the Department of Health is that parenting behaviours can be described as a continuum, with very serious cases of abuse falling at one extreme end of the dimension of behaviour. Thus parenting behaviours defined as abuse and neglect are those that children ordinarily encounter 'but which in certain circumstances could be defined as maltreatment' (Department of Health 1995). If it is accepted that the majority of abuse and neglect is part of a continuum of parenting behaviours then, until we have more research information, it is reasonable to use the views of the general population as a rule of thumb when engaging with fathers of abused and neglected children.

Legislative and Policy Context

For a comprehensive overview of the law relating to fatherhood in England, including that which applies to new reproductive technology, see Cronin's excellent review (1997). When a father and mother are married they both have equal parental responsibilities (although they may not always be treated the same, as discussed below). A father who is not, or has not been, married to the mother does not automatically have responsibilities. The spirit of the European Convention on Human Rights requires that states take positive steps to strengthen the legal position of unmarried fathers (Bainham 1989). The thrust of international developments is to link paternity rights with cohabitance with the mother. For example, in Sweden, an unmarried father has no automatic rights, but automatic shared custody for unmarried fathers living with the mother is being considered. The Domestic Relations Act of Alberta states:

47(1) Unless a court of competent jurisdiction otherwise orders, the joint guardians of a minor child are

(a)   the mother, and

(b)   the father, if...

(iii) he cohabited with the mother of the child for at least one year immediately before the birth of the child...

In some states of the USA (for example Utah) the unmarried father has to have demonstrated his commitment to the relationship with the mother and to have applied for paternity, before he can be granted parental rights.

However, it is still the case in Britain that fathers do not have legal parental responsibility unless they are married to the mother. Although it is possible for unmarried fathers to obtain parental responsibilities, this occurs for less than 4 per cent of births outside marriage in England and Wales (Lord Chancellor's Department 1998). What is concerning is that three-quarters of men questioned in a survey on this issue were unaware of the implications for fatherhood of marriage or non-marriage. Further, the majority of the men surveyed saw marriage as irrelevant to fatherhood and no differences in attitudes to fathering were found between married and unmarried fathers. The great majority thought the law outdated and unfair (Pickford 1999). Neither the international examples nor the local position support an aspiration for fathers in their own right to be involved with their children; instead, fathers are linked with children only by virtue of their relationship with the mother (Speak, Cameron and Gilroy 1997).

Conversely, the setting-up of the Child Support Agency in Britain allowed for the recovery of financial support for children from fathers not married to the mother. As F. Williams (1998) points out, the Child Support Act 1991 seems to be drawn from a discourse of 'bad fathers'. The advent of DNA testing has provided a means for men to prove a direct biological relationship with the child, regardless of their relationship with the mother. This, along with an increasing recognition of the rights and responsibilities of fathers, has driven plans to change the law to make it more straightforward for unmarried fathers to be accorded parental rights, but at the time of writing these have not been progressed into legislation.

If the Child Support Act is premised upon the notion of 'bad' fathers, the UK Children Acts are drawn from a discourse of 'good fathers' (F. Williams 1998). The Children Act 1989 and the Children (Scotland) Act 1995 present 'parental' responsibilities, partnership with parents and encouraging contact with both parents after divorce and separation as key concepts. Parents are expected to make and supply the court with details of arrangements for the care of children. F. Williams (1998) suggests that there are two assumptions underlying the English Act: that children are best cared for by both parents and that parenting is always shared in a complementary fashion. As will be discussed throughout the book, the reality does not always match either of these assumptions.

Another aspect of child care legislation is the principle of decision-making on the basis of the welfare of the child. This has allowed for the recognition that a range of people may be important to the child. This is expressed in the Children (Scotland) Act, Section 11(3)(a)(i) which states that *anyone* who 'claims an interest' can apply for a number of orders dealing with aspects of parental responsibilities and rights. The signpost here is, therefore, towards a broadening of the notion of parenting, not only away from mothers, but away from mothers and fathers.

The last three decades have seen an increase in policy development within Europe aimed at paternal involvement in child care. Britain, until recently, has been one of the slowest to implement such developments. Sweden was the first to introduce paid parental leave that included fathers back in 1974 and since then others in the EU have followed suit by implementing provision for paternity leave or male access to parental leave (for example to care for a sick child). Paternity leave has a fairly high take-up rate, ranging from 88 per cent in Sweden to 52 per cent in Denmark and 34 per cent in Finland. Male take-up of parental leave is much lower. Economic factors can affect the level of take-up of such provision and the remuneration varies in different countries (O'Brien 1995).

A range of legislative and policy developments have been initiated by the current government in the UK to tackle poverty, social exclusion and child care and many of these will affect the context of fathering over the next decade. For example, European regulations giving fathers a right to 13 weeks' unpaid leave for children born on or after 15 December 1999 have been implemented. However, the fact that this will be unpaid is likely to reduce significantly some men's ability to make use of this right. Similarly, the Working Time Directive (*Fairness at Work*, 1998) limits working hours (unsocial and social) and sets standards for paid leave.

A government paper setting out 'to analyse the inequality of opportunity' describes the extent to which poverty limits opportunity for employment (HM Treasury 1999). The paper analyses the gap between the rich and poor and demonstrates the link between poverty and lack of employment opportunities, and also highlights the damaging impact of poverty upon children in the short and long term. Measures to promote a move from welfare to work, for example New Deal, Child Care Tax Credit, Sure Start and Working Families Tax Credit, are described. The specific link between lone parenthood and poverty is also mentioned, with strategies to support employment being described as the most effective approach to this.

This is therefore a time of much legislative and policy development which is likely to have a significant impact upon the context of practice.

Child Care and Child Protection Context

Health visitors and social workers are in the prime situation to turn the theory of engagement with fathers into practice. Health visitors, particularly because of their direct role in supporting parenting, are in a position either to marginalise or to involve fathers. Their role involves visiting *all* families with children from the time that the midwife discharges the mother and new infant, approximately ten days after the birth. Their role in parental support is predicted to expand following the publication of the Government green paper *Supporting Families* (1998). Intervention, however, concentrates on mothers, either as providers of nurture or as protectors from abuse (O'Hagan and Dillenberger 1995).

There seems to be a broad social acceptance of a discourse of paternal involvement with children, albeit in a number of versions. There is also an increasing recognition of the potential role for fathers in the care and nurture of their children. Indeed there is general agreement that fathers should be more involved in the care of their children (Beail and McGuire 1982). But the actual shifts in the structuring of child care are minimal. Traditionally, caring has been regarded as a female task (Turney 2000) and health visitors and social workers do not appear to be prepared to challenge that traditional expectation.

As is shown in Box 1.2, the research suggests that men tend to be regarded by both health and social care practitioners as problems, whether they are present or absent (Edwards 1998). When absent, fathers are seen to be irresponsible, when present they are viewed both as making demands upon the mother and as possibly violent. This furnishes adequate excuse for screening them out. Edwards's study demonstrates the gulf between rhetoric and reality. Although her interviewees emphasised the importance of engaging with men, when observed in practice they reinforced traditional messages that child care is women's work and they regularly missed any opportunity to engage with the men they did encounter. This is especially starkly demonstrated with black men (Harrison 1988), whose role as fathers is devalued in data analysis, policy and theoretical models. Agencies can become 'locked into' a conscious or unconscious 'risk view' of all fathers (Gilligan 1998). Child care and protection practice is characterised by its consistent marginalisation of the father, both as a potential asset and as a potential risk (O'Hagan and Dillenberger 1995).

Box 1.2 Screening out men: or 'has mum changed her washing powder recently?'

This study was undertaken in two areas of Greater Manchester during 1991 and 1992, and aimed to explore the concept of social support from the perspective of community health and social service workers (Edwards 1998). There was a particular focus on pre-school age children, so community midwives, health visitors, social workers and voluntary sector workers were interviewed. The caseloads of those interviewed comprised families in dire circumstances. Low income, poor educational attainment, unemployment, family breakdown and domestic violence seemed common.

The majority of those interviewed expressed the opinion that it was beneficial to work with both parents if both were involved in the care of their children, and that health and social care professionals should encourage them in this. However, several interviewees contended that these same professionals deliberately excluded men, even though they agreed there were benefits to including them. The reasons men were excluded can be summarised as follows:

1. Culturally specific ideas of men dominated: if a father was absent, he was ignored. Fathers were seen as synonymous with cohabitation. The stability of the mother's relationship with the father was seen as a positive influence on the lives of children and women.

2. Professionals did not view men as either interested or forthcoming in issues concerning child care.

3. Men can monitor or inhibit the interactions of their partners with health and social care professionals.

Edwards poignantly highlights the differences in the ways professionals deal with men and women as parents. The title of this box is a question a health visitor posed to a father who showed her a rash on his child's skin.

The overall message that parenting is domestic work and women are more capable of this emerged strongly from the interviews.

There are a number of possible reasons for this. The first is that society as a whole still operates within a traditional model of child care. As more women work outside the home, the scene would appear to be set for men to assume more responsibility within the home. However, in reality there is little evidence that the role of men has shifted in a complementary fashion so that they are more involved in child care. There may be discussion about 'shared care', but the discourse is not reflected in action. It is not easy to work against the tide of common understanding. This also means that workers are not likely to come across many situations in which roles have been reversed and which could give them direct experience and models of different ways of doing things (Rolfe 1997). When families are not apparently struggling and the children appear to be happy, then the impetus to challenge the status quo is low. In other words, there appears to be a self-reinforcing cycle in which mothers expect to be the focus of attention, fathers expect not to be involved, and child care practitioners expect to engage with mothers.

The second, linked, reason lies in the extent to which 'parenting' is equated with 'nurturing' which, in turn, is equated with mothering. Although there are many aspects to the successful raising of emotionally and physically healthy children, good parenting is often judged according to the physical care of the child and it is on this measure that mothers are often assessed (Swift 1995). Further, the 'benchmark' of good parenting is perceived by both men and women as parenting carried out by women, who are perceived to be more 'naturally' caring and better able to communicate with children (Warin et al. 1999).

The third reason lies in the lack of theory to guide practice. To be fair to practitioners, there has not been clear guidance on this issue from statutory bodies, or from the literature and training establishments. The marginalisation of the father has a number of effects:

- The mother necessarily becomes the focus of intervention.
- The potential of fathers as risks is minimised.
- The potential of fathers as assets is overlooked.

Focus upon mothers

The tendency for social work practice to concentrate on mothers has been well rehearsed, detailed and documented elsewhere (see for example O'Hagan and Dillenberger 1995). In summary the research suggests that the child protection system tends to concentrate on intervention with mothers, regardless of who is the alleged perpetrator, as for example with cases of physical abuse, which is perpetrated equally by fathers and mothers (Farmer and Owen 1995). Even in cases of sexual abuse the work tends to concentrate on the mother's ability to protect the child from further abuse (Dempster 1993).

It is with cases of physical and emotional neglect that social work and health visiting intervention is most skewed towards the mother. In a detailed analysis Swift (1995) demonstrates the extent to which neglect is characterised as a failure of mothers to 'mother' properly. It is mothers who are overwhelmingly identified as perpetrators of neglect. Many children referred for neglect are being cared for by women on their own, but somehow the man's ultimate neglect – his absence – is not labelled as such.

In cases of child sexual abuse a large component of the risk assessment focuses on whether the mother failed to protect her child, and on her apparent ability to provide ongoing protection. Longer term intervention usually involves meetings with the mother.

However, given that society is still structured around the mother taking primary responsibility for children this is hardly surprising. What are social workers and health visitors supposed to do? On the one hand their theoretical rhetoric espouses engagement with fathers. On the other hand, when they visit the family it is the mother who answers the door and it is the mother who sees her own role as that of primary caretaker.

Failure to assess men as risks

Paradoxically, although child protection practice tends to be focused on issues of risk (Department of Health 1995), there is often a lack of explicit attention to the risks that men may potentially pose to children and to their mothers (Munro 1998). Even when a father or father-figure is clearly identified as a perpetrator of abuse the focus of assessment and ongoing intervention is with the mother and her ability to protect her child (Farmer and Owen 1998). This issue will be explored in detail in Chapter 6.

Failure to assess men as assets

Just as there is a failure to make an assessment of, and engage with, the risks that fathers may pose, there is a failure to assess and engage with the positive attributes that fathers may offer. Fathers feel excluded from child protection proceedings (Whitfield and Harwood 1999). Information about fathers is often missing from case files. By excluding men from the process of assessment and intervention, practitioners effectively exclude the possibility that men may have something to offer their children. In Chapter 7, different ways in which men may be assets to their children will be considered.

Need for guidance

Child care and protection professionals, therefore, are practising in a climate of confusion and mixed messages. They are increasingly being urged to engage with fathers in a purposeful way. However, what is lacking is specific guidance on how to engage with men and to what precise end. The contemporary context is one of majority father presence. Practitioners need not necessarily see themselves as changing social structures, but they do need to be able to interpret the structures they encounter and find ways of working with them. They need to move from the recognition that current practice focuses on women and begin to explore practical and realistic suggestions for broadening practice to include fathers. It is essential for health and social work practice that practitioners are absolutely clear about:

- the *role* terms they are using and what they mean, especially when using the term 'father'
- the *aim* of engaging fathers.

Key Issues from Theory

1. Despite concerns about family disintegration, the majority of fathers live with their children. Children referred because of child care and protection concerns are more likely to be living apart from their fathers.

2. The father–child relationship can be considered separately from the father–mother relationship.

3. Financial provision (breadwinning) is expressed by men, women and children as the absolute bedrock of identity as a father.

4. The legal position with regard to fathers is confused. A number of policy and legislative developments are emerging which aim to support parenting as carried out by both women and men.

5. In child care matters, British society is still largely structured around the traditional role divisions between men and women.

6. Health and social care professions have not developed a sufficiently sophisticated theoretical framework to guide practice with fathers.

7. Child protection investigations tend to focus upon mothers, whether they are the alleged perpetrators or not.

8. Longer term intervention following abuse and neglect centres upon mothers.

9. The potential risk that fathers and other male figures may pose both to children and women tends to be minimised in child protection.

10. The potential for a father to be an asset to his child is consistently overlooked within child care and protection practice.

Practising within the Contemporary Context

Fathers are, clearly, present in the majority of families. Although this book is not specifically focusing on families where there are no presenting problems, there is still a challenge for practitioners to take account of fathers in all circumstances.

It is important that practitioners actually have information about the context within which they are working. This will involve gathering information about fathers in their locality and what services are already available for them. An example of comprehensive information gathering is an audit carried out by the Fathers Plus project of Children North East, a children's charity covering the North East of England (Richardson 1998). Fathers Plus aims:

> To support men as fathers through a period of transition, enhancing the father's connection with his children, and helping them find new

directions as parents which are valued and relevant to the social, economic and cultural needs of Britain in the new millennium. (p.3)

This excellent audit of group work with fathers throughout the North East of England uncovered a wide range of projects which are grouped under community-based group work, work in custodial settings and academic and research activities. One conclusion from the survey is that the most effective group work should not try to be 'all things to all men' but should target men with specific needs, such as young fathers, separated fathers and so on.

For health visitors the majority of their work is with families where there are no child care concerns. However, it is still important that they make the role of the father visible and find out what fathers want and need. For example, in Liverpool the regional midwifery unit conducted an exploratory study with first-time expectant fathers to find out about their knowledge and feelings about labour (Lavender 1997). On the basis of a questionnaire and interviews three main themes of concern emerged: support, information and role conflict. The authors conclude that fathers must be included in the birth experience as part of a three-way partnership.

The fact that there is a considerable amount of debate about fatherhood could help this process. A discussion with the parents about this current debate could open up the whole issue for consideration. In other words, asking a simple question of each parent signals a willingness to understand their particular viewpoint:

> People nowadays have different views about the roles that fathers and mothers should play in the lives of their children? What do you see your role as a parent to be?

Professionals may well find that they have been making unwarranted assumptions about the parenting roles that the parents see themselves adopting.

The same lack of assumptions should characterise work with families where children are considered to be vulnerable. Again, one simple starting point is to gather basic information about the families that are known to the service. For example, a team, local office or council could do a simple exercise of looking at all the open cases and collating what information is known (or not known) about the fathers. Box 1.3 gives examples of such local surveys.

Box 1.3 Social work practice with fathers: two examples of getting the information

The social work services team that works with under-12s in Perth and Kinross identified a need to come up with new ways to engage with men who are part of the families the team works with (Millar 2000). The first step was to ask all the social workers to fill out a questionnaire about their current casework. The questionnaire asked about the number of men they were in contact with and how many of these men have been, or would potentially be, interested in some form of parents' group or activity. From the 20 returns approximately 50 men in families were identified, mainly parents, co-carers or grandparents. There was an impression that more men are now involved in the care of children than had been the case in the past.

Workers felt that there was a need for some group work or individual work on issues such as parenting, money, self-esteem and anger management. A small number of men already attended some form of voluntary parenting group. Workers noted the existence of domestic violence and physical and sexual abuse and were concerned about the difficulty of engaging with the perpetrators of such violence and of persuading them to attend groups on these issues.

The next stage is to interview as many of the men as possible to gain their views about what group or individual services they would find helpful, and to develop practice from there. The aim is, by starting to ask men about the services they may want, for practice to move towards a more inclusive approach.

An initiative such as this can be carried out in any team, and indeed would be an ideal project for a student social worker on placement.

Contact: Gareth Millar, Perth and Kinross Council, 01738 643 066.

The following is an extract from a description of a study carried out by a family centre worker into the views of the fathers of children attending the centre (Rogers 1994).

> Twenty-five fathers were interviewed, using first a structured interview to elicit demographic details (childhood experiences and possible links to present relationships with partners and their children, preparation for fatherhood, getting support, information and advice, and what kind of help they saw themselves as needing), and second a questionnaire to gain an impression of participants' attitudes towards fathering and their actual involvement in child care and housework.

Although some researchers report on the difficulties of recruiting men for research purposes, I found the men appeared to value the opportunity to talk about themselves as part of process of forming an identity as men, partners and fathers.

Most of the respondents were unemployed, having left school with no qualifications. A fifth were receiving treatment for chronic medical problems, while a further fifth had received, or were receiving, psychiatric treatment, mostly for depression. Most saw their extended families as their main source of support, and they had limited knowledge about who else to consult for help or advice and felt reluctant to use even resources they were aware of, in spite of a generally positive attitude to the notion of seeking help if required.

Whilst most mothers of respondents were viewed positively, their fathers were generally viewed negatively. Nearly half of the respondents reported difficulties in their parents' relationship, and these difficulties appeared to be replicated in their own current relationships.

Similarly, their own childhood experiences did not seem to equip the respondents for their fathering role. Most were keen to do something different and better, but were not clear how to achieve this. Few were prepared for fatherhood, and nearly half experienced some difficulties with the behaviour management of their children, often seeing their partners as having the main disciplinary role.

On the other hand, most respondents reported being quite highly involved in child care and in domestic chores, although there was some selectivity in what chores were undertaken.

It was clear that many of the fathers experience some awkwardness in involving themselves in the work of the Family Centre.

As to services for men, there was a roughly even split between those who prefer to seek advice on a one-to-one basis, those who wanted a self-help group, and those who asked for options for both kinds of help. Most men were reluctant to approach people they had not already met. The men identified as needing help with relationships with their partners and their children, knowledge about children generally, and behaviour management ideas. Those asking for group based help were keen to find out other men's ideas and experiences. The men demonstrated an awareness of the social changes that have occurred, and they showed an interest in the implications for their roles as men, partners and fathers – in masculinity, in fact.

Contact: John Rogers, Scottish Borders Council, 01896 754751.

Fathers are often not resident in homes where there are child care and protection concerns. This makes the challenge of assessing their understanding of their role more difficult, but that does not mean that careful consideration should not be given to how best to obtain their views. It should be possible to explore the mothers' and children's views, and such a discussion could open up important issues. The surveys reveal that men themselves do not automatically assume that their relationship with their children should end if the relationship with the mother ends. It is therefore crucial that practitioners bear in mind the point that *physical* absence does not necessarily equate with *psychological* absence (Burghes *et al.* 1997). Again, it can be helpful to consider the father–child relationship separately from the father–mother relationship.

Whilst guarding against assumptions, it seems reasonable to expect, on the basis of survey information, that the majority of families encountered by practitioners will consider the male role of providing to be central. In families where men are employed this should be respected and taken account of. Social workers and health visitors tend to emphasise the attachment and nurturing aspects of parenting, but they must not render the financial aspect invisible. Many parents do expect fathers to exhibit caring and nurturing behaviours as well, but it should be remembered that this is often overlaid upon the providing role. With all families, practitioners need to look at the whole range of parenting activities carried out by both mothers and fathers.

The position of fathers of children about whom there are child protection concerns are again a little different from the majority picture. The rates of unemployment, poverty and material deprivation are much greater amongst the parents of children referred to child protection services. For example, in one study (Pitcairn *et al.* 1993) 85 per cent of mothers and 75 per cent of fathers were found to be unemployed. Not being able to provide affects a man's confidence severely as a father and it is important to take account of the impact of this upon esteem. Although an unemployed father may have more potential time to spend with his children, it is as if he hasn't 'earned' the right to be a proper father: 'You ask blokes what they feel their role is as a dad, it is to provide for their kids. You take that away and you've got problems' (Warin *et al.* 1999, p.25).

Simple exhortations for the man to take a more active role in caring may be perceived as patronising, or as 'writing off' the man as a provider. Given that men, women and children all tend to hold the value of father as provider, intervention with the whole family may be necessary to help the family to re-assess the father role. Men who are unemployed or low paid should also be given as much support and advice as possible about regaining employment, or training to improve prospects. There may be a tendency to accept that unemployment is the norm in vulnerable families, especially for women. There are political arguments about women and work, but it is essential that all get equal access to information about their rights with regard to employment. It is now the norm for both parents to be in some form of paid employment, so both mothers and fathers may value employment-related information and support.

Practising within the Legislation and Policy Context

All child care professionals must work within the statutory context, as mediated by policy documents and professional guidelines. Unfortunately, the legislation does not give a clear direction for developing a coherent response to fathers. The message for practitioners is one of engagement with 'parents' with no distinctions on the basis of gender. The difficulty with this is that it does not match practice experience in which women assume the main role of caring for children. Further, many of the children referred because of abuse and neglect have biological fathers who are either abusive or who are absent. In these kinds of cases the expression 'parent' becomes synonymous with 'mother', largely because the tasks of parenting that are of primary concern to health visitors are those nurturing tasks so often carried out by mothers anyway.

Social workers can switch between the discourse of 'bad' or 'good' fathers. Many of the children encountered in child care practice have fathers who do not hold parental responsibilities. When the father is viewed as a potential risk to a situation the lack of parental responsibility can allow him to be eliminated from the process. However, if the father is seen as a potential asset, biology may be given precedence over legality. This is clearly an unfair use of the legal anomaly, particularly as children may know who their father is, but do not grasp the legal niceties.

Within child protection proceedings it has been found that non-resident fathers are rarely involved in enquiries, assessments or case conferences (Ryan and Little 2000). If the spirit of working in partnership with parents is to move beyond partnership with mothers, then the issue of residence is a red herring; it does not excuse lack of attempts to, at the very least, inform the father of events. Of course, when the father is considered a risk to the mother, child or professional, caution has to be exercised about how this is managed. Although fathers without parental responsibility do not automatically have a right to be included in accommodation proceedings, they must be informed, consulted and where appropriate, be provided with arrangements for contact with their children. Adoption orders cannot be made without the consent of a father with parental responsibility (unless his agreement is legally dispensed with); a father without parental responsibility may be involved in adoption proceedings and may prevent an adoption (Ryan and Little 2000).

Ideally, practice should aim to reach the position whereby the automatic assumption is that the father will be involved in proceedings unless there is a specific and well-documented reason to justify his exclusion.

Practising within the Current Child Care and Child Protection Context

The fact that the mother is the primary point of access to the household can shape the whole subsequent practice. Of course, social workers and health visitors have to work with the reality of current family structures, so it is not surprising that mothers are the pivotal feature of child care practice. Often the mother herself will request support with parenting; frequently the mother is living on her own with the children; often fathers will absent themselves from discussions about children. It is perfectly possible to accept the status quo and continue to work primarily with mothers. However, the premise that runs throughout this book is that to concentrate intervention upon mothers is a severe limitation upon practice because:

- to focus principally upon mothers runs counter to the principle of anti-discriminatory practice

- currently the burden of expectations to care, protect and nurture children falls upon women

- the potential for men to be involved in a meaningful way is lost

- it is dangerous to ignore the potential risks that men may pose to their partners and their children

- practitioners should be exploiting every possible resource on behalf of the child; to ignore the father is to ignore a possible resource.

Whilst urging practitioners to engage with fathers, there has to be a recognition that this may not be straightforward. Contemporary family life is complex, and practitioners are confronted with this complexity in all its forms. Although, as described above, only a minority of fathers have very complicated family histories, it is precisely within child care and protection practice that complexity is likely to be encountered. Once the practice focus is broadened beyond the sharp focus on the mother, the complexities abound. As an example consider the fictional situation of two young children, Jill, aged 18 months and Ann, who is six months. The two children are referred because of concerns about physical neglect. In the standard referral information these children are described as the daughters of Jane. In some situations of this kind that may be the limit of the recorded information. However, on further assessment it emerges that the children's father, John, is also in the household and that there are two older children, Alison and Davie. Unless somebody explicitly asks the appropriate question it may not be known that Alison and Davie's father is not John, but a previous partner, David. Finally, with further prompting it may come to light that Jane has two older children, Janet and Dan, who live with their father, Peter. At this stage, therefore, assuming that all the questions have been asked, the genogram depicted in Figure 1.1 can be drawn in the file.

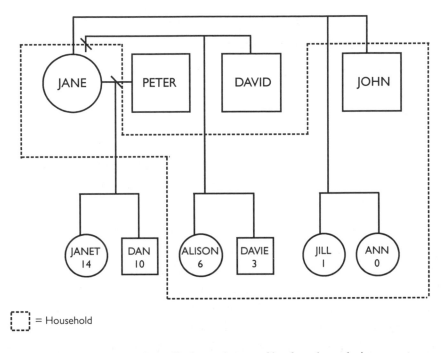

Figure 1.1 A genogram as traditionally depicted in case files, from the mother's perspective.

In practice, Jane can remain the focus of attention. So, it is decided that she is in need of parenting skills and she is referred for parenting classes. Jill and Ann are provided with a place in day care and Jane is encouraged to attend, to learn how to interact better with her daughters. Jane is offered counselling to help her come to terms with the loss of her two older children. Jane and John are offered relationship counselling.

But what if the genogram is drawn from John's perspective? If this is done a completely different picture of the family emerges, as shown in Figure 1.2, because John has other children, who live with their mothers. The focus of practice shifts to an exploration of the role that John plays with all his children. It emerges that John spends a considerable amount of time with his other children, leaving Jane to struggle to cope with the four children in the household without support. Intervention is aimed at encouraging John to spread his time more evenly between his children and to offer more practical support in the home.

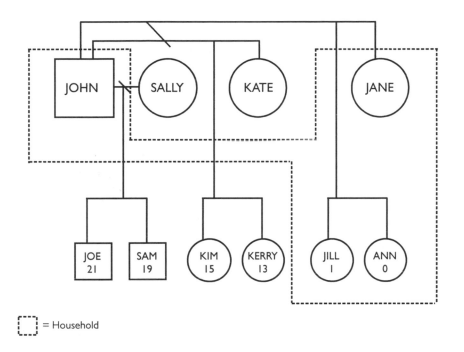

= Household

Figure 1.2 A different way of drawing a genogram, from the father's perspective.

A glance at a cross-section of files will show how unusual it is to see a depiction of the family from the father's perspective. Of course, it would be just as problematic to swap one skewed picture for another. The illustration is used simply to show that the 'normal' depiction is not the only way of looking at a family. Our preconceptions and expectations shape how we view a family unit and then may shape the subsequent intervention.

To take the illustration a step further, the genogram can be drawn from the perspective of Jill and Ann as in Figure 1.3.

This is not a completely unusual scenario for practitioners to encounter: it is based upon a number of real referrals for neglect. Once we view the family from the children's perspective, another set of issues emerges. It may be that the children themselves are unaware of the full extent of their sibling and half-sibling network. It may also be the case that some, or all, of the children are uncertain about the biological connections. It is not unusual to hear children describe a half-sibling as a step-sibling, for example. Jane's children Alison and Davie may not be

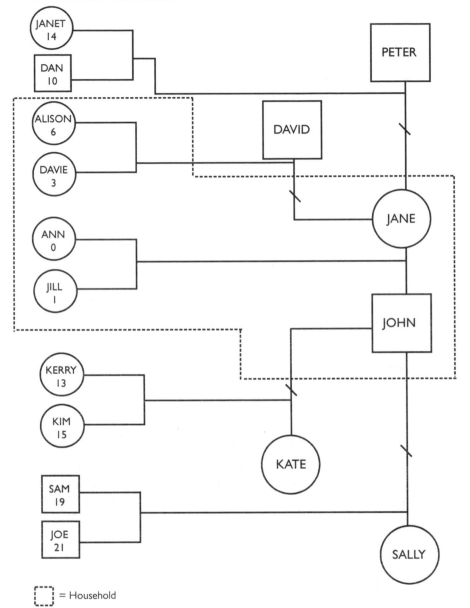

[⌐] = Household

Figure 1.3 A genogram drawn from the perspective of the children.

aware that John is not their biological father. Perhaps the mother will tell the social worker or health visitor that David is their father, but that the children do not know this and she does not want them to know. A number of ethical questions result:

- How is such information to be recorded?

- What potential is there for a future worker to glance at the genogram and to say something to Alison about her dad, David, unaware that Alison thinks John is her dad?

- Do children have the right to know who their biological father is, regardless of the wishes of the mother and the new father-figure who is carrying out the 'fathering' role?

Box 1.4 Case example

George is accommodated away from home. His biological father is Frank, a man he knew for years as a family acquaintance. The man he believed to be his father was not his biological parent, but his mother's partner of many years, Brian. George has one half-sibling, Brian's child. The family received support from the social work department over the years in managing what they described as George's difficult behaviour. All the professionals involved believed Brian to be George's father. As George entered adolescence there were many tensions within the household and arguments centred on George and his behaviour. He and his mother, Kay, had violent physical fights which Brian tried, with little success, to defuse. Kay and Brian had a reasonably good relationship, although Kay accused him of being too soft on George.

When George was 13 he found out that Frank, not Brian, was his father. For George the revelation was completely devastating and it undermined his sense of self and his trust in both Kay and Brian. He immediately sought out Frank and asked to live with him, in the hope that he would provide him with the 'perfect family life'. Frank was angry that he was drawn into what he viewed as another family's argument. He felt no real connection to George and told him to go back home. The arguments escalated until the police were called and George was removed from home. Despite continued attempts at family-based intervention George was unable to return home to live and remains with a foster family.

Throughout all of this, it is Brian who shows the most commitment to retaining contact with George. The social worker supports him in this by helping him with finance to visit, by including him in review meetings and by arranging joint activities for George and Brian. He remains the point of access for George to the rest of his family, especially his sibling.

It is, perhaps, because of an awareness of the intricate nature of family life that social workers and health visitors often confine their attentions to the mother. After all, in some circumstances it may not seem appropriate to probe into matters that are not obviously relevant. However, these issues can be explosive within families (see Box 1.4). If the welfare of the child is placed at the centre, then it may be appropriate to explore the family relationships in more detail. It may be that parents and children are harbouring feelings of loss, confusion and hurt. Conflict may develop from misconceptions and misunderstandings about loyalties, family ties and responsibilities. These are all factors that have the potential to undermine the quality of the parenting atmosphere for the children. There may be other practice benefits from exploring the extent of the network in more detail; for example, it may reveal a member of the extended family who is prepared to offer practical or emotional support in child care.

Key Messages for Practice

1. The role that the father has with his children, whether resident, or non-resident, has to be rendered visible. The impact of separation from the father, under whatever circumstances, should form part of the enquiry and assessment.

2. Practitioners need to ask about the relationship between each child and his or her father. Such questions need to be separated from questions about the relationship between the parents.

3. Children referred because of child care and protection concerns are more likely to be living in situations of poverty and deprivation with unemployed parents. This should not be accepted as inevitable, but should be tackled head on with advice, guidance and support.

4. The legal anomalies surrounding unmarried fathers should not be used in a discriminatory fashion to exclude some fathers from child protection proceedings.

5. Even though mothers still tend to carry out most caregiving, practice should aim to reach the position whereby the

automatic assumption is that the father will be involved in proceedings unless there is a specific and well-documented reason to justify his exclusion.

6. The guiding principle of intervention is that the child and his or her needs must be placed at the centre of every assessment of family relationships.

7. Practitioners must look at the structure of the family from the perspective of all its members without making assumptions about roles.

8. If there is to be direct communication with children, then it is essential to be clear about what they have been told, have inferred and know about who is their father.

9. If a man is considered to be a risk this should be dealt with explicitly and not hidden behind the fact that he may not have parental responsibilities.

10. Children benefit from having a network of support. Any way in which the father may be an asset to the child should be explored.

Try it for Size

Try to examine your own views honestly:

- What would be your own views about the roles that men and women should play in their children's lives?

- Consider what your own values are about mothers and fathers working. Do you regard men's and women's jobs in the same way, or do you differentiate between them in your own mind?

- What does your own work mean to you and how does it interact with your own gender identity?

- What messages may be given to mothers and fathers encountered in practice by male or female practitioners? Consider all combinations: for example, what may be the impact for an unemployed man of a visit by an employed female practitioner, or an employed male practitioner? What may an unemployed mother make of an employed mother visiting her and examining her child's development?

- Monitor the implicit and explicit messages that you convey to mothers and fathers about paid employment and child care.

Chapter 2

Fathering Roles

Introduction

How can fathers be engaged with purposefully and to what end? In order to engage effectively with men as fathers, child care practitioners need to be clear both about what role they anticipate the man playing and about what role he himself considers appropriate. This chapter concentrates on exploring the roles of men and women as parents by disentangling the tasks associated with 'mothering' and 'fathering' from each other and from their assignment to a particular gender.

Trends in Fatherhood

A review of a number of surveys 20 years ago showed that many men believed in 'maternal instinct', that women 'naturally' made better parents (Parke 1981). Nonetheless, it has been established that most people these days do not support the idea of traditional marital values, such as only having children within marriage. Rather, it is the context of family life as opposed to its structure that is seen as most important (Buchanan and Ten Brinke 1997). Studies that have tried to understand paternal behaviour have examined paternal involvement in 'non-traditional' families as well as in 'traditional' ones, but the results are contradictory and difficult to interpret (C. Lewis 1986).

Policy debates remain dominated by a negative view of fathers based on an economic view of (absent) fathers (C. Lewis 2000). It is still too early to know whether attempts to limit the working week will have any effect on this, but trends have changed. Such trends have an important influence on fatherhood roles and are summarised by C. Lewis (2000):

- Whilst in the early 1970s fewer than half of all mothers worked, two-thirds of women with dependent children now work.

- In the 1960s and 1970s there was a steep rise in divorce rates and these have remained at high levels since.

- There are also declining marriage rates and an accompanying rise in cohabitation, which has more than doubled since the early 1980s.

- More babies are born outside marriage: 8 per cent in the early 1970s, increasing to 38 per cent in 1998.

C. Lewis (1986) acknowledges that it is undeniable that men shirk many aspects of child care, but argues that the feminist perspective alone does not explain why most fathers are less involved with their children than mothers. He suggests another three trends that have affected fatherhood:

- Working arrangements outside the home. These can result in less time and less energy for fathers. Additionally, the costs of child care, particularly in the early years, can mean men often take on extra work at this time.

- Stereotyping of providers. The amount men participate in child care depends in part on how much women let them do, as women gain a psychological advantage from having the major role in this domain.

- Children's needs change. When they are younger for example, children often need to be in bed before the father returns home. It is not therefore a simple matter of shirking responsibility. Men's participation is only necessary if their wives also work.

Statements such as these, which could be interpreted as: *Poor man, doesn't he work hard, no wonder he doesn't have time for the children; and his wife won't let him do much anyway* are not particularly useful in a discourse regarding fatherhood. Yet they are clearly popular views and cannot be dismissed outright. If fathers and mothers and professionals hold similar views to these, then we need to consider how to engage with fatherhood within this very context.

Male Gender Roles

In a study of lone fatherhood it is argued that male gender roles are often ignored (R. Barker 1994). Whereas in the eighteenth and nineteenth centuries children were seen as the property of their fathers, the twentieth century began to focus on a strong ideology of motherhood, and in terms of role theory, there is a much clearer shared definition of mothering than there is of fathering (R. Barker 1994).

R. Barker argues that both men and fathers operate within a patriarchal context (i.e. male power and the way it is exercised), and this requires some explanation. Walby (1990) suggests that there are a number of patriarchal structures where male gender roles are promoted and centred, including waged labour, culture, male violence and sexual relationships. Together, these encourage a complicated and multi-faceted system of oppression. However, whilst all men benefit from a system of patriarchy, not all men are involved equally in all of its structures and patriarchy is better understood as relationships in various settings, such as the home and the community (R. Barker 1994). R. Barker suggests that masculinities are better understood in terms of a continuum, with traditional patriarchal masculinities at one end and pioneering and progressive masculinities at the other. This is confirmed by Burgess and Ruxton (1996), who suggest that there are three stages in the public acceptance of the notion of children and fathers:

- Stage One: traditional values concerning mothering are paramount and fathering is seen as something essentially different.

- Stage Two: ambivalence. Fathers are seen as valuable and perhaps even necessary, but mothering remains superior.

- Stage Three: the value of fathers is not only accepted, but the means to achieve this full participation are in place.

Burgess and Ruxton argue that whilst the Nordic countries, for example, are well into the third stage, Britain is just entering the second. This suggests that male gender roles are inextricably bound up in societal and cultural notions of fatherhood and placing the emphasis on individual male behaviours is not particularly useful.

Sex-role theory essentially suggests that humans learn from society's various institutions about how to behave in ways appropriate to their sex (Trigiani 1998). Despite the serious influence that sex-role theory brought to understandings of fatherhood, a study of family change more than two decades ago was already finding a move away from traditional sex-role preferences (Scanzoni 1978). This was not only because there were huge changes in the meaning of work for women and the consequences of their work, but also in the way women would negotiate or conflict with their husbands (Scanzoni 1978). Despite a recent spate of populist literature that still tends to emphasise sex-role theory (e.g. the *Men are from Mars, Women are from Venus* books), by the 1980s it was realised that sex-role theory was too rigid for real life for a number of reasons (Trigiani 1998), because it:

- does not address individual behaviour differences in diverse situations

- refuses to admit that masculine traits are valued more highly in society than feminine ones

- does not explain why certain characteristics become attached to a particular gender

- assumes that gender forms the core of a person's identity

- seems to endorse passive learning.

Fatherhood in context

Once a woman has given birth, her motherhood is never in doubt, whereas a man's fatherhood is always a matter of presumption (McKeown, Ferguson and Rooney 1999). What is actually meant by fatherhood? Different men might perform different paternal functions in the child's life – the provision of sperm, a sexual relationship with the mother, social interaction with the child, economic support of the family or child, and legal obligations to or rights over the child (Warin *et al.* 1999). LaRossa (1989) argues that the institution of fatherhood has two distinct elements:

- the culture of fatherhood, i.e. the shared norms, values and expectations that surround men's parenting

- the conduct of fatherhood, i.e. what fathers actually do.

What becomes clear is that the *culture* of fatherhood has perhaps changed somewhat, but in reality, the *conduct* of fatherhood has changed very little.

When we talk about parenting it becomes quite clear that mothers are more central than fathers in contemporary British society – a fact that many object to. Partly this is due to gender role differentiation and it may be changing – whilst men remain with more overall power and status in society in general, in terms of child care it is mothers who are probably seen as most important. Box 2.1 describes a survey of men's views about health visiting.

Box 2.1 Going the distance: Fathers, health and health visiting

Robert Williams (1999) undertook an audit with 66 fathers in Birmingham to ascertain their views about parenting and the local health visiting service. Qualitative interviews were undertaken with the men, who were from a range of ethnic backgrounds. The findings indicated that most fathers perceived that health visitors provided a valuable service to women and children. A minority of the fathers had used the child health clinics and had generally found them welcoming. Some men also explained how health visitors had involved them in addressing family health issues (for example, post-natal depression). However, many men expressed concerns about their exclusion from health-visiting assessment and care delivery and also concerns that their health as men was rarely addressed by the health visitors they encountered.

Williams found evidence that men's identities as men may also limit their ability to access services. Most men conceptualised fatherhood as being about differing forms of responsibility. Indeed, many also conceptualised health as being a functional capacity ('going the distance'), with particular reference to their responsibilities for children and for household income. Some of Williams's themes are summarised below:

- Many men had strong feelings of love for their children but did not always find these easy to express.
- For many men the love and pleasure they experience as fathers is very important in how they see themselves.
- Many men suggested they had concerns for their children regarding financial security, crime, too much or too little

> freedom in society, and for some men, the potential threat to
> their daughters' sexual integrity.
>
> - A dominant theme was that of responsibility: to the children, to
>   their partners and to their communities.
>
> - For many men, their religious and spiritual beliefs are very
>   important in the way they see their roles as fathers.
>
> Contact: Robert Williams, Department of Professional Education in
> Community Studies, University of Reading, Earley, Reading RG6 1HY.

It has been worked out that the cost of replacing a mother killed in an
accident would be based on the price of paying someone to look after
her sons (Lewenhak 1992). In 1991 this amounted to £3910 per year
and of course this would be an even higher figure now. The replace-
ment value of the father though, killed at the same time, was based
entirely on the children's dependence on his wages, excluding any
other contribution he might have made to their upbringing. In
monetary terms then, a father's 'value' is likely to be three or four times
that of the mother. But is the father role still completely entangled with
a societal view of fathers as providers?

Father as provider – a notion of involvement?

Historical analysis reveals a socially constructed nature of fatherhood
that still emphasises the 'breadwinner' notion as central, despite being
complemented at various times by moral overseer, sex-role model and
nurturer (Marsiglio 1995). There is no longer such a consensus on what
the role of fathers either is or should be. Central to such a discourse
seems to be the receding role of fathers as providers. Studying fathers in
Northern Ireland, McKeown, Ferguson and Rooney (1999) illustrate
this point by arguing that the main factors affecting fathering include:

- the growth in the number of women working

- the threat to the breadwinning role of men in Northern
  Ireland by high rates of unemployment

- the growth of lone-parent families

- a change in expectations regarding what constitutes a good
  father.

Also writing within a Northern Ireland context, Harland (1997) confirms that the traditional routes to acquiring male status are less attainable (and by this he means particularly employment), so boys prove their manhood through deviant and risk-taking behaviour. Of 25 boys interviewed, all differentiated between male and female roles and all believed they had to provide for the family. Women, these boys believed, were much better at parenting skills than men.

So what seems to have happened over the last 150 years is that fatherhood has been deskilled (Burgess and Ruxton 1996). Perhaps because the 'father as provider' role has been eroded, the 'playful' aspect of fathers is emphasised continually, promoting fatherhood as 'special' and play as 'natural', even where it has been shown that fathers in other cultures are not particularly playful.

Many or most adults in the USA believe the role of fathers has changed (LaRossa 1989). According to Levine (1993), this is due to two trends in fatherhood:

- the large and increasing number of families where children are being raised without the continued presence of a father (in the United States this has increased by 51 per cent since the 1970s)

- the growth in the numbers of fathers who take an active, even primary, role in child rearing.

As have many others, Levine (1993) argues that both trends are tied to changes in women's economic and social status since the 1960s. Competing with such trends though, fathers often receive harsh treatment in the press. 'Bad dad' images are not new, but media attention has drawn attention to such negative exposure (Marsiglio 1995). Although there is little data to demonstrate whether or not public opinion is in line with such images, we do know that perceptions of black fathers are even more negative than those of white fathers (Marsiglio 1995).

Even where women work, their income is rendered invisible and they are first and foremost defined in their carer role (Warin *et al.* 1999). A survey of 200 men and women confirmed that the gender divisions of labour remain entrenched in the values of modern society (Dench 1996). In this study, the majority of interviewees were classed as 'traditional', i.e. following the usual divisions of labour and family role, but a significant minority were classed as 'alternative', emphasising personal choice, resisting convention and negotiating family roles. The final group were classed as 'mixed' – they expressed alternative views but in fact lived within a traditional pattern of parenthood. Breaking some cultural stereotypes, Dench (1996) found that whilst non-European cultural communities showed the least overall support for an alternative family culture, Afro-Caribbeans born or raised in the UK demonstrated the most. Nonetheless, for British men, even where they are ideologically attempting to break free from traditional notions of fatherhood, the idea of father as provider is very powerful.

The parenting–mothering–nurturing chain

It is a major methodological flaw in child abuse intervention research to use the word 'parenting' when in reality it is mothers who are studied (Gough 1993; Gough, Taylor and Boddy 1988). Although caution needs to be exercised in making any generalisations, this argument is illustrated in a recent systematic review of the literature on the links between parenting, social factors and failure to thrive. (Failure to thrive is where a child does not grow according to population norms and where no organic basis for the child's condition has been detected (Taylor 2000). In the past this has been referred to as non-organic failure to thrive.)

Of 138 studies that met the inclusion criteria, only one attempted directly to include fathers. The remainder looked at either maternal behaviours or mother–infant dyads. Most subsumed these under the term 'parenting', though. In the single study that did try to involve fathers (Dubowitz et al. 1989), the attempt was abandoned because it was too difficult – fathers would either not comply with the research protocol or they were always absent. This might seem a stark example, but it is probably not uncommon. There are likely to be many such instances, where studies of 'parenting' are in fact studies of 'mothering'. Research on the long-term effects of home visitation and *parental* caregiving, important though this is, actually uses a sample of 400 *women* (Olds et al. 1997a; Olds, Henderson and Kitzman 1997b).

This reinforces a chain of attitudes that is evident in both the research and assessment. Pregnancy prevention programmes, for example, almost always concentrate on females (Levine 1993). Such examples lead to what we term the parenting–mothering–nurturing chain: *Parenting actually means mothering, which is a female activity.*

Mothering implies nurturing which, as carried out by women, includes domestic tasks.

It has been argued cogently in the literature that the role of mothering is synonymous with the role of nurturing. Warin *et al.* (1999) have sug-

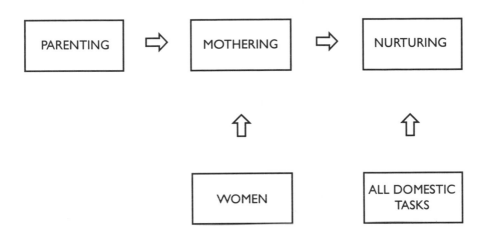

Figure 2.1 The parenting–mothering–nurturing chain in which 'parenting' is used to denote 'mothering', which is carried out by women and includes all domestic tasks.

gested that the way women parent is seen as *the* way to parent, because women are seen as more sensitive, better at communication, calmer and more patient (a very debatable point, but one commonly heard). Nurturing tasks are seen as mothering tasks and mothering tasks are in fact nurturing tasks. These nurturing tasks, when synonymous with mothering, include domestic and household chores. There is a different connotation for men who nurture, however, where 'nurturing' for them tends to focus on direct child care responsibilities. 'Men do work, women do housework' (R. Barker 1994, p.107). There is no equivalent chain when considering the role of men as fathers.

The literature abounds with examples of this chain, and it is not just found in the research – women themselves may contribute to the disparity. One study reveals that many women do not trust men to be good enough at the parenting role, a view often shared by the fathers themselves (Clarke and Popay 1998). It is perhaps an indictment that some practitioners do not consider the father to have a role in child care at all. Chalmers (1992) gives an example of a health visitor who had worked with other professionals for a number of years in attempting to prevent abuse and neglect with one family. On being questioned though, the health visitor had little to offer as regards the father: she had conceptualised the mother as caretaker, and the father, in her view, was not considered important.

We would like to believe that such instances are isolated examples. Modern fathers do not want to be peripheral figures in their children's lives and although full-time mothers may spend more time with their children, there is a tendency to exaggerate the amount of actual interaction they do with the children (Lamb 1981b).

A qualitative study on parenthood (Clarke and Popay 1998) highlighted three types of father: the 'nouveaux traditionalists', who talked enthusiastically about parenting but whose parenting was difficult to discern in practice; the 'pragmatists', who saw their role as that of provider; and the 'egalitarians', who actively pursued equality in parenting. Even when fathers were committed to a parenting role, they expressed more reluctance to be involved in the routine labour of parenting. Clarke and Popay highlighted the important point that there are less class differences than might be anticipated, in that working-class men were as likely to seek 'new fatherhood' as middle-class fathers were to be traditionalists. Similarly men interviewed in a sample of 30 new husbands and fathers articulated a large and involved notion of fatherhood (Cohen 1993), again with little reference to their socio-economic status. Work-centred definitions of fatherhood were inadequate for their beliefs.

A Framework of Roles

There is a plethora of possible roles, all of which either overlap with, or complement the mother role. We suggest that different discourses about the different roles for a father tend to fall into one or more of the following categories:

1. A partner with the mother; this can either take the traditional form where the mother carries responsibility for nurture and the father for financial provision and discipline, or the non-traditional role in which both parents share both roles.

2. An 'alternative mother', where the man is the primary caretaker for the children.

3. A luxury, where the father is 'good with his children' and offers support to the mother.

4. A unique father role, where the man offers something that a mother cannot, such as offering a good male role model.

These different accounts tend to describe the role of the father in different ways. Fathers may describe their own role in one or more of these ways. Practitioners may attempt to engage with a father with one or more of these roles in mind. Being aware of these categories may begin to expand our assessment of what is meant by fatherhood within the particular families that health and social care professionals deal with. With a clearer view about what they mean by the role, practitioners can extend the narrow slots which can be used to pigeonhole both men and women in parenting debates, and embrace a wider framework. If our own views of fathers cannot be challenged, they cannot be expanded.

The father role – in partnership

In the first description of fatherhood, a child-rearing relationship based on partnership, there are the subdivisions into traditional or non-traditional roles (see Figure 2.2). It is assumed that fathers take more responsibility for child care now than in previous generations and that such child care is more than ever before seen as partnership. One way of viewing partnership is embodied in the dominant traditional notion of the father as breadwinner and disciplinarian. This is seen as complementing the mother's nurturing role. Another model of partnership is the emerging 'new fatherhood' which consists of shared care, usually referred to as 'non-traditional' fatherhood. The rhetoric suggests that this non-traditional type of partnership is increasing, but in reality such partnership models are uncommon. So whilst unemployed men may take on more housework and child care, they still tend to view themselves as 'failed providers' (C. Lewis 2000). As discussed earlier in the chapter, although the view of the father's role as that of provider is changing, it remains a common understanding of what is meant by a traditional partnership.

Partnership	
Traditional	*Non-traditional*
Provider	Equality in all child-rearing tasks
Disciplinarian	May include shared domestic tasks
Role model	
Play and homework	

Figure 2.2 The aspects of fatherhood associated with 'traditional' partnership and 'non-traditional' partnership.

In a study of intact families of which half were 'non-traditional' families (where the primary caregiver was the father), the non-traditional families believed in equal sharing, whilst the traditional ones also expressed a belief in sharing, but not always on an equal basis (Geiger 1996). It has been shown that the more mothers become involved in the labour market, the more fathers become involved in parenting and domestic tasks, *but* the major responsibility for child care remains that of the mother (Ferri and Smith 1995). Whilst women may embrace androgynous notions of fatherhood, not many men actually practise them, and there is little evidence that practice has changed at even half the rate of the apparent ideological shifts that go with it (LaRossa 1989).

This traditional role division is deeply entrenched and it is not unique to Britain. For a quarter of a century Sweden has promoted gender equality by policies designed to encourage men to be more nurturing and women to be more involved in paid employment (Haas 1993). This has proved to be reasonably successful – women are almost as likely to be employed as men are and men have an increased participation in child care. Even in Sweden, however, it is rare to find fathers who have assumed an *equal* responsibility for care of children. As in Britain, more women than men work part-time and women continue to take the main responsibility for children, especially when they are unwell.

Walby (1990) cautions against the generous interpretation of studies which show that men are more involved in child care. More women than ever are involved in the labour market and consequently they spend less time on housework, so of course statistics for women involved entirely in child care have reduced. This does not mean that the numbers of men involved in child care are necessarily greater however, and interpreting such statistics as indicating a fair division of household duty is probably false.

However, it is not always acknowledged that, even though it is generally women who hold the main responsibility for *organising* child care, the father is the most common source of child care for working women in Britain and the USA (Ferri and Smith 1995). It should not be presumed that men are reluctant or incapable of looking after children, but that the mother needs to recruit them into that role. In fact, it has been shown that fathers are just as involved as mothers with their children and do not differ in the frequency with which they engage in the majority of behaviours (Parke and Tinsley 1981). The amount of stimulation and affectional behaviour depends, though, on the opportunity afforded fathers to hold the child. It is interesting, however, that Parke and Tinsley showed that during stressful times (for example, around giving birth), families, no matter how egalitarian, all reverted to traditional role. The parenting styles of mothers and fathers have been shown to be remarkably similar and where they differ, this tends to be related to situation as opposed to gender (Burgess and Ruxton 1996).

By exploring some of the 'tasks' of parenting, it becomes clear that 'partnership' does not extend equally into the spheres of mothering and fathering. The research about whether the partnership role (in either traditional or non-traditional form) is of benefit to children is unconvincing. One study that focused on whether or not men were good for the welfare of women and children (Oakley and Rigby 1998) concludes that children can benefit materially from the presence of fathers. However, in part this is due to the ability of the mother to buffer the child from the more negative aspects of the father's role. Men in this study could cause as much stress as they relieved and were not always seen as an asset (see Box 2.2).

Box 2.2 Are men good for the welfare of women and children?

The Social Support and Pregnancy Outcome (SSPO) study was under-taken between 1985 and 1989 to test the hypothesis that providing extra social support in pregnancy would improve the health of women and their babies. Oakley and Rigby (1998) explored five subsets of the SSPO to throw light on the question 'Are men good for the welfare of women and children?'

One in five mothers cares for children in one-parent households, even though 90 per cent had the child within marriage or cohabitation. Lone mothers were socially different to those living with a partner, with considerably less family income, lower educational levels, no access to a car and tending to live in rented accommodation. The health of children in households with men is better than those in households without. Women living without men appear to have poorer health than those who have a partner.

Within households where a father is present, material resources are not always divided equally between mothers and fathers. The control, management and budgeting of financial resources are gender-differenti-ated functions.

Domestic participation by men is generally low. Even where they were described as 'very helpful', the primary responsibility for taking care of the home and the children falls to women. As children get older, men get less helpful both around the house and in relation to child care. There is also a hierarchy of male preference, where helping with child care is far more likely than doing the cooking.

Even where men were not seen as particularly helpful with domestic and child care arrangements, they provided a level of social support to the generally disadvantaged women in the SSPO study. However, this too declined over time.

Living with a man does not necessarily mean being helped or sup-ported by him. Women are exposed to his problems as well and need to support him too. Women who reported problems in the relationship were 6.3 times more likely to have poor psychological health.

It has been suggested that whilst 'new fatherhood' is seen positively and is encouraged, its dangers must also be exposed. 'New fatherhood' perhaps also insidiously strengthens men's control over women (Segal

1990). In engaging with and assessing the parenting roles of the families they deal with, health visitors talk about their 'mums' with some frequency. If we begin to talk about 'parents' instead, it is possible that partnership roles will be acknowledged for the strengths and weaknesses they can bring to child care.

The father role – as alternative mothers

The father role can also be conceptualised as an alternative 'mother' role. Although there is limited research evidence about this type of role, it again highlights the potential and limitations of the reality. The alternative mother position is illustrated well with reference to the Dustin Hoffman film *Tootsie*. Here Hoffman not only makes a better mother than most women, he makes a better woman as well (Segal 1990). A spate of similar films have cast 'strong' men into child care roles, but rather than emphasising how fathers 'parent', they highlight (often through humour) the alternative role fathers have when they take on a 'mothering' role.

If men have primary responsibilities, either permanently or temporarily, for child care arrangements, the question posed is this: do they or can they also take on all the obligations that are embodied in concepts of motherhood? The research indicates that even men who have the primary responsibility for child care rarely do so from the moment of birth (Geiger 1996). Evidence from a number of sources suggests that men who take on the 'alternative mother' role do not do so in the same way as mothers do (Clarke and Popay 1998; Geiger 1996; Johnson 1988). Even when fathers are committed to a parenting role, they express more reluctance to be involved in the routine labour of parenting (Clarke and Popay 1998). For example, the priority given to domestic chores is much less than one expects from a traditional mother, but time allocated to play and having fun is increased. There is a lack of empirical evidence to suggest whether this is a negative or a positive experience for the child.

It is very clear, though, that if women were to dismiss household, organisational and nutritional responsibilities in the same way that men – who may still be perceived as good fathers – can when looking after children, society and professionals alike would view them as poor mothers. Figure 2.3 represents one way of illustrating the difference between mother as mother and father as 'mother'. 'Fathering' thus

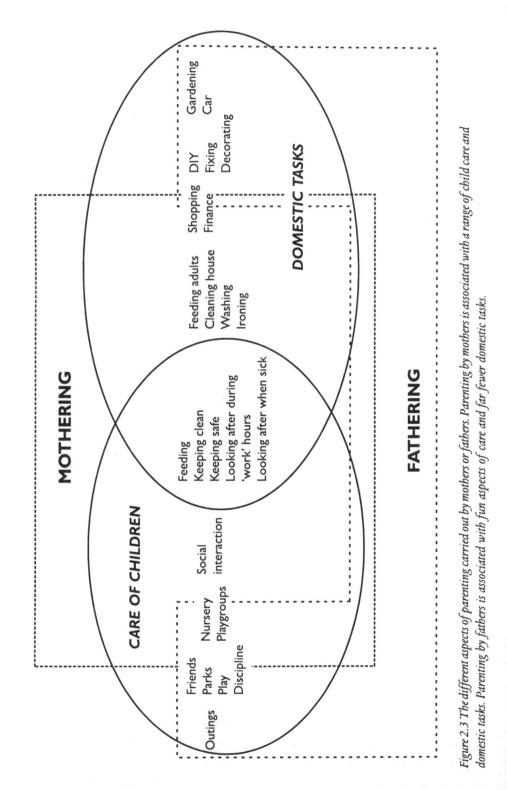

MOTHERING

FATHERING

CARE OF CHILDREN

DOMESTIC TASKS

Outings
Friends
Parks
Play
Discipline

Nursery
Playgroups

Social
interaction

Feeding
Keeping clean
Keeping safe
Looking after during
'work' hours
Looking after when sick

Feeding adults
Cleaning house
Washing
Ironing

Shopping
Finance

DIY
Fixing
Decorating

Gardening
Car

Figure 2.3 The different aspects of parenting carried out by mothers or fathers. Parenting by mothers is associated with a range of child care and domestic tasks. Parenting by fathers is associated with fun aspects of care and far fewer domestic tasks.

clearly does not mean taking on the mothering role as carried out by women. Interestingly, in a study of 35 lone fathers, R. Barker (1994) found that all had been involved in reshaping their gender roles, but were not self-made 'new men'.

There has been a significant growth in the number of lone parents in Britain (Rowlingson and McKay 1998),which has triggered a focus on lone mothers as a social problem. However, the number of mothers being approached by the Child Support Agency to provide financial support for children being cared for by fathers has trebled since 1994 (*Daily Telegraph* 1998). Many of these fathers may have new partners, but the implication is that there are an increasing number of lone fathers. Hansen's (1986) study of single fathers suggests that men can develop very effective interactions with their children, and 'exhibit the potential that all men have for a more involved, caring, primary relationship with children' (p.193). This is probably true, although it should be pointed out that in this case the single fathers were a volunteer sample and interpreting the results too generally may be unwise.

The roles that men can and should play in their children's lives are not clear-cut. On the one hand there is increased recognition of the potential for men to nurture and care for children in the ways that mothers traditionally have. However, on the other hand, social structures do not appear to have shifted sufficiently to facilitate this potential. Men who are not main earners in a family and stay at home to look after children receive little compensatory recognition for their contribution to the social fabric as parents (C. Lewis 2000). Fathering continues to be defined in terms of activities identified with mothering.

The father role – as a luxury

In this discourse the father is perceived as a luxury or as an add-on extra in parenting (Daniel and Taylor 1999). As Oakley and Rigby (1998) suggest, even bad men are perceived as having their good sides and are often viewed as better than no man at all. It is not uncommon to hear women speak of their partners as being 'a good dad', or saying 'he's great with the kids', as if this were not only quite a surprise, but an added bonus. Women who talk like this are often envied.

Mothers are not ascribed the same terms with the same regularity however. It appears that society generally expects so little from fatherhood that if a man takes any practical interest in the child's welfare and adopts a purposeful role in the parenting responsibility, many women regard him as something of a hero. Unlike mothers, fathers are not assessed negatively for their poor housekeeping, and are appraised positively if they are seen undertaking such tasks (Swift 1995). For example, when meeting fathers who express knowledge and ability in child care, health visitors have been known to shower these men with praise and credit them with exaggerated levels of expertise (Williams and Robertson 1999).

Another aspect of the 'father as luxury' discourse is demonstrated in a study of lone fathers. None of the men in this study felt that their masculinity was diminished by the experience of becoming a lone father and most felt that others respected them for being lone fathers (R. Barker 1994). There is a different societal and governmental response to lone mothers. So while lone fathers may attract sympathy and respect, lone mothers are blamed for a range of adverse child behaviours, from classroom disruption to criminal activity. Within 'good enough parenting' debates, this raises an interesting question. Is it easier for men to get a 'good enough parent' badge than it is for mothers?

Such findings strike a chord with us. During the process of putting this book together we attended a conference dedicated to fatherhood. One of the delegates was the father of an infant and he brought the child with him. It was announced by the convenor that this man was the primary caretaker of the child and at a fatherhood conference this was perceived as wonderful. (We point out that we have no idea whether the father was consulted about the announcement.) As about half of the delegates were female, it could be assumed that more than a few also had children and took primary responsibility for them most of the time. Such aspects about women are never announced and there would usually be a certain expectation that alternative child care arrangements would have been made. At the very least, conference organisers rarely boast that women, present with their children, are those mainly responsible for child care. So the very idea of a man able to be the primary caretaker of a child is not perceived as a luxury just by women and by society, but also by professionals.

The 'father as luxury' dimension is likely to exist in parallel with other father roles, but more than any other aspect of fatherhood it reinforces the domesticity of women that often undermines and disempowers them. Health visitors and social workers who comment on men being helpful around the house or taking their share in the school run are usefully documenting an assessment of the family environment. It is suggested, however, that this dimension not only disempowers both parties, it can sometimes create a barrier within child protection work, resulting in risk going unnoticed. A father as a 'luxury' may be perceived synonymously with a 'good' father and consequently important aspects of a child–parent relationship may be missed. Despite the rhetoric then, who is the 'luxury' really for?

The father role – as unique in itself

'To father' literally only means 'to impregnate' (M.M. Johnson 1988) and it is difficult to disentangle the father role as something unique of itself from the alternative mother or add-on extra roles. In unpicking the role of fathers though, consideration needs to be given to such a unique father role. Writing about masculinity in crisis, Clare (2000) asks if men still have a role as fathers, what is it that they are? What can they bring to society that society cannot do without, and how do they become good fathers? Clare argues that as a social role fatherhood has shrunk. Despite attempts to resuscitate this with the emergence of 'new men', most men remain 'old'.

Contained within the debate surrounding lone parents is an inherent accusation that women cannot be 'good' mothers unless there is also a father in the household. Alternatively, is it possible for men to be fathers without there also being a mother? This discourse could include ideas of role modelling, playing or taking a turn in changing or washing nappies. It could also contain expectations for training sons for their own future role as fathers or daughters as mothers. It is difficult, however, to envisage a unique role that is fatherhood in the absence of an incumbent motherhood in partnership.

Edwards (1995) offers clues in this debate. She discusses the significant notion of teaching 'parenting skills' that is used by both health and social care professionals. Such sessions tend to focus on single mothers, but as Edwards questions, why are single mothers more in need of being taught parenting skills than women who live with men? The unique role of the man inferred here appears to be that he somehow imbues the mother with the essential parenting skills and knowledge that she lacks without him. It is acknowledged that many health visitors encourage men to be involved in parenting classes, but there is a lack of a firm evidence base to show how universally this is practised.

Researchers have often overlooked fathering activities because they are so diverse (Warin *et al.* 1999). Whereas the father's provider role is visible through his comings and goings, mothers fit their work around child care and their work is consequently more invisible. Warin *et al.* (1999) argue that women want men to be more involved, but on their terms. Where they have cornered the market on aspects such as listening, men have found alternatives, such as helping with homework. However, playing remains the main role men see themselves as having ownership of (Warin *et al.* 1999). As Burghes *et al.* (1997) point out though, this may be artefact and stereotypical: it is what people *think* fathers do.

In one description of being a man (Keen 1992), scant attention is paid to fatherhood, although Keen suggests that the most important thing a father can do is to create a sense of welcome for the child. He sees children as 'playmates' of the father. Keen's results reveal that 75 per cent of men surveyed rate being a good husband and father as central to their perception of ideal masculinity, but 70 per cent are unready for this view to be translated into that of househusband. As has been pointed out: 'acting as a wife and assuming her duties is seen as demeaning for a man, while "wearing the pants" does not demean a woman in the same way' (Johnson 1988, p.7).

If there is a unique role that is fatherhood, then it should be possible to state the extent to which fathers are a resource for their children, regardless of any relationship they may have with the child's mother. Within this particular discourse, the unique role of fatherhood apparently concerns the improvement a father gives to mothering roles. This is limiting in two ways. First, it undermines women by regarding them as better mothers in the presence of a father and second, it weakens men because their 'uniqueness' is not generally defined as useful.

A man, of course, can be a 'male role model' for his son. This term frequently occurs in the literature about fathers. But the concept is not well defined. Who defines what a 'good' role model is? Some might suggest that a good male role model is a man who is prepared to show his 'feminine' qualities, others that it is a man who provides his son with an example of 'masculine' traits.

Key Issues from Theory

1. Within current child care provision there is an absence of theoretical frameworks to provide coherence between theories of fatherhood and the real world of practice.

2. Although more women now go out to work, there are few signs that men are more involved in child care.

3. Fathers are not less talented at child care than are women, but are more reluctant to take on this role.

4. The majority of people emphasise the context of family life, rather than its structure (e.g. married or not).

5. There are clearer definitions of mothering than there are of fathering.

6. Male gender roles are bound up in societal and cultural notions of fatherhood, so emphasising individual behaviours is not always useful.

7. The culture of fatherhood may have changed, but the conduct of fatherhood has remained much the same.

8. The provider role of fathers remains a dominant theme.

9. There is an implicit chain in descriptions of parenting: for women this includes domestic tasks.

10. There are many overlapping roles for fathers: partner, 'alternative mother', luxury and unique. All can coexist and all can be challenged, but consideration of different notions is important in assessment.

Defining the Father Role: Issues for Practice

In practice, child care professionals may call upon the different roles of fathers in different ways. This is not necessarily a problem; however, it is not always clear that the underlying assumptions are made explicit or that they chime with the values of the family involved. The gulf between the rhetoric and reality of engaging men is not confined to health visitors or social workers. Child protection language emphasises the value of engaging with fathers, but in practice, child care structures continue to reinforce traditional models of role segregation.

The first step in providing a theoretical framework for practice is to break into the cycle of expectations. This may entail changing the language of engagement with all parents, both men and women. Once it is recognised that a number of unspoken assumptions are made about parenting roles, then these assumptions can be brought into the open. It may be that it is the mother who carries the main responsibility for child care; even so, this should explicitly be explored and acknowledged with the parents. Fathers may in fact be much more involved in the parenting of their children than is obvious to the practitioner. If the concept of parenting tasks is broadened to include all aspects of physical and emotional care of children there is more scope to ask questions about who does what. Thus, even if it is established that the mother provides the main nurturing care, there is still considerable scope to explore the role or potential role of the father (or other male partner). The greater involvement of a father is only of benefit to the individuals involved if they hold this as a value themselves (Lamb, Pleck and Levine 1986).

How can practitioners use the four role categories that were explored earlier in assessment and support of families? Although the roles overlap, taking them separately may provide a useful framework to guide practice.

As a partner with the mother

Fatherhood as partnership can either take the traditional form where the mother carries responsibility for nurture and the father for financial provision and discipline, or the non-traditional role in which both parents share both roles. When considering the impact of socio-economic disadvantage, this category is extremely important, as it is so often the father who provides financial support. Whilst he may be psychologically and/or physically absent, this aspect of his partnership role in child rearing requires explicit exploration. For example, a child may be bullying other children at school in order to take their lunch money. This money is then used to feed the gas meter. Because the mother has taken control of the 'housekeeping', the father may not have realised that rates have increased and no one may have dared ask him for more. Although it would be simplistic to suggest that this may be the only reason for the child's bullying behaviour, using a partnership model may provide a partial solution to one immediate problem in this family.

Another example is provided where a child protection referral concerns the problem of a child out of control. At the case conference there may well be discussion about the 'lack of a male role model'. What is sometimes ignored is that this kind of debate centres on the assumption that it is a father's job to discipline children. However, it is necessary to ascertain whether or not the family hold this value and if they do, then the aim of involving the father may be to support him in the traditional role as a father in partnership with the mother. On the other hand, families may prefer a more non-traditional approach in which parenting tasks are shared. In these families the child protection professionals need to discuss with both parents how best to support both of them in these roles. This might entail arranging to meet always with both parents together. Gilligan (1998) has described the potential benefit of fathers who give support to their partners in their roles of respite giver, mediator, protector's supporter, perspective giver and source of discipline. So within this category, practitioners need to ascertain what the views of the parents are regarding parenting roles, then work with them in supporting and exploring these.

As an 'alternative mother'

In this category, fathers could be seen as 'alternative mothers', taking on some or all of those tasks generally assigned to women. This can happen in both traditional and non-traditional families, although practitioners need to work with the values the family themselves hold. If the child protection referral concerns neglect for example, then there may be an opportunity to involve the father in sharing the child care tasks. This may be counter to the traditional role values he holds and he may need support in entering into this new type of partnership position. Alternatively, if the child's mother is unable to 'mother' according to societal expectations, then the purpose of engagement of the father may incorporate elements of him becoming a father who 'mothers' by encouraging him to take on the prime responsibility for the child. This may include support with his self-esteem, as this is as yet a relatively unusual situation. Although men typically receive more practical support from friends and family when they take on the 'alternative mother' role, it is nonetheless fraught with potential difficulties that must be acknowledged. For example, it may be troublesome to find public nappy-changing facilities and many so-called parents' groups tend to involve only mothers. This may be an irritation or an embarrassment, but it can also lead to severe social isolation when fathers are excluded from activities such as 'mother and baby' swimming classes or nursery parent days. As men have been shown to use more internal coping strategies than mothers do (Becker *et al.* 1993), practitioners need to recognise and support the different gendered responses to parenting (Brown and Barbarin 1996; Mack and Trew 1991).

As a luxury

The father as luxury category is where the father is 'good with his children' and offers support to the mother. Some families are structured in such a way that the father is not able or willing to take on such a role. Nevertheless, he should not be excluded automatically from taking on an indirect role in the protection of children from further harm. For some women the male partner is someone who can offer support and encouragement. Practitioners need to assess this and if this role appears to be the main asset he can offer, the limits and extent of this support need to be explored openly. Practitioners also need to reflect on whether their assessment of a father as a luxury (he helps with the feeds/nappies/school run) means there is a danger that a full assessment of any risk he also poses is overlooked. For example, a health visitor may have concerns about the poor development of the youngest child in a family of six. The assessment has included asking the mother about the father. The mother's view is that he is very good with all the children, even though they may not all be his biological offspring. He always baths them, prepares most of the meals, gets up in the night when one of them is crying and is, in her view, wonderful. There are a number of possible implications to this scenario that the health visitor might want to consider. For example, if he is really so wonderful, is the mother losing her bond with the youngest child by allowing him to do everything with the child while she does little herself? Is he more used to older children and thus, unknowingly, providing the wrong kind of stimulation or nutrition to the youngest? Does she feel guilty and inadequate because although he is a 'better dad' than any others she has met, she still feels unable to cope? Although he might be 'wonderful' with the children, is he wonderful with her or psychologically or physically abusing her? And in the worst case, even though rare, is he abusing the child behind the facade of his helpfulness? All of these possibilities (and of course many others) could be overlooked by immediate categorisation of the father as a luxury.

As contributing something unique

In this category the man offers something unique that a mother cannot; for example, he may offer a good male role model. For all child protection referrals there should be the scope to assess the male partner in terms of what he can offer uniquely to the child. There is a tendency to consider a man to be a father only when he is in a relationship with the mother and to ignore him when he is not (Edwards 1998). As part of the process of breaking the cycle of expectations, practitioners can play a vital role in exploring explicitly what the father may be able to offer the child, regardless of any relationship with the mother (Daniel and Taylor 1999). If the child protection referral has arisen because of adolescent identity problems for example, there can still be a role for even an absent father in answering questions about a child's heritage (Ott 1997; Owusu-Bempah and Howitt 1997).

Figure 2.4 provides an assessment of a family where the father's role has been more clearly defined by using these categories. Mentally using such a framework and documenting the results may provide a more holistic approach to supporting such a family.

From Discourse to Practice

Writing 20 years ago, Parke and Tinsley (1981) identified a number of opportunities to improve fathering. They advised:

- Increase the opportunities to learn fatherhood skills.
- Teach the economic realities of fatherhood in school.
- Give men time and practice to implement these skills.
- Give paternity leave wider support.

Parenting Assessment: Towards a Fuller Assessment

Child problem	*Ten-year-old boy accused of vandalism and unruly behaviour. Six-year-old sister has become aggressive at school*	
		Possible action
Partnership (state whether traditional or non-traditional)	Traditional values. Father unemployed, sees the loss of identity as breadwinner as an erosion of his status as father. Mother working at supermarket, but still prefers to take responsibility for child care arrangements and most domestic chores. Father responsible for discipline, but since losing his job is no longer interested.	Parenting classes. Advice on discipline. Work with father's self-esteem. Job clubs. Renegotiate domestic chores in the household. Refer to GP for possible depression.
Alternative mother	Father takes the children to school, but they are often dressed inappropriately and do not appear to have had any breakfast. Father often forgets to pick them up from school as he has fallen asleep because of late nights watching television. Mother cooks and cleans in the evening.	Breakfast clubs. Encourage preparation of clothes etc. the night before. Home help. Encourage to fill days differently, e.g. take on a vegetable plot and prepare vegetables for cooking.
Luxury	Father used to help with the homework, but this now interferes with his television routine.	May need to undertake parallel learning as homework may be too difficult? Can entertain children by reading to them. Reframing views by showing how helping children and mother is a positive role for the father.
Unique	A strong father who always felt he was a good role model, especially to his son. Imaginative and creative, usually provides fun-filled days out. Used to be captain of local football team until a knee operation five years ago.	May need referral for physiotherapy for knee. Are there local fun activities that he can be involved with? Emphasise benefits.

Figure 2.4 A fuller assessment of a child care problem by using different descriptions of the role 'father'.

- Modify maternity ward visiting.

- Support couples in their own ideology of role definitions as much as possible.

How many of these are now reality? Boys need separate programmes, unique to them and not just tagged onto programmes for girls, as illustrated for example by the strong message used in the USA (Levine 1993): *Don't make a baby if you can't be a father.*

Burgess and Ruxton (1996) more recently suggested a number of ways in which father roles can be emphasised:

- Cultural images of fathering need to be widened.

- Education and support for fathers needs to be improved.

- Post-separation conflict between mothers and fathers needs to be reduced.

- Contact between children and parents must be maintained.

Additionally Milner (1996) suggests that there should be an obligatory inclusion of fathers on official forms, not one that is subsumed under parenting and is therefore likely to include only mothers.

Any analysis of fatherhood, though, must consider the differing gendered perspectives on relationships and family life (Marsiglio 1995). Sometimes these will be inhibitory. Fathers may be unwilling to seek help from support services, but this may arise from a lack of awareness of either their existence or of what they actually do, especially as so many are targeted at mothers (Burgess and Ruxton 1996). There is a real need to work with fathers as men, not just as fathers by only offering help with their child care arrangements (Ghate, Shaw and Hazel 2000). The attitude of professionals is absolutely crucial. Box 2.3 describes one attempt to address the needs of fathers.

Box 2.3 Men as fathers:
The Pilton Community Health Project

Pilton Commmunity Health Project has been running since 1984 as a community development project concerned with raising awareness and action on health issues. The area of Greater Pilton has high levels of unemployment, with those in work being poorly skilled and qualified and being in low-paid work. Most of the population survive on low incomes and are dependent on benefits. Consequently poor levels of health associated with poverty are clearly discernible and are amongst the worst in Scotland.

Part of the work of the Pilton Project focuses on men, in recognition that they experience poor levels of health and are less likely than women to make use of community-based resources. Fathers in particular are focused on as a group because their role has been changing. The traditional male breadwinner role, especially important in a working-class community, is being eroded. The Project undertook work with a group of local fathers to determine and address the issues and support available for them in this role, specifically to:

- look at their needs
- provide a forum for discussion
- improve access to resources and information
- explore and challenge male attitudes and values in response to the role of men in family relationships
- increase confidence and self-esteem through work and leisure-based activities.

Recruitment to the Project was low. Of 34 contacts made through nursery classes, 15 men expressed an interest. On average, four men attended each session, and a total of five made use of the child care on offer. Sessions were varied, focusing on health needs, childhood accidents and fatherhood, for example. Feedback was entirely positive, with particular mention made of the sessions on fatherhood and child development. Although there were no objective measures that any of the aims had been met, the fathers felt that it was a success.

Contact: Kate Burton, Pilton Community Health Project, The Health Hut, 3 West Pilton Park, Edinburgh EH4 4EL.

Health visitors and social workers are in the unique position of being able to engage with both men and women in child care and protection. However, in practice 'parenting' tends to imply 'mothering'. Not only does this marginalise men as parents, it places an undue burden on women. Fathers are therefore not being engaged with purposefully within the child care and protection arena. We contend that there are two main reasons for this. First, practitioners have not fully explored what the father role actually means and second, they do not fully assess men's potential as either risk or asset to the child. If we are to move this debate on, health and social care practitioners are in a front-line position to challenge the current disempowering notions of parenting and change rhetoric to reality.

Indeed, if government schemes are to work, we need to understand the diversity of fatherhood as an experience and then concentrate on policies that allow positive father roles to develop (Williams and Robertson 1999).

Key Messages for Practice

1. Practitioners need to be clear about the role they anticipate the man playing and what role he himself considers appropriate.

2. Child care structures need to be reappraised – they currently reinforce traditional models of role segregation.

3. Practitioners need to change the language of engagement with parents.

4. Supporting families should take place within the family's own notions of fatherhood, traditional or non-traditional, not the practitioner's.

5. Where fathers need to be encouraged to be involved in child care counter to their own role or gender values, they may need support and specific advice.

6. There are different gendered responses to parenthood: practitioners must recognise and support these.

7. Any assessment of fatherhood roles must not overlook the element of risk the father may pose.

8. Practitioners should include fathers who do not necessarily have any relationship with the mother in their assessments of what is in the child's best interest.

9. Fathers need to be included specifically in assessments, not subsumed within the parenting category.

10. We need to allow positive fatherhood roles to develop – in practice and in policy.

Try it for Size

Identify three fathers and three mothers from at least three different generations (they don't have to be couples). Ask each of your 'participants' to list the three most important things that a father does or is. This will generate a list of 54 statements. Transfer these onto separate pieces of card, and on the back code them according to generation and gender (e.g. born 1930s, male number two, could be recorded as m30/2). Now ask two colleagues to read only the statements and see if they can identify both gender and generation. Are there any surprises? What does this exercise say about gendered and historical perceptions of the fatherhood role?

Chapter 3

Attachment

Introduction

In this chapter we consider the relevance of attachment theory for working with fathers. In the first part we give an overview of the main components of attachment from the perspectives of the child and the parent. In the second part of the chapter we explore the practice implications of these issues in detail and set out a framework for intervention with fathers based upon attachment theory.

Attachment theory focuses on the primacy of early attachment rela tionships for physical and emotional well-being. It is used both to understand problems in the parent–child relationship and to guide practice (Fahlberg 1991). For example, if a child is showing challenging behaviour, the theory may suggest that the child's attachment to the main carer is insecure. After close attention to the carer–child interactions a health visitor may make specific suggestions aimed at helping the caretaker to foster more secure attachments.

Unfortunately, attachment theory has a poor historical record with regard to fathers. The early writings of Bowlby (1951) concentrated on the role of the mother as the primary caretaker and the vast majority of empirical and observational studies have been of mother–child dyads. Although this view has since been challenged (Rutter 1981), the notion of the importance of attachment to the *mother* has been tenacious, both in general society and specifically within the child care professions. Also, although there have been some cross-cultural studies, the majority of the detailed empirical work has been with white, nuclear families.

Attachment theory has been refined and developed to incorporate the potential not only for primary attachment to the father, but for there to be multiple attachment figures (Schaffer 1996; Schaffer and Emerson 1964). That different ethnic groups may have different cultural approaches to the organisation of primary child care has also been recognised. So, it is now established that there is nothing intrinsic about mothers to make them primary attachment figures; rather, the social order places them in the position of being the most likely to become primary caretakers and main attachment figures. Fathers can successfully become main carers, and, if they do, can become primary attachment figures (Geiger 1996). Further, children can demonstrate close attachment to a number of different adults at the same time as well as showing strong ties to siblings (Dunn 1993; M. Lewis 1994).

Therefore the main message for practice that emerges from current attachment theory is that it does not matter who the attachment figure is, as long as there is at least one (Schaffer 1996). This provides a theoretical basis for the recognition of fathers, either as supplemental or main attachment figures. It also allows for different cultural experience. However, this message has not been incorporated into current practice in other than a piecemeal way.

It is ironic that a theory with such sexist roots has developed into one that is gender-blind. Paradoxically it is this gender-blind aspect that is a limitation for meaningful practice development. Without attention to the different structural influences upon men and women in society it is difficult to shift practice to embrace fathers fully as attachment figures. It is not enough simply to swap the term 'mother' for 'parent'. To illustrate, in a major text on fostering and adoption based on attachment theory, terms such as 'parents' and 'carers' are used throughout the text (Fahlberg 1991). However, the overwhelming majority of 'parents' described in the numerous case examples are mothers. Of the few fathers mentioned, several are described as violent or abusive. What message are practitioners to take from this? Perhaps that the rhetorical use of 'parents' cannot override the reality of practice with 'mothers'.

Attachment theory principally focuses on the development of relationships, but without attention to the different structural influences upon men and women in society the theory is limited in the guidance that practitioners can take for practice with fathers. Knowing that fathers can potentially be attachment figures is one thing, translating this into practice with individual mothers and fathers is quite another.

Further, consideration of structural, cultural and ethnic issues and an understanding of the roles of fathers and mothers in our society are essential. The overwhelming picture is one of potential: potential that with all the right circumstances can flourish, but which is often missed or thwarted.

The Main Components of Attachment

An understanding of the child's role in attachment is as important as an understanding of the adult's role, because attachment is essentially an interactive process. First we shall look at attachment theory from the perspective of the child and propose that there is nothing to suggest that attachment to the father need not be of a similar quality as attachment to the mother. Then we shall look at attachment from the perspective of the father and suggest that it is this aspect that can lead to differences in attachment relationships.

From the child's perspective

It was the biological basis of attachment that was drawn on by Bowlby (1969) when he first set out a systematic analysis of attachment theory. According to the theory, attachment evolved to promote children's survival. For a child to become attached to a particular adult, to seek them out when threatened, to discriminate between them and a stranger and to use them as a safe base from which to explore the world of objects and other people is clearly biologically sensible. Young babies and children are highly dependent and consequently highly vulnerable. A mechanism that binds them to a more mature being is adaptive.

However, as with so many human biological functions, attachment also has an emotional component. There is now an overwhelming body of research that links emotional well-being with the quality of attachments.

Children seem to be innately prepared to make attachments from infancy and attachment behaviours are demonstrated in various forms throughout life. Most empirical research has been carried out with young children and, as a result, attachment has been classified into different types which will be briefly summarised. (For a more detailed discussion of attachment types see Howe's (1995) text.)

Attachment is a natural human phenomenon which is not easily pinned down experimentally. However, Ainsworth *et al.* (1978) developed a fairly robust methodology for classifying attachment. It is known as the 'Strange situation' and has stood the tests of time and replication. The principle classification is of *secure* and *insecure* attachment (the categories can be seen either as discrete types, or as two ends of a dimension). In summary the methodology involves observing caregivers and children at home and during a series of standard 'laboratory' tests, of which there are a number of variations.

In one sequence the toddler and caregiver are brought to a room where there are toys, and the child's behaviour is observed in the presence of the caregiver. A stranger enters and attempts to engage with the child. The caregiver leaves the baby alone with the stranger for a short time and then returns. The stranger leaves and, after spending some time with the baby, the caregiver leaves the child alone, the stranger enters and is alone with the child. Finally the caregiver returns and the stranger leaves. This sequence allows observation of the child's exploration of the room and toys with the caregiver present or absent or in the presence of a stranger. The child's willingness to explore is an indication of how relaxed they feel. The sequence also allows observation of the child's reaction to separation from and reunion with the caregiver and reactions to a stranger. Such observations provide insight into the quality of attachment to the caregiver and whether the child shows some discrimination in their behaviour towards known adults and strangers.

Children who are classified as showing *secure* attachment will play happily when their caregiver is present, will protest when they leave and go to them for comfort on their return. They will show some wariness of the stranger and choose their caregiver for comfort. Children who are classified as *insecure* may show one of three patterns. If *avoidant* they tend to shun the caregiver on return and show similar behaviour towards a stranger as the caregiver. If *ambivalent*, children appear to want comfort from the caregiver on reunion, but at the same time show resistance to comfort, for example by squirming out of a hug. A further form of insecure attachment, known as *disorganized/disoriented* is demonstrated in a mixture of reactions.

Secure attachment is therefore an emotional tie which, it is largely agreed, comprises a set of well-established components:

SECURE BASE AND SAFE HAVEN

Children require a secure base from which to set out to explore the social and physical world. This can be observed when a young child crawls away from his or her attachment figure to play with some attractive toys, but glances over occasionally to check that the caregiver is still there. In adolescence the attachment figure can provide the 'base camp' from which gradually to move away from home (Gilligan 1997).

As a corollary to providing a secure base, the attachment figure must also provide a safe haven that can be crawled back to quickly when a stranger enters the room, or retreated to following the first heartbreak.

PROXIMITY SEEKING AND SEPARATION PROTEST

Children's attachment can be demonstrated by the extent to which they seek proximity to the attachment figure or protest when forcibly separated from them and mourn their loss. A baby left alone whose cries bring the attachment figure running has effectively brought about proximity. A young adult who frequently phones home is finding another form of proximity.

Protest and grief at the loss of an attachment figure is an all-pervasive phenomenon. The toddler screaming when left at the nursery is a graphic illustration of separation anxiety.

The majority of attachment studies have been carried out with mothers and they tend to show about 60 per cent of children to be securely attached, 25 per cent to be insecure avoidant, 10 per cent insecure ambivalent and 5 per cent insecure disorganised (Howe 1995). Longitudinal studies have demonstrated the endurance of early patterns of attachment.

Far fewer studies have been carried out using other potential attachment figures, in particular the father. The first question is whether a father can act as an attachment figure at all, the second is whether the patterns of attachment to the mother and father are similar, and the third is whether the type of attachment to the father is related to the type of attachment to the mother.

Can fathers be attachment figures?

As long ago as 1964 Schaffer and Emerson found, on the basis of maternal report, that by 18 months most infants will protest at separation from the father (Schaffer and Emerson 1964). Other studies have also suggested that by eight months most infants are attached to both parents (Kotelchuck 1976; Lamb, Pleck and Levine 1986).

The answer to the question is, therefore:

- Infants can indeed form attachments to fathers.

ARE PATTERNS OF ATTACHMENT TO FATHERS SIMILAR TO PATTERNS OF ATTACHMENT TO MOTHERS?

As to whether patterns of attachment are similar, there is some evidence that when under stress, and in a position to choose between the mother and father, infants will turn to the mother. However, there is also some evidence that infants will show more smiling and vocalising to fathers (Lamb 1981b; Parke and Tinsley 1981). As has been discussed in more detail in the previous chapter, there is a tendency for fathers' and mothers' roles to diverge very quickly after birth, with mothers taking the primary responsibility for caretaking and fathers for play and fun. Although it is dangerous to generalise, where such a role divergence occurs it would not be surprising for there to be differences in patterns of attachment.

Geiger (1996) carried out a direct comparison between families where the mother acted as primary caregiver and the father worked, with families where the father acted as primary caregiver and the mother worked. He found the primary caregiver behaviour to be very similar in both settings, although the fathers still engaged in a little more rough and tumble and play than mothers. Under stress and in a position to choose the children tended to go to the primary caregiver regardless of whether male or female. So, potentially, and given the appropriate circumstances, infants can behave towards fathers just as they do towards mothers.

The answer to the question is, therefore:

- Patterns of attachment to mothers and fathers can be similar, but it depends on who is the primary caregiver.

IS THE TYPE OF ATTACHMENT TO THE FATHER RELATED TO THE TYPE OF ATTACHMENT TO THE MOTHER?

There is debate about the extent to which the attachment style to the father depends on the attachment style to the mother. Attachment theory states that the child constructs an inner working model that represents a template for their relationships. However, there is considerable discussion about the distribution of such inner working models. One position is that there is a hierarchy of attachment models, with the one derived from the primary caregiver at the top. This inner working model then defines the overall style of interaction, but there are also others that are more specific to the particular relationship (Collins and Read 1994). For example, a child's secure relationship with her mother could be at the top of the hierarchy and in general the child might tend towards secure attachments but show insecure attachment to her grand-father. Another position is that children can simultaneously hold differ-ent working models for different people which operate as a network of attachments rather than a hierarchy (M. Lewis 1994).

A number of detailed comparisons of infant behaviours towards the mother and father have been carried out. For one such example, see Box 3.1. Fox, Kimmerly and Schafer (1991) took 11 such studies and carried out a meta-analysis in which all the data was brought together to examine whether there was a relationship between attachment style to the mother and father. They showed, rather differently from Main and Weston (1981), that there was a significant relationship between the styles, so that a child who was secure in relation to the mother was more likely to be secure in relation to the father. However, although the relationship was significant, there was still a substantial proportion of the children (31 per cent) who were secure with one parent and insecure with the other. Both these findings are important for practice. They suggest that if one attachment is secure, then the other is likely to be. But if one relationship is insecure, the potential is there for a secure attachment to be made.

Seen with Father				
Seen with Mother	Avoidant	Secure	Ambivalent	Unclassified
Avoidant	9	9	–	1
Secure	11	15	2	1
Ambivalent	–	2	1	2
Unclassified	2	4	–	2

Figure 3.1 Classifications of infants seen at 12 months and at 18 months with different parents. Table of results reproduced from Main and Weston (1981), with the permission of the Society for Research in Child Development.

Box 3.1 The quality of the toddler's relationship to mother and to father

Several studies have employed Ainsworth's Strange situation methodology to study the patterns of attachment to mothers and fathers and to explore the extent of relationship (concordance) between them. Not only have these studies produced different results, the results can be interpreted differently.

Main's (1981) study aimed to address a number of questions, including:

...whether infant–father attachment relationships resemble infant–mother attachment relationships in terms of Ainsworth's security classifications.

...whether a given infant's security classification with one parent is related to, or is instead independent of, the security classifications with the second parent.

...whether security of attachment to mother and to father, considered separately and jointly, influences social interactions with new persons. (p.932)

Sixty-one infants and their mothers and fathers were recruited through birth records in California. At 12 months the Strange situation was carried out with either the mother (48 infants) or the father (15 infants). At 18 months the Strange situation was carried out with the other parent (48 with father, 15 with mother). This meant all infants had been observed with both the mother and the father. At 20 months 30 infants were seen in the Strange situation again, each with the same parent they had been observed with at 12 months, the aim being to test the stability of the type of attachment. In addition, at 12 months each child was observed in a play session with the mother or father, during which an unknown adult dressed as a clown entered the room and attempted to engage with the child, thus providing a measure of readiness to establish new relationships.

Security classifications were (see Figure 3.1):

- with the mother – 67.4 per cent secure, 28.3 per cent avoidant, 4.3 per cent ambivalent
- with the father – 58.7 per cent secure, 34.8 per cent avoidant, 6.5 per cent ambivalent.

Thus the profile is similar for fathers and mothers. However, no significant correlation was found between classification with the mother and with the father: an infant could show a secure attachment to the mother and an insecure attachment to the father.

Finally, the children most ready to establish relationships with a stranger were secure with mother/non-secure with father; followed by non-secure with mother/secure with father; whilst those insecure with both showed least readiness.

We perhaps tend to think of parents as performing their main function during childhood. However, the research into adult attachments suggests that parents remain as significant attachment figures (Feeney and Noller 1996). A study to explore the hierarchy of attachments in young adults found that over time partners take over from parents as being at the top of the attachment hierarchy for safe haven and secure base (Trinke and Bartholomew 1997). However parents remained as important attachment figures, particularly as a secure base, and although mothers had a key place, fathers also figure highly. A high proportion desired to use father as a secure base, and 58 per cent actually did. Males wanted to use their fathers as a safe haven. The father was ranked as the top in the network by 11 per cent. But for some, although there was an expressed desire to see the father as a secure base, the actual relationship did not facilitate this. One girl described her father as 'emotionally sterile'.

As well as it being known that different inner working models can coexist (whether in a hierarchy or network), it is also known that an inner working model can be self-perpetuating. So a child whose main attachment experience is avoidant is likely to appear stand-offish and to bring about the same kind of relationship with others. What is also known, however, is that, with experience of different kinds of relation-ships, it is possible for the predominant inner working model to change.

The answer to the question is, therefore:

- Types of attachment are usually related, but need not always be.

The need for, and demonstration of, attachment develops from birth and is the expression of a powerful biological imperative. It is a primeval and, at least initially, involuntary and instinctive behaviour. The important conclusion is that, from the tiny baby's point of view, the gender, and indeed the familial relationship of the attachment figure, is beyond their capacity to consider. From the point of view of the child, the essential requirement is for another human being, preferably one who is more mature, to be the object of attachment.

From the adult's perspective

From the point of view of the adult the situation is rather different. As well as being a biological event, the birth of any baby is also a social event and is given its social meaning by the people involved. A child is born into a society with structures and role expectations and to people who carry their own interpretation of social structures and expectations.

For the adult the situation is more complicated than for the child. The child is obviously at the mercy of adult circumstances; the adult, however, is subject to biological, social, cultural, emotional and experiential forces. The attachment role the father takes depends on a range of factors. The factors that contribute to the adult being in a state of readiness to become an attachment figure who will promote secure attachment have been studied. Most of the work has been carried out with women and more research focused specifically on men is needed. The findings, though, can be examined from the male perspective.

In a succinct concept analysis of attachment Goulet *et al.* (1998) set out a model which provides a useful framework within which to consider the factors that promote secure attachment (see Figure 3.2).

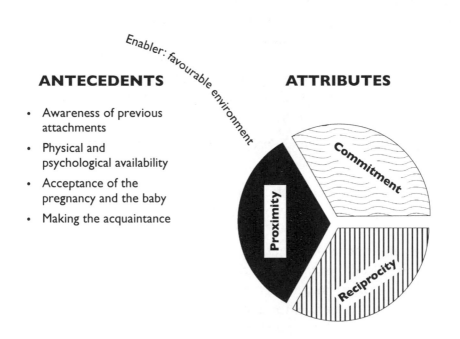

Figure 3.2 The antecedents of parent–infant attachment, adapted from Goulet et al. (1998) with permission of the publishers.

AWARENESS OF PREVIOUS ATTACHMENTS

A person's ability to parent sensitively and to promote secure attachment is closely associated with his or her own attachment history, and more specifically with his or her insight and understanding of past experiences (Howe 1995). A harsh or insecure childhood need not automatically intrude upon the developing relationship with the child as long as there is some opportunity to process that experience and set it at a distance from the new generation.

PHYSICAL AND PSYCHOLOGICAL AVAILABILITY

Attachment is not entirely related to the amount of time spent with the child, rather the quality of that time. Nonetheless, the adult must be able to set aside sufficient physical and emotional space for investing in the relationship with the child.

ACCEPTANCE OF THE PREGNANCY AND THE BABY

Whether the pregnancy is planned or unplanned, the process of attachment is facilitated if the person is not ambivalent about becoming a parent.

MAKING ITS ACQUAINTANCE

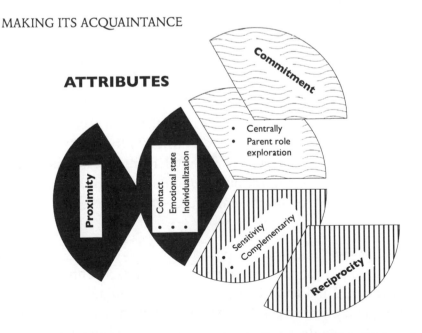

Figure 3.3 The critical attributes of parent–infant attachment, adapted from Goulet et al. (1998) with permission of the publishers.

The cycles of interaction described above enable the parent to acquaint him or herself with the particular child as an individual, an essential antecedent to close attachment, which is, after all, a relationship between people with unique personalities.

In the central part of the model Goulet sets out the critical attributes of attachment that help to explore the adult perspective (see Figure 3.3).

PROXIMITY

Adults seek proximity with their babies and it is expressed through the sensory experiences of physical closeness and intimate contact. Positive feelings that the adult has towards the child and to their caring role are an emotional attribute of attachment. The adult also has, to some extent, to detach him or herself from the child and to see the child as a separate being with individual needs.

RECIPROCITY

Attachment is a two-way process and ideally the adult demonstrates sensitivity and responsiveness, whilst the infant actively responds and takes part in the human exchange. Fahlberg (1991) describes this process as two cycles that promote the development of attachment: the 'arousal-relaxation' cycle where the adult responds to the infant's expressed need and the 'positive-interaction' cycle where the adult sensitively initiates social interaction.

COMMITMENT

As part of an enduring commitment to a child the adult accepts the centrality of the infant in their life, takes responsibility for their well-being and finds a way to 'integrate the parental identity into their self' (Goulet *et al.* 1998). Again, ideally, the adult would need a sense of well-being in the role of attachment figure.

The man as parent

What are the implications of the attributes and antecedents of attachment for expectant and actual fathers? Men can potentially be as excited about a pregnancy as women. Both women and men can show ambivalence, distress or delight at pregnancy. Assuming he wishes it, the extent of intimate access that the father has to the developing foetus will, though, depend largely on the relationship with the mother. Attachment to the foetus has been shown to be related to attachment to the infant (Ferketich and Mercer 1995 cited in Goulet *et al.* 1998).

Potentially, also, fathers can make the child's acquaintance and move on to demonstrate proximity and reciprocity. Greenburg and Morris (1974) use the evocative term 'engrossment' to describe the delight and preoccupation expressed by the new fathers they interviewed, 'a feeling of preoccupation, absorption and interest in their newborn' (p.526). These men already saw their infant as unique and different from other babies. Parke and Tinsley (1981) have carried out a number of observational studies of fathers with their infants and have shown them to exhibit a whole range of attachment-promoting behaviours such as holding, rocking, kissing and feeding:

> as shown by a wide variety of parenting behaviours such as touching, holding, kissing, exploring and imitating the infant, fathers were just as interested in their babies as were mothers. In fact, fathers tended to hold the infant more than mothers and to rock the infant in their arms more than mothers. (Parke and Tinsley 1981, p.40)

The more opportunity the father has to hold the baby, the more these behaviours are shown. Fathers have also been shown to modify their speech patterns when talking to babies just as mothers do and to be sensitive to contextual cues, for example, slowing speech during feeding.

Many of the antecedents and attributes of attachment can therefore be shown by men. The studies tend to demonstrate the potential for men to become important attachment figures, but the potential seems to be very vulnerable to thwarting or extinction. This is partly due to the structural gender divisions and role divergences described in Chapter 2, which are part of an interactive dynamic process.

On an individual level many factors impact upon the bonding and attachment relationship and some of these effects may be different for men and women. Again, much of the relevant research has been carried out with mothers, but the indications are that a parent's relationship with their child can be affected by the parent's own attachment history, by their attitudes to being a parent and by their psychological availability towards the child.

The cycle of attachment is not a simple one, so that an adult who has had poor childhood experiences of attachment will not necessarily have children who are insecurely attached to them. On the other hand, there does appear to be an association between the way that an adult will describe their early attachment relationships and the attachment pattern demonstrated by their child. Main and colleagues devised an 'Adult Attachment Interview', which asks people to recall their early attachments (Main, Kaplan and Cassidy 1985). Responses tend to fall into one of three patterns which have been shown to be associated with their own child's attachment patterns. Adults described as *autonomous-secure* give a coherent account of their early relationships, whether positive or negative, that is, they show reflection and insight. In turn, their children are more likely to demonstrate secure attachment to them. Adults described as *preoccupied-entangled* give an account that is confused and inconsistent, with preoccupation, anger and unresolved conflict. Their children are more likely to show insecure ambivalent patterns of attachment. Finally, adults who are *dismissing-detached* do not recall attachment experiences easily and the impact of attachment experiences is dismissed. Their children are more likely to show insecure avoidant attachment.

There is little direct evidence about the impact of gender upon the responses given in the Adult Attachment Interview. Some clues may be gained from a different set of studies into adult attachment, primarily aimed at studying adult romantic relationships. In infants there are no sex differences in inner working models: baby boys are as likely to show secure attachment as baby girls. Studies of adult attachment behaviours, on the other hand, have shown some gender differences which tend to be in line with generally understood sex-role stereotypes. People are given four descriptions of attachment styles, described as *secure, dismissing, preoccupied* and *fearful* and asked to indicate which best describes them (Bartholomew and Horowitz 1991). Men tend to show higher ratings of dismissing attachment, a pattern that describes the importance of independence and comfort without close relationships (Feeney and Noller 1996).

Thus, within the context of these studies, men are more likely than women to be dismissing of attachment, that is, to describe themselves as preferring to be independent and not to need a close relationship, suggesting that by adulthood men's inner working models may have shifted (Feeney and Noller 1996). Men's emotional development has also been described as a process of differentiation, whereby they define themselves as 'other' by distancing themselves from their mother, and thereby from human connectedness (M. M. Johnson 1988). It would be unwise to draw strong conclusions from such studies, but they do raise interesting questions about whether a dismissing style of adult attachment extends to affect men's relationships with children.

How men think about themselves, about children and about fatherhood does seem to have an impact upon their relationships with their children. The attitude to being a parent is therefore important (Bretherton and Waters 1985).

Cox *et al.* (1992) observed mothers and fathers interacting with their first-born at three months and in the Strange situation at 12 months. At three months parents were interviewed individually about their parental role. For both parents the more positive and physically affectionate the interaction at three months, the more secure the attachment at 12 months. But for fathers only, the 'attitudes about the infant and his parenting role predicted significant variation in infant–father security of attachment' (p.480).

There are a number of complexities about how a man may view masculinity, fatherhood and parenthood. What is most salient for the child is that the person is a human being. However, the man may see himself as a man first rather than as a father first. He may have a specific attitude to being a man that does not incorporate the antecedents and attributes for the promotion of close attachments to babies. Men can have very different ideas about what being a father means: for some the main element might be warm attachment, for others it might mean providing. Practitioners therefore need to be aware simultaneously of the potential in all men and the specifics of the individual situation.

As Cox *et al.* conclude:

> We suggest that looking at the parent's cognitions and reports about the infant and about the parental role may be particularly important in understanding the development of the infant–father relationship. (p.480)

The important conclusion when looking at the situation from the adult's point of view is that although there is potential for the attachment relationship to be secure, gender, attitudes and social structures impact upon whether that potential is developed. In the second part of the chapter we draw out the messages for practice from this complex theoretical picture.

Key Issues from Theory

1. Men and women's roles in society are different; they are not usually interchangeable in a straightforward way.

2. Fathers cannot be considered as a homogenous group.

3. Fathers can be attachment figures.

4. Children can show separation anxiety at the loss of the father.

5. Early on, men's and women's roles tend to diverge, with women adopting more caretaking tasks and men taking part in fun and play activities.

6. Infants tend to develop similar inner working models towards more than one attachment figure; but they have the potential to develop different working models for different people.

7. Inner working models of attachment tend to become self-fulfilling.

8. Attachment patterns need not be written on tablets of stone; they are amenable to change through experience or therapeutic input.

9. The parent's own attachment history, and the sense they make of it, can impact upon their relationship with their child.

10. The father's attitude to the parenting role can affect the quality of attachment.

Exploring Practice Implications

It is likely that, if asked, most child protection practitioners will say that fathers can be attachment figures. All around them in general society the whole spectrum of father–child relationships can be observed, from violent to rejecting to loving and close. There has been a considerable increase in interest in fathers and the contemporary debate about their role has been given extensive media coverage. But, perhaps because of the very range of possibilities of father–child relationships, attachment theory has not provided practitioners with a clear framework for practice.

Part of the problem lies in the gap between the potential and the actuality. Children can form secure attachments to fathers, but not all do. Fathers can act as primary attachment figures, but not all do. It may be that social workers and health visitors are not entering situations with high expectations of the fathers and father-figures. They often encounter men who are violent to children or women; they frequently encounter women who are parenting alone; they are keenly aware that men are more likely to sexually abuse than women. Perhaps, if one is jaded by such knowledge and experience, it is easy to miss or overlook evidence of men who are significant attachment figures, even when attachment is not expressed in exactly the same way as it is by women.

Social workers and health visitors are as subject to social convention and role structures as anyone else. Unless these conventions are explicitly explored and challenged they may not even be obvious. The frontline workers are, after all, usually women carrying out the traditionally female task of caregiving. They and the women they encounter in practice may well share views about who acts as the primary caregiver. Further, there is also potential for an element of collusion with the notion that women are better at being the primary caregiver; a tacit agreement with the view that men are just no good at it, as expressed by one mother:

> He attempted once (to bathe her) and he didn't get on very successfully and he offered to do it again, but I said I'd do it (laughs). I think he's quite happy to keep away from that side of it, quite honestly (laughs). I don't want to force him to do it. (McKee 1982, p.130)

In moving practice forward with men, therefore, it is first essential to develop a sophisticated understanding of the overt and subtle forces that operate upon both men and women to shape and direct their roles with children. There is a need to balance the requirement to see the person first, before the gender, with the need to understand the impact of gender upon life opportunities. Practitioners need first to be able to recognise and appreciate existing attachment relationships between fathers and children. If there are child care or protection concerns, such an attachment relationship could be an important strength to build upon. Practitioners also need to be able to promote secure attachments between fathers and children where they do not exist. For all children, whether at risk or not, there are significant advantages to having a network of attachments. Box 3.2 summarises the approach at the NEWPIN support project.

Box 3.2 NEWPIN

The following is a direct account from a practitioner at a fathers' support centre about their work:

> The NEWPIN Fathers' Support Centre works with the view and understanding that fathers play, have, and make a life-long impact on the lives of children; that every child has the right to a healthy, tender and loving relationship with a dad or father-figure.

> We work mainly with fathers in the development and enhancement of their relationship with their children, partners, parents and their community. Research supports that where fathers are better involved with their children, breastfeeding is more successful, post-natal depression is less likely, educational achievement is enhanced, as well as criminal conviction being less likely by the age of 21.

> At the NEWPIN Fathers' Support Centre we offer a wide range of free and confidential services for fathers from all aspects of our society and are accessible to the culturally diverse community within which we live. Services include a black ethnic support group, a general fathers' support group, counselling, a drop-in service, summer play schemes and trips, education and training (NVQ), parenting programmes and befriending.

>> 'Just three weeks into a 12-week group has made me change the way I communicate with my children. I can now play and have some really good times with my children without getting angry' (a father using the NEWPIN Service)

> We are constantly working to change the negative ways in which fathers have been portrayed within our society.

> One of our visions is that one day soon every child and father will have equal opportunity, rights and access to have and develop good healthy relationships with their father/child as with their mother.

Contact: The Amersham Centre, Inville Road, Walworth, London SE17 2HY. Tel: 020 7740 8997 Fax: 020 7740 8994 Email: fathers@nationalnewpin.freeserve.co.uk

Assessing the Main Components of Attachment

Children's perspective

Experienced practitioners are usually very familiar with the concepts of secure and insecure attachment and skilled in assessing them. But the template for such assessment is the mother–child dyad and has been for decades. As practitioners are also more likely to see children with their mothers, they may have no direct observation of them with their fathers. Mothers may not discuss the role of the father, either because they do not see it as important, or because they are not asked.

CONSIDERING THE POSSIBILITY THAT THE FATHER IS AN ATTACHMENT FIGURE

There is a dilemma inherent in looking for father–child attachment: from the research it is not at all clear whether to look for something that resembles attachment to the mother, or for something different. Although father–infant attachments can look very similar to mother–infant attachments, especially in relaxed conditions, there have been findings that suggest that they may be to some extent different. Babies may show more affiliative behaviours to fathers, and the relationship may be more based on rough and tumble or play. If this is the case it may also be that the mother (understandably) feels some resentment at this division and discounts the father's input as less important. This may also be the case for practitioners. If the main concern is about physical neglect then it is caregiving which is the primary concern, and again, other types of activity may be discounted. It may also be that a father would feel reluctant to give up this aspect of the relationship in order to assume a more caretaking role.

From the point of view of the child, the care and fun aspects of attachment are both important. Obviously being physically nurtured is essential and underpins other development, but a full assessment should also pay attention to the child's social experiences, whoever provides them.

A way through this dilemma would be to look for *all* aspects of attachment to *all* significant figures. For example, closer attention to the fun aspect of mothers' relationships with children could also yield important information that may have been missed. In other words, assessment currently often starts with the mother and assesses her relationship with the child and whether she meets the child's needs. Instead a fuller picture will be gained by starting with the child and making no assumptions about the adults. The issues then are:

1. What attachment needs does this individual child have?

2. Who, among the network of adults and other children around this child, meets which of these needs?

The way to gather this information is by asking questions and by observing behaviour.

ASKING THE QUESTIONS

In all cases, therefore, practitioners should aim to ask as many questions about the attachment of as many significant people in the child's network as possible. Even if the father is absent such questions must be asked. The questions should reflect the broader aspects of attachment to include the 'fun' aspects of parenting.

If the family is happy with the traditional role divisions, then these can be worked with, valued in their difference and enhanced. If one or other or both parents are unhappy, then work with both should focus on exploring all the possible options. Appendix I contains an activity about parenting tasks that may be helpful. In it parents are asked to explore who is prepared to do what.

OBSERVING BEHAVIOUR

Children can tell us a lot about their attachments by their behaviour towards people. But the behaviour has to be observed and recognised. Opportunities to observe the child's interactions with significant people should be taken. Both play and caretaking situations should be observed. A wide range of activities should also be observed. So, for example, in their study Cox et al. (1992) broadened the observation to include:

- sensitivity
- warmth
- reciprocal play
- activity level
- physical affection

- appropriate encouragement of achievement.

In observation it should be possible to look at the extent to which parents are used as a secure base and safe haven and the extent to which children are willing to engage with strangers.

TAKE SERIOUSLY THE IMPACT OF LOSS AND SEPARATION FROM FATHER AND FATHER-FIGURE

The strengths of children's attachments, even to people who have been abusive to them, is often remarkable. Workers often encounter mothers who are looking after their children alone. In fact, this is so often a feature of referrals that it may almost be taken for granted. In reports the fact can be encapsulated in the simple phrase: 'single mother, no contact with father', sometimes even without the second part.

When making assessments however, it is essential to unpick that statement and to consider:

- Under what circumstances did the parents separate?
- Had the child made a significant attachment to the father?
- Does the child have unresolved grief feelings about the father?
- Can the absent father still act as an attachment figure?
- Have other father-figures been present and then moved on, and if so are the above issues relevant?

CONSIDER ALL AGE GROUPS

The majority of attachment studies have been carried out with infants and young children, but, as discussed, people retain attachment needs throughout life. Older children are also more likely to be able to reflect upon their attachment experiences and to realise the significance of whether they know their father or not.

Therefore older children or young people should be asked for their views on their attachments to men:

- Do they know their father?
- If not, would they like to?
- Have they fears about their father, for example that they may 'turn out just like him' or that he will find them and hurt them?

- Are there other significant male figures that they currently know or have known in the past who are important to them?

When the mother is unable to look after the child, either by her own choice or by the judgement of others, the father should be considered as a potential caregiver. Even if that is not possible, contact arrangements with the father should also be considered. Even if the father has not previously made significant efforts to see the child, he should still be considered. The lack of contact may be a function of a difficult relationship with the mother, not the child.

When children leave local authority accommodation as young adults the majority seek some form of family contact. A father who has not been able to provide care for a younger child might be able to act as part of the young adult's attachment network.

CAPITALISE ON DIFFERENT WORKING MODELS

The fact that children can simultaneously hold different inner working models for different people may be a real asset in practice. If a child's attachment to the mother is insecure, there is still the potential for attachment to the father to be secure. If there is a glimmer that this is the case, then practice should be aimed at nurturing the security of that relationship.

By the same token, if the relationship to the mother is secure it should not be assumed that the relationship to the father or father-figure is also. If it is insecure, then this should be taken seriously as it is likely to reflect the child's experience of the father. It may help with assessing whether the situation is abusive. It may indicate that therapeutic relationship work with the father and child might be helpful.

Adults' perspective

As the findings discussed above indicate, it is not possible to generalise from attachment theory about practice with men. Each situation is unique and many of the suggestions for practice would apply as much to mothers as fathers. Practice will obviously also vary according to whether the man is assessed as being an asset or risk to the child. Here the guidance will be based mainly upon the presumption that the father does not pose a physical or sexual risk to the child (for discussion of working with men who are considered risks to their children, see Chapter 6).

Some of the main suggestions are set out in a table in Figure 3.4.

READINESS FOR SECURE ATTACHMENT RELATIONSHIPS

If it is the case that men tend to show greater discomfort with closeness and intimacy, then fathers, even more than mothers, may need help in exploring previous attachment relationships. As described above, Main and her colleagues have carried out extensive research, using her Adult Attachment Interview, in which parents are asked to reflect upon their significant attachment relationships. The bulk of the research has been carried out with mothers. However, in practice the same principle can be adopted in helping potential and actual fathers to reflect and gain insight into the possible impact of their experiences. They may benefit from the opportunity to reflect on the relationship they had with their parents.

In exploring attitudes towards becoming a parent the practitioner can consider:

- How would this man describe himself first – as a person, a man or a father?

- How would he describe the role of father?

- What is his attitude to becoming or being a parent?

If possible, both parents should be seen and asked how they envisage their separate and joint roles developing as parents. Both could be asked to describe the essential aspects of parenting and then to describe the essential aspects of mothering and fathering. Any discrepancies offer points for discussion.

Teenage pregnancies are currently a matter of some concern, especially as young mothers can become extremely isolated and can feel unsupported. The evidence suggests that the parental relationship rarely survives the pregnancy, but that teenage fathers do express a wish to be involved with their children (Speak, Cameron and Gilroy 1997). If the parents could be encouraged, helped and supported in organising for the continued involvement of the father with the child, regardless of the parents' relationship with each other, then all could potentially benefit.

Aim of intervention with the father/father-figure	Younger child/father present from birth	Older child/father meets child later
Promote readiness for a secure attachment relationship with the child	• Support in becoming aware of previous attachment relationships • Explore and help develop positive attitudes towards becoming a parent • Provide with information about factors that are known to promote attachment • Explore with both parents how they wish to divide tasks and what roles they envisage taking with the child.	
Promote the development of secure attachments	• Help with acceptance of the pregnancy • Encourage father to organise time and space for a child in his life • Maximise opportunities for the father to be involved with the baby in the womb • Build upon the 'engrossment' that the father shows towards the new-born • Encourage, advise and support factors in sensitive, reciprocal interaction with the child	• Help the father to make the child's acquaintance • Provide the father with as much information as possible about the child's life to date • Help the father to get to know this individual child's likes and dislikes, mannerisms, characteristics and so on • Teach the father any identified missing parenting skills, e.g. appropriate discipline
Repair or change unhelpful attachment patterns	• Encourage situations of play and fun between father and child • Use games, video, role-play and so on • Refer to/or consider setting up fathers' groups • Encourage both parents to take part in a range of activities with the child • Provide information and give feedback	• Advise the father of ways in which the child might try to repeat unhelpful patterns of attachment • Encourage joint fun activities • Support the father in carrying out caregiving activities • Make use of neutral contact centres and supervised access settings

Figure 3.4 Examples of practice situations for working with fathers, based upon attachment theory.

PROMOTING THE DEVELOPMENT OF SECURE ATTACHMENTS

There is much overlap between this area and the previous one, as aspects such as physical and psychological availability, acceptance of the parental role and commitment depend so much upon attitudes to becoming or being a parent. The fact that children can demonstrably exhibit secure attachments to fathers has to inform practice. Expectations of fathers whose children are subject to child care and protection concerns should be no lower than expectations of any men. From this starting point intervention should be aimed at maximising opportunities for the father to be involved with the foetus and the new-born child.

If the family are happy with and prefer a division in roles whereby the mother takes the primary responsibility for caregiving, then this should be respected. Equally, the role that the father plays should be appreciated and nurtured.

REPAIRING AND CHANGING INSECURE ATTACHMENTS

Two key aspects of inner working models should be kept in mind: first, that different models can coexist and second, that people tend to impose existing patterns of attachment onto new situations.

In many cases the primary focus of intervention for health visitors and social workers is the attachment between mother and child. Specific programmes have been developed with this in mind (Binney, McKnight and Broughton 1994). There has been little practice attention to the attachment with the father. Perhaps the mother–child attachment is seen as the priority, but as discussed above, from the child's point of view there is no intrinsic reason for this. For the child the priority is secure attachment to *someone* (See Box 3.3 for a case example). Again, many of the techniques in such work with fathers may be similar, for example using video cameras to record interactions and explore them with the father; developing joint games and activities and modelling interaction with the child.

Box 3. 3 Case example

Anne has a child, Jane, aged eight months. Anne split up with Jane's father during the pregnancy and they have no contact. When Jane was one month old Anne began a relationship with Peter and they now live together. Neither is in paid employment.

Anne asked her health visitor to refer her to the social services. She said she felt isolated, alone, was not able to cope with Jane, had on several occasions felt like hitting her and was thinking about asking for her to be 'taken into care'.

The social worker and health visitor met together with both Anne and Peter. It emerged that Anne had been afraid to ask for Peter's help with Jane, fearing that he would resent looking after 'another man's child'. She never left Jane alone with Peter as she did not trust him to know how to look after her. Peter admitted to feeling very nervous of Jane, wanting to offer help, but having no idea of what to do. He felt that he had never really got to know her.

A short intensive period of intervention was agreed. In a series of co-ordinated sessions, the social worker would take Anne away from the house and support her in exploring local community resources for parents and children. On the same occasion the health visitor would go to the house and spend time with Peter, supporting him in learning child care skills and giving him basic information about feeding, appropriate toys and so on.

However, aspects of this kind of work may not be so accessible for fathers. Often such work will be carried out in a family centre or day care setting. Work with fathers in such settings is extremely patchy and may often be in the form of groups of adults, rather than father–child dyads.

If the work is carried out in the day, the father may not be available if he is working. Similarly, if the father does not live with the mother and child there may be logistical difficulties. But once such work is recognised as important, arrangements can be made to accommodate different times and places.

When a father is being helped in establishing relationships with an older child, perhaps one who is being looked after away from home, he needs as much information as possible about the child's earlier life. He also needs the opportunity to make the child's acquaintance. The blood relationship does not magically enable this process to be short-circuited.

Key Messages for Practice

1. A father may be an attachment figure, but his ability to carry out that role may be influenced, shaped or hampered by societal expectations.

2. Assumptions should not be made about the nature of the child–father relationship.

3. The quality of attachments to all significant people of all ages and both genders must be assessed.

4. The impact of separation from any father-figure should be assessed.

5. It should be taken into account that the father's attachment relationship with the child could be based on rough and tumble and fun. In fact, if this is the case it might be possible to capitalise on it.

6. Secure and insecure inner working models can be held simultaneously for different people. This information is important as it indicates the nature of the relationships and also suggests possible avenues for intervention.

7. Inner working models tend to be self-fulfilling. Children may try to impose an insecure working model upon a father-figure. Similarly, a man may impose his insecure working model upon the child.

8. Insecure inner working models are susceptible to change through the experience of new, more satisfying relationships, or through therapeutic support. Opportunities to help either children or fathers with insecure inner models should be explored.

9. The parent's own attachment history impacts upon parent–child relationships, therefore the father's attachment history should be taken.

10. The father's attitude to being a parent, and more specifically a father, should be assessed and discussed with him.

Try it for Size

Health visitors are frequently involved in setting up parent groups with the aim of helping with problems of attachment and behaviour.

If you are involved in such a group, or intend to set one up, why not consider creating one that is father-friendly?

Some issues that you would need to consider are:

- What are fathers themselves saying that they want? Pilot research is essential.

- What is the best time to hold such a group?

- Where is the best place to hold such a group, where do men feel comfortable, what images are on the walls, etc.?

- Are there specific aspects of father–child attachments that you could incorporate?

- Should the group be mixed or men only?

- Should at least one group facilitator be male?

Chapter 4

Anti-discrimination

Introduction

In this chapter we explore what is not so much a unified theory of practice, as an anti-discriminatory value system, built upon a collection of theoretical approaches. If we accept that practice has been skewed towards mothers, then we have to accept that it has been discriminatory. It has been discriminatory against mothers because of the assumption that they should be the main carers, and against fathers because it has marginalised their role. Some might argue that there is no problem with traditional role divisions on the basis of gender. However, as we showed in the first chapter, many people now agree with the concept of more father involvement, even if they find it hard to put into practice. Running with one of the main themes of the book we argue that, in practice, discrimination against either the mother or the father restricts the choices of the adults involved, and also limits options for intervention on behalf of abused and neglected children.

We shall devote the large part of this chapter to feminism: the theory of oppression that has the most direct relevance to gender issues. Both of us would describe ourselves as feminist, and, indeed, it is feminist principles that have prompted our interest in the roles of men in children's lives. We shall augment this with a wider view on oppression. However, as we acknowledge in this chapter, feminism does not offer one clear, coherent message for practice with fathers, rather a collection of helpful pointers. In the second part we draw from different strands of feminist theory to make suggestions for practice. We do not want to be prescriptive; instead we want to widen the choice of intervention options as much as possible.

In the era of what is described as 'post-feminism' many would argue that some gender battles have been won. It can be also be argued that the concept of equal opportunities and anti-discriminatory practice has been incorporated into social work practice, with the emergence of the 'backlash' as ironic evidence of its purchase. The consideration of gender issues is a requirement within qualifying and post-qualifying social work training, and feminist theory is taught routinely within social work courses (Phillipson 1992).

In nurse training the ideology of anti-discriminatory practice does not have such a high profile. But in both professions there is an assumption that it is a 'good thing' to take account of fathers when assessing the situation of children at risk and in need. For decades the practice literature has espoused the importance of working with both men and women in such a way as actively to encourage men to be more involved in the care of their children. The rhetoric, therefore, might suggest that there is a spirit of readiness for the place of fathers in society in general and in child care practice in particular.

However, the reality of health and social work practice looks different from the rhetoric. In a text to aid social work educators, Phillipson (1992) points out that social work assessments can be 'riddled with gendered assumptions about roles in families' and that intervention is typically aimed at supporting women in their gendered roles and not recognising the full range of their resourcefulness and strengths. It is likely that this is often the case in health visiting practice as well. Women, as mothers, tend to be central to a health visitor's caseload whereas fathers may be somewhat peripheral.

The Impact of Feminism

Impact on society

Contemporary social work has an explicit value base of anti-discriminatory practice. For gender issues the obvious theoretical input is from feminism. But feminism is not a unified theory itself and we need to look in more detail at its development before we can draw out clear messages for practice.

North American and European feminism is usually described as having two 'waves' (Fox Harding 1996). During the end of the nineteenth and beginning of the twentieth centuries, the first wave concentrated mainly on the public sphere, that is on fighting for women's rights to vote, to higher education, to equal property rights and so on.

Less challenge was made of family structure and women's and men's roles in the home.

Starting during the 1960s, the second wave was broader in scope; it addressed the public sphere with the impulse towards rights for abortion, contraception, maternity rights, state child care, and protection against men's violence. The Equal Pay Act came into force in 1970 and the Sex Discrimination Act in 1975. In addition there was a more conscious questioning and challenging of the gender-relations status quo. The traditional family structure and patriarchy were identified as operating at all levels of society to the detriment of women. Thus there was an articulation of woman's oppression and exploitation in both the public and private spheres. The fundamental meaning of 'masculinity' and 'femininity' was questioned. With more women entering paid employment, the fact that they had to retain the bulk of home responsibilities as well began to seem more like exploitation than fair role division. During the 1980s the prominence of feminism declined and the 'backlash' emerged. But feminist theorising is ongoing, and in particular, there is an increasing interest in the implications of feminism for men as fathers.

Feminism has lead to changes in consciousness in society, and it has challenged a number of assumptions about parenting, for example:

- that women are biologically prepared for mothering
- that the nuclear family is essential for adequate child rearing.

It has also pointed out some of the realities of women and children's lives:

- that the nuclear family can be the site of violence and sexual abuse perpetrated by men
- that women are economically disadvantaged in comparison with men.

Feminism has also challenged the assumption that parents always make decisions together on an equal footing (Walby 1990).

In the previous chapter we looked at developments in attachment theory. Some of these developments were driven by the feminist challenge to Bowlby's idea that young children need their mother on a full-time basis. The post-Second World War 'Bowlby era' in Britain put the onus on women to be at home and look after their children (Fox

Harding 1996). A feminist challenge to this was that more, good-quality child care provision should be made to allow women to continue to work outside the home. But developments in state child care have been very slow in Britain. The National Childcare Strategy aims to improve this state of affairs, but fairly recently there was still only one registered child care place for every six children aged under eight in England (Pullinger and Summerfield 1998). State child care tends to be reserved for vulnerable families.

> Broadly, the state's expectation in Britain is that parents/mothers will care for young children during the day, and this is conveniently reinforced by post-war theories of child development which suggested that day care outside the family was damaging. (Fox Harding 1996, p.171)

So, feminists have been influential in encouraging the notion that women can find fulfilment outside the home and that they should not automatically be expected to care for children. But, and it is a big but, this leads to a potential child care vacuum that is not being filled, either by fathers, or by the state. And, in a dramatic shift, UK policy now actively encourages lone mothers to seek work rather than draw state benefit. This policy is mainly based upon an economic argument (HM Treasury 1999), but the suggestion that women will find this more fulfilling clearly borrows from feminist thinking. The fathers of the children of these lone mothers are rarely mentioned, other than in the context of the Child Support Agency; 'support' in these terms is seen in financial terms. It is hard for feminists to know how to respond to this. It is considered to be 'good' for women to work, but at the same time the neglect of children's needs cannot be condoned, and there is discomfort with the whiff of compulsion. Thus, while feminism has articulated women's right and ability to work, there has been no consistent counterbalanced argument for men to take responsibility for the care of children.

There is a real dilemma for feminism in formulating an effective response to fathers, particularly non-abusing fathers (Trotter 1997). The driving impulse of much feminism has been the exposure of the extent to which women and children have been systematically disadvantaged, have been on the wrong end of the power imbalance and have been subjected to abuse and violence. But the solution to this is not agreed upon. Some argue for mothers to change the way they bring up their sons to encourage them to be more caring. Others that women should separate themselves from men and form alternative ways of living. Others that men should take more part in child rearing, which would encourage them to be more caring and egalitarian. The call for more 'shared parenting' is powerful, and is not only a feminist demand. Organisations lobbying on behalf of fathers, especially non-resident fathers, may use some of the same arguments to argue for fathers' rights to more contact with their children (F. Williams 1998).

The idea that gender role divisions be loosened, that men be enabled to use their nurturing and caring sides and that women be released from the 'double shift' of paid work and work in the home is appealing. However, some feminists argue that this is a dangerous position to advocate without women's position first being bolstered further. It has been argued that to strengthen the role of the father is to run the risk of strengthening the control that men have over women (Segal 1990). M. M. Johnson (1988) also argues that fathers' parenting styles are different from mothers' and in fact reinforce traditional sex-roles in their children (a view that is, to some extent, supported by the research (McGuire 1982)). Johnson maintains that it should be accepted as a fact that women will take on the main responsibility for children and that policy should aim to support women with child care. Interestingly, this view has been politically articulated in West Germany with the publication in 1987 of a Mothers' Manifesto by a section of feminists from the West German Green party. The manifesto makes little mention of fathers, but concentrates on demands for payment and pensions for women who choose to remain at home, flexible working hours for mothers and more public provision for mothers (O'Brien 1995).

The impact of feminism upon general society, and the suggestions for solutions, are therefore mixed and if there is no obvious guidance for society, then it is perhaps not surprising that the messages for child care and protection practice are not coherent. But there are two messages coming from different strands of feminism that perhaps need not be seen as mutually exclusive:

1. As both men and women are now involved in paid
    employment there must be state-provided or state-subsidised,
    high-quality, plentiful, child-centred, child care provision.

2. There is no intrinsic reason for mothers to be the main carers for children and a more equal sharing of the parenting roles between fathers and mothers is something for society to aim for.

Impact on child care and protection practice

In formulating any practice guidance for engaging with fathers it is crucial first to recognise ways in which feminism has influenced theories that guide child care and protection practice. As yet, feminist scholars have made only a beginning in the analysis of child physical abuse (Featherstone 1997). The main impact has been upon that most problematic intersection of power and gender: child sexual abuse. There are three main strands of understanding about child sexual abuse that have been influenced by feminist analysis (MacLeod and Saraga 1988).

1. *Child sexual abuse is predominantly committed by men and the explanation must therefore be sought in the social construction of male sexuality as a biological imperative which is associated with power and the right to expression.*

   That this has been accepted in social work is evidenced by treatment programmes that explicitly challenge these aspects of masculinity and require men to take responsibility for their actions.

   Related to this understanding is the challenge to the 'cycle of abuse' which assumes that people who have been sexually abused will go on to abuse. Once it is pointed out that at least half, if not more, child victims are female whilst over 90 per cent of perpetrators are male, the simple cycle theory makes no sense. The recognition that a cycle of abuse is not inevitable is extremely helpful to men who have been abused as children, go on to have children and harbour a fear that they will repeat the sins of their fathers.

2. *The concept of the 'collusive' mother, especially as viewed by family dysfunction theorists, is simplistic and ignores the power differentials in family structures.*

    The notion of the 'collusive' mother who somehow allows her daughter to be sacrificed in order to keep the family together is no longer so prevalent, although it does, on occasion, surface in child protection proceedings. There is no doubt that some mothers are aware of the sexual abuse, and some take part in it, but it is no longer considered to be an essential element in the phenomenon.

    Self-help groups for mothers of children who have been sexually abused continue both to support women and to reiterate the message, on the basis of lived experience, that the vast majority of mothers are not collusive in the abuse of their children.

3. *The voice of the abused person must be heard.*

    Largely through the support of feminist organisations, created upon feminist principles, women who were abused as children have been able to articulate themselves as 'survivors', not merely as 'victims'. They have also been able to express, in their own words, the trauma they experienced and challenge any suggestion that children may 'ask for it' or be 'provocative'.

    It is now a fundamental element of all work with children who have been abused to emphasise their complete lack of blame and to place responsibility with the adult abuser.

Despite these vital shifts, feminism does not provide one clear, obvious model for anti-discriminatory practice across the range of child protection practice (Featherstone 1999). One reason for this may lie in the uneasy tension between a socialist feminism that is inclined towards viewing state intervention as 'soft policing' and the recognition of the needs of vulnerable children for protection. Another lies in the very range and diversity of feminism: there is no one dogma that can be translated into a model for practice (Thompson 1997). There are more questions than answers:

1. Should practitioners concentrate on liberating women from the constraints of the mothering role?

2. Should they provide sufficient support to allow women to continue with the mothering role?

3. Should they try to bring fathers back into the picture?

4. Should they support women's rights to bring up their children without fathers?

Oppression, Empowerment and Anti-discriminatory Practice

The men, women and children encountered by child care practitioners may be subject to a range of oppressions including disableism, ageism, homophobia and racism. When gender issues are being considered it is sexism that is under the spotlight. Essentially feminism is a challenge to sexism, which is defined as:

> a deep-rooted, often unconscious system of beliefs, attitudes and institutions in which distinctions between people's intrinsic worth are made on the grounds of their sex and sexual roles. (Bullock and Stallybrass 1977, p.571, cited in Thompson 1997)

The aim of anti-oppressive practice is to:

*   recognise and challenge the impact of sexism upon male and female service users

*   deliver services without discrimination on the basis of gender.

The dominant model for practice that has emerged from the feminist theoretical strand is one of the empowerment of women, based on principles of equal opportunities (see Box 4.1). Underpinning this is the view that women are structurally disadvantaged and that this disadvantage is the cause of many child care and protection problems. So, for example, it is recognised that living in poverty, in poor housing and with little support from men makes it much more difficult for mothers to parent effectively. If it is accepted that many child care problems have their roots in the structural disadvantage of women, then the aim of empowerment is to support women to improve their situation, for example by entering further education and seeking better paid employment. The argument would be (although it is not always clearly spelt out) that empowering women would lead to better child care environments for children.

Box 4.1 Social work and power relations: towards a framework for integrated practice

McNay (1992) sets out a model for integrated practice that advocates empowerment. Once it is accepted that the basis of social injustice is unequal *power* relations, power can be used as a unifying concept for the understanding of *unequal* opportunities. Therefore the exploration of power relations will help in explaining social issues.

The mode of intervention is based upon empowerment, which recognises that 'everyone has basic needs...and that if these needs are not met, then certain functions will be harder to carry out' (p.59).

Rather than assessing the *problems* that people have, instead assess what material and emotional resources are needed to meet their needs. An analysis of power relations will help in understanding why resources are limited. Those with more power are likely to resist change, but practice means 'tackling the resistance of the more powerful to their loss of power but works with the potential gains of all' (p.61).

The work aims to 'identify what people want and how they propose to achieve the goals identified'. Commonly people lack self-esteem, confidence and frequently, communication skills. By enabling better communication within relationships, the power relations can be articulated and the needs of each explored. Often internal power struggles are actually the result of external forces such as poverty, and the recognition of this can reduce conflict.

There are strengths and weaknesses with this model for practice, both for men and women. There are three issues:

- It is by no means self-evident that empowerment will automatically lead to the protection of children.

- The principle of empowerment may be difficult to uphold in the statutory child protection sector.

- The empowerment model is underdeveloped in attention to the role of fathers.

We will look at each of these in more detail.

Protection of children

It is very difficult for practitioners to know how to deal with the knowledge that structural factors are likely to cause, or at least exacerbate child care problems. The most obvious solution lies in changing social structures in order to remove inequalities and disadvantage. But practitioners are not politicians and the main focus of their work is with individual families. They are expected to work at the level of the individual child who is neglected or abused by individual parents. Attempting to reverse the force of structural disadvantage within one family may improve the situation for the child, but it may not.

At heart, feminism is centred on the liberation of women, and rightly it concentrates on what is best for women. It does not fully embrace the needs of men and children. As a model for child care practice, empowerment is based on an assumption that women's and children's needs coincide; that is, if women are more fulfilled they will be better mothers (Featherstone 1999; McNay 1992). It may be sacrilege to suggest, but it could be true, that within current structural limitations, what is best for women may not be best for children. Feminism has not found a way to address fully the needs and rights of children (Alanen 1994; C. Parton 1990). As Featherstone (1999) suggests:

> feminist social work has often tended to assume that mothers and children are broadly on the same side in their battles with abusive men, and the complexities of the relationship between mother and child are not always addressed (p.49)

The undeniable fact about children is that they demand a huge amount of care and that to provide that level of care entails personal sacrifice. Currently it is women who, in their millions, make that personal sacrifice. It is asking a great deal of practitioners to expect them to reverse the force of structural disadvantage within one family. Practitioners are well aware of who it is that cares for children. It is undeniable that when looking for alternative carers for children, social workers frequently turn to grandmothers or aunts, who will often come up trumps.

Health visitors may well feel that it is beyond their remit to seek to empower women. Health visitors often provide advice and guidance to women that relates to self-development and educational opportunities. However, the main focus is and should be on the welfare of the child. Personal development of the mother would normally be seen in this context – that is, on the assumption that it is better for a child to have a mother who is fulfilled and happy – but this cannot be assumed.

The liberation of women from child care responsibilities and the empowerment of women to assert their needs will not necessarily lead to more men taking over the care of their children. Without parallel structural shifts in society's arrangements for child care, where the rhetoric of shared parenting is turned into reality, social workers and health visitors who attempt to empower women may be struggling against the tide. This is particularly the case for families where there are child care and protection concerns, because they often have the least material and social resources. Even well-resourced and supported families find it difficult to reverse the trends: 'Numerous families who attempt to break the mould...find that they are thwarted in the process' (Warin et al. 1999, p.17).

Empowerment and the statutory sector

Empowerment in its purest form may not always be appropriate or possible in practice in statutory work. Wise (1995) describes an essential incompatibility between the power imbalance inherent in statutory child protection work and the empowerment model. She points to the roots of empowerment that lie in the non-statutory self-help services for women based upon feminist principles (such as Women's Aid). Empowerment here is based upon the principle of shared oppression and egalitarian work. Statutory services, especially in child protection, are frequently imposed upon unwilling recipients, with the inherent power imbalance distilled into the power to remove children. The system itself may not feel empowering to the fathers, mothers and children it is aiming to help (Browne 1995).

The situation is complicated further by the fact that many men and women encountered by practitioners may not share their values about what is best for them. 'For women firmly committed to traditional roles, feminist ideas may be deeply threatening' (Fox Harding 1996, p.18). Similarly such views might feel threatening and alienating to fathers.

There is a real quandary for practitioners in trying to empower someone who either does not see him or herself as lacking power, or who does not agree with the solution. It is an added irony that often social workers are the most obvious wielders of actual or potential power in the parents' eyes. Is someone likely to want to be 'empowered' by a social worker who is saying that their parenting is not good enough and who has the power to recommend that their children be taken away from them?

It is perhaps not necessary completely to lose aspects of the empowerment model in statutory work if empowerment is seen in a broader sense. In the second section we will draw out messages for work with fathers, but in general there are principles of empowerment that are helpful:

- aiming to work in partnership with parents
- providing good information
- being clear and honest about statutory powers
- advising people of their rights
- referring to other support agencies
- avoiding assumptions
- linking people with others who are in similar situations
- encouraging and supporting self-help groups
- developing group work.

The role of fathers

The empowerment model does not provide guidance about practice with fathers. Fathers can be seen as part of the structural problem as oppressors of women and as benefiting from the patriarchal society. But the fathers of children referred because of child care and protection concerns may not feel any obvious benefits from being men. They are themselves likely to be oppressed by economic, material and educational disadvantage. They may lack social and peer support to assume joint parenting roles. Black fathers are likely to suffer the oppression of societal racism and the institutional racism of statutory services.

One message for practice could be to engage far more purposefully with fathers, to encourage them to take part in the care of children and provide support for them in doing so. However, it seems that this aspiration is far from being achieved in society in general, since again it means swimming against the tide.

Thus fathers may, at the same time, be seen as violent aggressors to children and as marginalised and excluded from the care of their children. Therefore, the anti-oppressive model raises the intriguing notion that social workers should be aiming to disempower men as *men*, whilst aiming to empower them as *fathers*. Such a position would require greater analysis of what the role of 'father' and the role of 'man' mean in our society.

The failure by both men and women really to tackle the issue of parenting means that the framework of anti-discriminatory practice cannot, in its current form, provide a fully fledged model for child care and protection practice with parents. Non-sexist practice certainly provides a starting point, but non-sexist practice that only focuses on women is not a coherent model. Also, does non-sexist practice mean that gender roles are not taken into account? For example, when professionals try to set up groups for fathers they often use traditionally 'male' activities to entice men in, so they may offer sporting activities, DIY, outdoor activities and so on. Is this non-sexist practice, or is it just sexist practice in another guise? Practice can be informed by feminism, amongst other ideologies, and services can be delivered in a non-discriminatory way. However, the point here is that a further analysis of the role of fathers and the aims of engagement of fathers is essential for the development of a framework for practice with men in child care work.

Key Issues from Theory

1. The focus of health and social care for children has traditionally been, and continues to be on mothers. This is to the detriment of both men and women.

2. Feminist theory was instrumental in challenging traditional gender roles.

3. Feminism challenged the assumption that young children need the full-time care of their mothers.

4. For many families, especially those on a low income, the issue of child care overwhelms other considerations and places limitations upon opportunities.

5. Feminism has not provided one clear framework for practice; rather it implies a number of possible options.

6. Feminism's major contribution to child care and protection practice has been to the understanding of child sexual abuse.

7. Service users are likely to be the victims of a range of forms of oppression, of which sexism is but one.

8. Any adequate model for practice derived from feminism must place the needs and protection of children at the centre.

9. Anti-discriminatory practice can be based upon empowerment, but the power differential between statutory services and their users has to be acknowledged.

10. Men may need to be simultaneously empowered as fathers and disempowered as men.

Practice Implications Drawn from Feminism

Can a path for practice be picked through this jungle of theory? As described, neither feminist nor anti-discriminatory practice has formulated detailed guidance for engaging with fathers. Nonetheless, whilst noting the limitations, and taking a pragmatic approach, the following discussion will draw from feminist theory, empowerment models and anti-oppressive and anti-discriminatory models. All will not be applicable to all situations; as we stress throughout this book, generalisations about fathers are dangerous and limiting. However, the aim is to provide a seed-corn of ideas that can be refined, developed or rejected as appropriate.

Feminism does not provide a clear analysis of the position of men and men as fathers. In some strands the preference has been to put energies into the situation of women; indeed, some would argue that men, not women, should address the issue of men as fathers. But each child whom the practitioner encounters has, or has had a father. It is therefore more productive to consider ways in which the insights of feminism can inform practice with men.

Feminism, along with other social changes, has already effected huge demographic changes in men's lives, as the number of women in paid employment illustrates. It is a myth that the increase in women entering paid employment is purely a recent phenomenon. Women have always been engaged in economically productive work. In fact Fox Harding (1996) describes the spread of the concept of 'housewife' at the end of the nineteenth and beginning of the twentieth centuries as 'a historical aberration'.

Nonetheless, in modern times, a combination of factors including feminism and economic necessity has resulted in a contemporary rise in the numbers of mothers entering paid employment. In 1973, in Britain, 27 per cent of women with children under five were in paid employment, in 1996–97, 53 per cent were. The number of women who return to paid employment by 9 to 11 months after the birth of a child has also dramatically risen, as is shown in Figure 4.1 (Pullinger and Summerfield 1998).

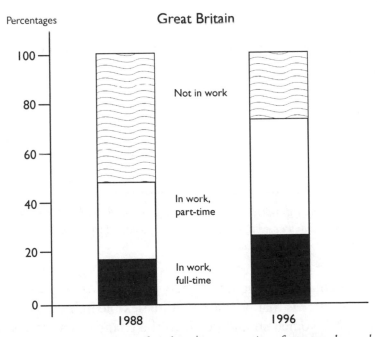

Figure 4.1 The employment status of mothers (as a proportion of women who worked during pregnancy) 9 to 11 months after the birth of their child, 1988 and 1996. Reproduced from Pullinger and Summerfield (1998) with the permission of the publishers. Source: Department of Social Security.

Of course, it would be too simplistic to argue that this is due only to feminism, and there are many women who would much rather stay at home to look after their children, but feel forced to work for economic reasons. Nevertheless, it is also the case that both men's and women's attitudes are changing, as is shown in Figure 4.2 (Pullinger and Summerfield 1998).

Great Britain				Percentages
	1987		1994	
	Women	*Men*	*Women*	*Men*
A husband's job is to earn the money; a wife's job is to look after the home and family				
Agree strongly	21	26	5	5
Agree	22	26	17	22
Neither agree nor disagree	19	19	17	16
Disagree	12	14	40	42
Disagree strongly	25	15	20	15
All	100	100	100	100
A job is all right, but what most women really want is a home and children				
Agree strongly	12	15	5	7
Agree	19	27	18	21
Neither agree nor disagree	20	23	23	25
Disagree	23	19	38	34
Disagree strongly	25	15	16	13
All	100	100	100	100

Figure 4.2 Attitudes towards women working, 1987 and 1994. Reproduced from Pullinger and Summerfield (1998) with the permission of the publishers. Source: British Social Attitudes Survey, Social and Community Planning Research.

Attitudes are changing in general society and the most important aspect of this for practice is that people are more flexible in their views about what men and women should do. With the change in attitudes comes more choice for men and women. Ideally (and some might say idealistically), a loosening of rigid gender roles should benefit both men and women. However, in reality, the changes in men's roles are less radical than those in women's. It is very telling that there is not a similar table showing attitudes towards men working. The question is not even thought worth asking. So although we know that there is potential for men to be more involved with their children, they may not actually develop that potential.

The question for practitioners then is whether they are considering all the options and choices. Child care practitioners need to be working towards the potential; they should aim to be at least as radical in their attitudes as the majority of the general public! The kind of questions that practitioners need to ask both themselves and the men and women they work with are:

- Does the family structure need to be the way it is?

- Would the father appreciate the opportunity for a different role with the children?

- Is the child protection practice focused on the mother only?

- Is there collusion with the father in holding the mother responsible for child neglect?

- Is there a need for a nursery place?

The family template is very powerful; so many hundreds of child care and protection reports begin:

| Mr Smith | Father: Unemployed |
| Mrs Smith | Mother: Housewife |

One of many alternatives would be:

| Mary Smith | Mother: Not in paid employment |
| Paul Smith | Father: Not in paid employment |

Above all, assumptions must be avoided. In many families roles are not rigidly divided by gender, but in times of anxiety, when being visited by a social worker, the family themselves may be at pains to present themselves as the 'ideal' family.

The ideology that the nuclear family is the best structure for all its members should be questioned. There can be a range of family structures, and different ethnic groups may organise family life differently. Many partnerships break up, many people are involved in extra-partnership relationships. Some gay men for example, may feel pressured into family life in order to appear or feel 'normal'; such a situation can lead to hurt and distress for all involved.

Once the message from feminism is embraced – that children do not necessarily need the full-time attention of their mother – then the way is open for involving fathers. Families themselves may believe that children will be damaged if separated from their mothers for too long. Sometimes grandparents can express grave disapproval of children being 'looked after by strangers'. It may be helpful to share the messages from research that it is the quality and stability of care that is most essential, not who provides it.

Two different messages about children have emerged from feminism: one advocates more state child care provision, the other more shared parenting. Of course these two strands need not be mutually exclusive and if brought together they increase the options. Many families now create a patchwork of care, but it is usually organised and kept together by the mother. An example of just one of the many ways in which the working day can be covered is shown in Figure 4.3:

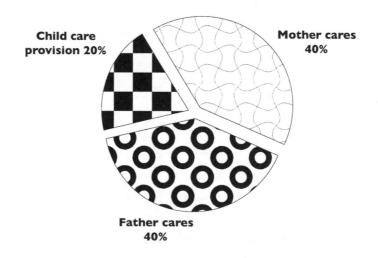

Figure 4.3 A chart to show one way in which child care during the working day might be provided.

If all the family members are happy with the mother taking the main caring role and this appears to be meeting the child's needs, then the arrangement should be respected. If, however, there are problems and stresses then other options to support the father's involvement can be considered, for example:

- discussing the details of what a shared parenting arrangement could look like, and whether it would need some financial support

- whether the father is present or absent, assessing the potential of all the paternal extended family (not just the female members) as providers of care

- finding out what the father's interests are and encouraging them to be shared with the children; if necessary, providing finance for activities for the father and child to do together.

Rather than the different messages from feminism being seen as limiting, instead they can be liberating in that they allow us to 'see' the huge range of options for family structure:

- shared parenting
- lesbian parenting
- gay parenting
- both parents working with the use of child care provision
- mother working, father caring for children
- father caring for children alone
- father working, mother living elsewhere, children in child care provision
- parents living apart, but sharing the care
- informal extended family arrangements.

At the same time social workers and health visitors must collate and disseminate information about the child care needs of their service users and lobby for better provision. Careful costing might show the provision of adequate child care earlier to be cheaper than accommodating children with foster carers later.

Messages from feminism about child sexual abuse

1. It is now recognised in social work that sexual abuse is primarily committed by men and male adolescents. Despite this, child protection practice still tends to hinge on the perceived ability of the mother to protect the child. In Chapter 6 we look in detail at ways to work with abusing fathers. In empowering practice, structural factors must be assessed and discussed with the mother, and it 'is equally important that social workers discuss all of these issues directly with the male parent or step-parent and seek to involve him in any plans to protect children' (Boushel and Farmer 1996, p.100).

   Prevention of future abuse is also important by, for example:

   - expanding the provision of treatment programmes for young men who sexually abuse
   - paying attention to the sexual development of boys, whether they are living at home or away from home, and developing methods for supporting sexuality that is not based upon power and force.

   When a child has been sexually abused by someone other than the father, the father should be engaged with as a non-abusing parent. His help in protecting and supporting the child should be explicitly enlisted. His specific needs for support should also be considered. Sometimes fathers channel their grief and anger into violence against the perpetrator. It is not always the case that the mother and father will be able to support each other precisely because of their different genders and the different meanings sexual abuse could have for them. If the parents are living apart the abuse can be a source of recriminations. Self-help groups for non-abusing fathers of abused children can offer an opportunity for them to explore the particular combination of feelings men may experience.

2. Men who sexually abuse their children will often play on the idea of the collusive mother. For example, fathers may use this as a way of ensuring the child's silence by saying, for example:

   'There's no point telling your mum, she knows anyway.'

'Your mum and I have discussed this, she thinks it is my job to teach you about sex.'

They may also try to excuse their behaviour when being confronted, for example:

'A man has his needs.'

'I was frustrated because she wouldn't have sex with me, I had to turn to someone.'

'Of course she knew, it saved her having to do it.'

All the professionals involved need to be united in challenging and refuting this message. Health visitors may be in a position to support women with coping with their feelings of grief and guilt.

3. Now that we are listening to the voice of survivors there is an increased awareness of the prevalence of sexual abuse of boys. A proportion of the fathers encountered during sexual abuse investigations will themselves have been abused. Alertness to this possibility might help explain confusing reactions on the part of the father.

    Having experienced abuse as a child could also impact upon a father's parenting. Men who have been sexually abused, therefore, may benefit from therapeutic support, perhaps from an appropriate non-statutory agency.

Recognising and Countering Sexism

Anti-discriminatory practice necessitates recognising sexism in the practitioner, in the statutory systems, in the family system and in society. For an activity that explores practitioner sexism, see Appendix II.

There are aspects of health and social care that mirror gender divisions in society. The majority of health visitors and social workers are women, whilst the majority of managers are men. This is a structural issue which urgently needs attention. There is an awareness of the need to recruit more men into child care work, but there is a long way to go. It is often still the case that male workers are allocated what are seen to be 'dangerous cases' and male workers are also still taken as 'minders' on visits to known violent people. Such practice only serves to reinforce and validate traditional notions of masculinity.

Fathers can be the victims of a range of discriminatory behaviours which interact with images of 'normal' masculinity:

- Black fathers may be subject to racist assumptions that devalue their role within the family.

- Teenage fathers can be seen as irresponsible and feckless.

- Gay fathers have extreme difficulty in gaining access to their children and are also subject to the totally false belief that they are likely to sexually abuse boys.

- Disabled men can find that their masculinity is questioned.

- Unemployed fathers are stigmatised as not 'providing' for their children.

In other words, there can be no hierarchy of oppression; instead, forms of oppression interact in particular ways for different people of both genders.

The challenge for practitioners is to be aware of and alert to discrimination of all types. They should observe the following guidelines:

- Make no assumptions about any ethnic group's child rearing systems, instead be respectful and enquiring.

- Provide support for teenage fathers to maintain meaningful contact with their children. Such support might involve arranging a place for them to see the child, liaising with the housing department to make the case for the father to have a suitable house for a child, providing finance for transport for visits and outings, referring both parents for mediation to discuss child contact and so on.

- Contact and residence arrangements are often made by courts, but their decisions are based upon the assessments and recommendations of child care professionals. When asked to assess the suitability of a gay man for contact it is essential to assess the father, not his sexuality. It is also important to recognise that to recommend against contact because 'the child might be subject to bullying or teasing at school' is to perpetuate and legitimate the prejudices of society.

- When organising case conferences, child care meetings, foster placements and placements in children's homes, it is essential to consider accessibility. This includes physical accessibility, as well as timing and cost of travel and so on.

- Unemployment affects a significant proportion of the fathers of children about whom there are child care concerns. When those concerns are being assessed, the emotional and material impact of unemployment upon parenting ability should be explored.

There are messages that can be taken from the empowerment model for work with fathers. In particular, the emphasis upon working with strengths is important (Dubois and Krogsgrud Miley 1999).

Of course the needs of children have to be paramount and statutory powers must be used assertively to protect children as necessary. For example, domestic violence is now recognised as being extremely damaging to children and as often accompanying physical abuse (Farmer and Owen 1995; NCH Action for Children 1997). However, even when working with conflict, those elements of empowerment associated with partnership can be drawn upon (Boushel and Farmer 1996).

Boushel and Farmer (1996) describe the ways in which the current British child protection system concentrates more on immediate protection from risk and less on providing support and assistance to families, especially over the longer term. They advocate an empowering practice that 'acknowledges the imbalances of power *within families* and in society'.

This links with McNay's model (1992), which advocates the analysis of power imbalances as a starting point (see Box 4.1 on p.107). The suggestion that assessment should centre on unmet needs and the material and emotional resources required to meet them rather than on problems can be applied to men, as the case example in Box 4.2 illustrates. At the foundation of all anti-discriminatory practice must be a careful consideration of the child's views and wishes.

Box 4.2 Case example

A child is referred as a victim of physical abuse. The father has recently lost his job and thereby the breadwinning role that he played, but retains the disciplinarian role in the house. His partner bolsters this role by leaving all discipline to him, and indeed 'saves up' lists of misdemeanours for him. Discipline is harsh but ineffective and escalates into physical abuse. Amongst the father's needs are:

- a job
- self-esteem
- a satisfying role in the home
- a more effective form of discipline.

Within the home realm the power has been skewed towards the father and this is discussed in joint sessions, with the external cause (unemployment) being pinpointed. The father is referred to a local community training resource. The primary need in the home is for safe discipline skills that also redress the skewed balance of power. A series of sessions to teach both parents how to implement behavioural techniques jointly provides them both with the skills required to regain control of their son.

Distinguishing Maleness from Fatherhood

A number of measures can be suggested to enable men as fathers whilst confronting unhelpful aspects of masculinity:

- Challenge sexism in children's homes, foster homes and schools.

- Encourage male foster carers to carry out more of the nurturing and caretaking tasks (Gilligan 1998).

- Challenge any form of sexual harassment, whether from service users or colleagues to professionals, or by fathers to their partners or children.

- Do not allow aggressive men to intimidate professionals into avoiding them.

- Offer support to raise self-esteem amongst men who feel disempowered.

- Provide or refer men for anger-management programmes if they are saying that they want help with their temper.

- Provide or refer men for self-control programmes.

- Provide or refer couples for relationship counselling if there appear to be communication difficulties.

- Offer validation for nurturing impulses that men show or express towards their children.

- Expect the best, rather than the worst, from fathers.

We conclude, therefore, that working in a non-sexist way is possible (see Box 4.3). Whilst there is still some thinking to be done about gender in our society and the way it interacts with power, there are very useful messages that can be taken from the simple challenge to the view that gender automatically prescribes roles and ways of behaving.

Box 4.3 Case example

Sarah and David are married and have three children, aged three, five and seven. David has a demanding full-time job. Sarah stays at home to look after the children. Sarah has a history of serious depression and has had a number of admissions to psychiatric hospital. As a child she was sexually abused. The family have been referred to the social work department by the health visitor who is concerned about the emotional and physical care of the children.

The social worker meets with both parents to discuss the child care concerns. Both partners are given the opportunity to express their views. However, Sarah finds it difficult to communicate her feelings and David tries to speak for her. The social worker has to encourage him to allow Sarah time to speak for herself. The worker makes clear the concerns about the children and between them they explore the options. Sarah comes to the decision to seek counselling from a sexual abuse survivors' support organisation. The social worker encourages David to make a commitment to take some time off work to help look after the children.

> During the interview the worker is aware of several gender issues:
> - Sarah has been the victim of abuse by a male relative.
> - Sarah needs some release from the expectations of marriage and motherhood.
> - David blames Sarah for the neglect of the children.
> - David takes his breadwinner status seriously.
>
> What is very apparent is that although, in some terms, David is controlling and holds the power in the partnership, both feel trapped, powerless and out of control of the situation and frightened of losing their children.

Key Messages for Practice

1. The focus of health and social care must be broadened to encompass fathers as well as mothers.

2. Practice should incorporate the knowledge that gender roles are not biological imperatives but social constructs.

3. It should not be assumed that young children will necessarily suffer if their mother is not the main caregiver.

4. The impact of the lack of sufficient child care facilities must be built into assessment, and intervention has to address the need for child care.

5. Feminism offers a range of options for practice with fathers and mothers. Flexibility is crucial.

6. Practice with child sexual abuse should continue to hold men responsible for their actions, eschew the notion of the 'colluding' mother and listen to the voice of the child and adult survivor.

7. Practitioners have to be aware of sexism, and other forms of oppression, both within themselves and their organisations and within families and society.

8. The views, wishes and needs of children must be placed firmly at the centre and they must never be eclipsed by the rights of mothers or fathers.

9. Feminist practice is not incompatible with the assertive use of statutory powers to protect children and to promote their welfare.

10. All unhelpful or dangerous aspects of masculinity should be challenged and their potential for nurturing reinforced.

Try it for Size

Have you ever found yourself in a situation where you felt prejudicial assumptions were being made about you on the basis of, for example:

- gender
- race
- physical ability
- age
- size
- class
- accent
- appearance?

Where you able to challenge the assumptions, and if not, why not?

What did the experience make you feel?

How do you avoid making similar kinds of assumptions about colleagues and about families you work with?

Chapter 5

Caring for Fathers

Introduction

This chapter will review some of the dominant themes that nurses, midwives and health visitors are familiar with. Although we acknowledge their differences, the term 'nurse' will be used in this chapter to denote nurse, midwife and health visitor. Such themes are examined in the context of their usefulness for formulating guidance for purposeful intervention with fathers. Whilst there is a particular focus on the role of health visitors, there are messages arising from this analysis for all professionals who may be engaged in child care and protection. Much nursing theory has been tested cross-culturally and can therefore be applied to a range of family settings. Whilst nursing lacks the overt anti-discriminatory emphasis embodied within social work training, the concepts of caring and reflective practice are dominant themes that will be explored in this debate.

Nursing ideology?

As we have described in Chapter 4, one dominant ideology of social work is anti-discriminatory practice, but this is not always an empowerment tool and indeed, can become a shackle when engaging with fathers in child care and protection practice. It is much harder to name the dominant ideology embedded within nursing. Ideologies are best identified in retrospect and JT once made an attempt to disentangle them (Taylor 1997). Accepting the social construction of nursing, her critique argued that nurses use patient-centredness to legitimate nursing ideology. In this view, any suggested change or belief is legitimated by the motive of improved nursing care, of patient-centredness. Thus it is difficult to argue against it as this then appears unprogressive and unholistic.

Such beliefs were described as complex phenomena, working both covertly and overtly to reinforce nursing ideology. The overall point was that nurses, perceiving themselves as 'caring' individuals, use the concept of patient-centredness to reinforce their arguments, but also to hide behind. This is demonstrated in nursing practice, education, management and in nursing politics. Although the dominant terms used have changed since that paper was prepared, we would argue that concepts such as caring and reflective practice are central to nursing ideology. These can be used effectively in engaging with fathers in child care and protection, but they can also be inhibiting.

Some clues from the classroom

Perhaps some clues from the classroom can be used to contextualise this debate. On numerous occasions where groups of nurses have been asked to define 'nursing', without exception they inevitably get to 'caring' (here we are drawing on our experience as lecturers). When pressed, they begin to flounder, unsure whether all nurses are in fact 'caring', if it is a prerequisite for the profession, if other professions could also be deemed 'caring', or what in fact 'caring' really consists of. Phil Barker and colleagues have provided an excellent critique of the concept of caring and it would be difficult to improve on this (Barker, Reynolds and Ward 1995). Nonetheless, it is raised here as an example of some of the underlying professional issues involved in seeking to untangle the ideology underpinning nursing, a problem exacerbated by the fact that this is not a homogeneous group. Indeed, midwives and health visitors tend to object when referred to as nurses and their distinctiveness is acknowledged. They are usually much clearer about their identifying roles than are nurses as a whole, who may struggle when defining their unique contribution. So the question 'what do you, as a nurse, do that no one else does?' can produce a varied response. This often culminates in 'bits of everyone else's job', from hairdresser to anaesthetist, from domestic assistant to physiotherapist, from porter to doctor. Essentially, however, the answer is 'caring'.

If the same exercise is then tried with a group of social workers there is usually a very different response. Social workers are much firmer, much less woolly in their responses regarding what social work actually is. They speak with clarity regarding overall roles and function, with little blurring of these roles. Nor are social workers a homogeneous group either, yet the underlying tenets of each tend broadly to produce a firm and clear role description. Without exception in the anecdotal examples presented here, social workers acknowledge the centrality that anti-discriminatory practice has in the ideology of their profession. It is much harder to identify the one core theme in nursing.

Remaining safely in the classroom, we have tried another exercise with the two professional groups. This one reveals another aspect of the difference between the underlying philosophies of both. Nurses should try this exercise first: brainstorm the characteristics of the unpopular patient. Without hesitation and needing no prompting, a list is soon produced. Although there will be slight variations, the list usually includes patients who are violent, demanding, who treat hospitals as hotels, who never say thank you, who are always complaining, and so forth. Groups of nurses appear to have few qualms about describing patient or client characteristics that they find distasteful. Equally, they are quite happy to describe those whom they do like and argue among themselves if they do not reach consensus about a particular characteristic. Although this is usually explored in debate, no one feels a need to explain that they would never show such feelings to the patients concerned – this is assumed. Of course we would argue with this assumption and that would form the basis of the rest of the lesson. Suffice it here as an illustration.

Now try the same exercise with social workers: usually it produces an immediate silence. Then someone will declare that social workers do not have unpopular clients, although some clients might be considered difficult. The session facilitator usually then needs to emphasise the confidential nature of the exercise and that it is difficult to believe that social workers actually like all of their clients. After some hesitation, there then follows a vigorous session that is in some ways unusual for these students, because they are now 'allowed' to say the same things that nurses 'can'. The lists they produce are in fact remarkably similar, probably because they are aspects of human nature that nobody likes, often intensified by the specific patient or client situations.

The teaching sessions drawn on for this chapter usually involve some debate regarding the respective stereotyping of health and social care professionals. Both groups are fully aware of the stereotypical images of their own profession and will acknowledge some truth to these. Naturally BD (a social worker) does not wear socks and sandals and long floaty dresses, is not always late if she even bothers to turn up, is not lazy or disorganised and is not always poking her nose in where things are not her business. JT (a nurse) is neither an angel nor a whore, is not always out partying before going to work, does not inveigle doctors into the linen cupboard and is not totally inflexible. Stereotypes such as these are widely held and can be inhibiting to both practitioners and patients or clients, but must be acknowledged in order to move forward. Having illustrated some of the debate by using rather lighthearted classroom experiences, perhaps this would be a good place to outline some aspects of ideological thought that may begin to unpick why nurses and social workers may not engage with men despite their rhetoric.

Acknowledging a Difference: Two Different Attitudes?

The concept of the 'unpopular patient' is discussed widely in nursing and reveals an interesting ideological difference between nurses and social workers (Johnson and Webb 1995; Stockwell 1972 reprinted 1984). Salmon and Manyande (1996), discussing pain management, suggest that nurses consider 'good' patients as those who deal with their pain. Johnson and Webb (1995) argue that the labels nurses give to patients (which can be both positive and negative) are not related to individual personality characteristics, but are socially constructed within a web of very powerful social influences. They contend that these evaluative labels can be an important way of managing interpersonal relationships. It seems then that nurses (and by extension midwives and health visitors) are 'allowed' to recognise the concept of unpopular individuals, whereas in social work there appears to be little public acknowledgement of such an idea. There are strengths and weaknesses in both approaches, but recognition of the essential difference begins to clarify some of the stumbling blocks that may dilute effective practice with men within child care and protection.

> A clear understanding of human values can be gained by becoming familiar with some of the existing conceptual value frameworks... They are important in health and social care because health and social care professionals need to make decisions about value-laden practice dilemmas on a regular basis. (Glen 1999, p.203)

Glen argues that values are usually expressed as behaviours, either verbal or non-verbal. She further shows how the professional socialisation of health and social care workers (through their training, profession and employing institution) is a source of their values, and these values may be covert or overt.

> One might argue that health and social care professionals do not reflect very often on the values that are peculiar to the professionalization or socialization through which they pass. (Glen 1999, p.208)

What is needed is a conceptual framework of tolerance, compromise and education for dialogue (Glen 1999).

Ideology in Practice

What then does this debate illustrate about engaging with men in child care and protection? Perhaps in nursing it suggests that being consumed by the notion of caring makes it difficult to acknowledge that practice may not always be so 'caring'. An emphasis on the individual client (mother or child) may mean that any caring aspect of practice that could be extended to fathers is blocked out. The primacy of patient-centredness can be destructive if fathers are mentally excluded in practice. Thinking in this way raises a number of questions:

- What is caring?
- Is it something that can be extended to men?
- If so, is it done in a different way?
- Is it something that actually 'turns men off'?
- Is it something in women that connects to what women do, or can it be extended by male professionals?

Reflecting on practice, as urged within all major texts, curricula and professional codes can be liberating, but it could also mean too much time is spent thinking and too little acting. It can be very difficult to challenge practice within a framework that is universally held to be caring. It may also mean that shades of grey are difficult to interpret, as clearly delineated situations are much easier to deal with. A situation may arise where a father is known to be alcoholic, with violent tendencies that are occasionally exhibited in front of the children. Within a caring ideology, the focus of the caring health care professional may be directed at the mother and the children, yet it is possible that engaging with such a man may sometimes be the most effective course of action.

Social workers may be so sure that what they do is anti-discriminatory that they are paralysed in their honesty. This could mean a failure to acknowledge a problem (i.e. not engaging with men), or engaging with them without a full assessment of the picture. In trying to be too fair they may not see what is best for the child in such cases. It is also possible that the rhetoric of Radical or Lesbian or Feminist or Liberal or a combination of such titles is presented to the client (either overtly or by implication). We suggest that this can be harmful, especially when trying to engage with men, who are likely to view such individuals with a high degree of suspicion. Indeed, would an 'ordinary' mother, cohabitant since the birth of her first child at 18, living on a large council estate and working part-time as a factory domestic assistant feel able to relate to such a person? Social workers (and to some extent nurses) are keen to discuss feelings. The feminisation of a profession can actually contribute to some of this alienation. If a male social worker asks a male client how he may feel about a particular situation, will a man used to discussing concrete issues have a response? Whilst nurses can be criticised for being too apolitical, the other side of the coin is the complete alienation between social worker and client if the politicised labels are too apparent. It is not hard to see where the notion of social workers as 'policing the poor' comes from, which creates an immediate barrier to effective practice.

Caring

The nature of caring in nursing has received much attention over the past decade and remains a popular focus for both research and discussion. P. Barker and colleagues' (1995) marvellous paper, mentioned earlier, is summarised in Box 5.1 and provides a thorough summary of the thrust of current thinking regarding the concept.

Box 5.1 The proper focus of nursing: A critique of the 'caring' ideology

P. Barker et al.'s (1995) paper takes issue with the way some nurse educators in the UK are following North American theorists in asserting that 'caring' is the core of nursing. Their critique focuses on the work of Watson, as she represents the development of the 'new caring' in the UK, and on the work of Kirby and Slevin, who appear to be 'Watsonian' in their orientation. Although the authors share a sympathy for humanism, they remain unsatisfied with the caring ideology, viewing it more as a theology. They ask the question 'what makes a difference to the course of the patient's health needs or problems?' contending that this is the essence of nursing, rather than a hypothetical component or quality possessed by the nurse. They argue that if caring is the essence of nursing, then first, nursing must always involve caring, and second, caring should only occur within nursing. As this is a patently flawed argument, they take issue with the language and philosophical basis of those who propound it.

If nursing is to find its proper place in an increasingly fragmented health care world nurses need to recognise that laying territorial claims upon age-old intellectual constructions, such as 'care' and 'caring', will create conflicts from which we may never recover (p.395).

A comparative analysis of the literature generated five conceptualisations of the nature of caring (Morse *et al.* 1991). These were: a human trait; a moral imperative; an affect; an interpersonal interaction; and a therapeutic intervention. Although each of these could be argued with individually, they provide a good springboard as to what nurses mean when they talk about caring. Sabatino (1999) has tried to answer the fundamental questions surrounding the meaning of care, summarising it as:

- sensitivity to the vulnerability of persons
- time spent both doing and being with others
- a special manner of responding to those in need
- the challenge to bring healing.

Although Sabatino focuses much of his reflections on caring for dying patients, there are some clear pointers here to what he means by 'caring'. Although it is perhaps taking Sabatino's reflections out of context to discuss what this might mean for health visitors who are attempting to engage purposefully with men, the underlying value is probably the same. Sabatino's central thrust concerns the balance needed between human struggle and the vulnerability of human life. For health visitors and social workers too there must be a balance between the human and resource demands of a service and the wider integration of assets and all that entails. If we really are to say that nursing is caring, we cannot marginalise a large population of those who help provide it.

In an American nursing text, a number of authors are brought together to write expressly about the concept of caring. Caring is 'being there well', it is about an overlap between individual and environment (Karl 1992, p.5). Karl goes on to explain that there are three categories within his perspective, those of being balanced, being held and being sustained (being held is described as the environmental issues that bring out the best in people). Later in the same book, there is an examination of the conflict between professionalisation and caring.

> Nursing needs to demonstrate to health care administrators and physicians that the caring practices will increase the well-being of patients and, thus, promote cost-effective quality care... Nurses need to make their caring practice visible... In addition, organizational models which facilitate the practice of caring need to be identified and created. (Gardner 1992, p.252)

Arising from such texts there are two interesting points of note in arguing for purposeful intervention with men in child protection. First, that 'caring' is concerned with whom we bring to practice; and second, that, individual and organisational changes may be needed to facilitate 'care'. The values and attitudes that individual practitioners bring to client relationships affect practice, and practice can also be impeded or enhanced by organisational and structural issues.

In an extension of the 'caring' debate, it has been argued that trust is a crucial mechanism in the power relations of caring (Gilbert 1998). Drawing on sociological theory, Gilbert's analysis suggests that other influential writers are mistaken in the identification of interpersonal trust in nurses, because it has no commitment and is also not an individual characteristic. 'Rather, it is the product of deliberate strategies (education, mentoring, supervision) which result from the system's reflexive activity' (p.1015). Currently few of these strategies promote engaging with men and thus cannot be called entirely 'caring'.

Nonetheless, it is espoused that the ideology of 'caring' is established in nursing practice (Woodward 1998). Using an ethnographic approach in palliative care and maternity care settings, Woodward demonstrates the commitment of nurses and midwives to contribute positively to their patient's quality of life and their determination to facilitate patient autonomy. Woodward concludes by acknowledging the fallible nature of humans in a caring relationship, but emphasising the promotion of patient autonomy in practice. This has not been tested with fathers in child care and protection practice, but if the findings are transferable, it would mean that the focus of commitment was to mothers and children because of the principles of autonomy. Where this means that fathers are not engaged with specifically, it could be easily defended.

Others have taken a more pragmatic approach to the concept of caring. Whilst admitting that this is an elusive and difficult concept to define, let alone measure, Beck (1999) sets out to review 11 caring instruments that have quantitative designs. Beck provides a useful commentary on each of these instruments and although none of them were found to be perfect, their designs offer further insights into what is actually meant by this notion of caring. Most of the instruments fell into Morse *et al.*'s (1991) category of caring as a therapeutic intervention (a patient-centred and task-oriented view). Most of the instruments Beck reviewed saw caring as actions, although three of them also attempted to measure the process of caring. As one can imagine, Beck unearthed a number of methodological problems in the use of these instruments, and concludes that caring remains a problematic concept, not least because of a lack of consensus regarding its nature.

The personal nurse–patient relationship is at the heart of nursing, and caring is described as a foundational condition of practice (Gastmans 1999). Interestingly, Gastmans argues that care can also be valuable in passivity. A caring attitude does not develop in a vacuum. Another study, this time Brazilian, attempted to describe care as a relationship (Sadala 1999). Although based on an isolation ward, the study converges with other reports that 'caring' becomes synonymous with 'being with the patient', the overall therapeutic relationship that nurses have with their patients/clients. Although this may have been hindered at the beginning by the students' preconceptions, they all demonstrated a willingness to engage with the patients, and used communication skills, reflection and nursing procedures to enter into this therapeutic relationship: 'it became possible to administer nursing care in an empathic and human way' (Sadala 1999, p.816). The reflective process, argues Sadala, enables student nurses to perceive patients as persons and relate to them in a humanised way. If this is possible with terminally ill and HIV infected patients, then surely it is possible in engaging with men. So whether or not we accept the concept of caring to be a core component of nursing, what must be acknowledged is that we cannot have a baseline of caring without fully considering the implications this may have for engaging with men in child care and protection.

Reflective practice

> The critical aspects that distinguish reflection from analysis of other kinds are that it involves self and leads to a changed perspective. (Lyons 1999, p.31)

Summarising the work of van Manen (1977) and Schon (1992), Atkins and Murphy (1995) suggest that reflective practice is another commonly used term in nursing. Within a chapter on ideological roots then, how can reflective practice be directed in the engagement of fathers in child care and protection? Reflection is summed up as:

- being a process whereby nurses (but one assumes anybody) have an awareness regarding their own perceptions and feelings
- when the reality of the work context is recognised
- when one's own value judgements are recognised
- when the impact of these judgements is acknowledged and their underlying assumptions are questioned.

Others have emphasised the experiential aspects of reflective practice: that is, reflective practice requires a critical review of actions and interventions (Bailey 1995; Jarvis 1992). The barriers to such practice are described as individual (e.g. perceived lack of time, low staff morale, staff shortages) and cognitive (e.g. lack of theoretical knowledge, lack of self-awareness and insight) (Bailey 1995). This report was based on an action research project, where six practitioners kept reflective journals and recorded critical incidents over a three-month period. There was a reported progression from descriptive functioning to a use of theoretical knowledge to inform decision-making and a perceived improvement in clinical reasoning. Similar findings were reported when midwives were asked to keep journals (Lyons 1999).

Although reflective practice has not been endorsed in the same central way in social work (although this is certainly shifting), critical thinking skills are firmly advocated as central to one means of incorporating the values expressed by the profession (Razack 1999). Journal writing in social work is used in some training establishments as a process aimed at highlighting struggles, different understandings and awareness of practice issues – and thus change (Razack 1999).

We do not entirely agree that encouraging all practitioners to keep journals is going to make a big difference to practice, although there is no doubt that for some people this is a very useful exercise. Within academic assessment for both nursing and social work, there is a growing emphasis on reflection, of relating the theoretical to the practical. In clinical practice there is increasing support for feedback, for debriefing after stressful events, for a continuous and managed helping relationship that encourages reflection. It is imperative within social work training and within the UKCC Code of Conduct for Nurses, Midwives and Health Visitors (UKCC 1992a) that we maintain, critically evaluate and develop our practice and knowledge. Social work adds values here too and both professions have a commitment to undertake continuing professional development. Perhaps neither profession sees engaging with fathers as a crucial issue, one that is worth reflecting on. We either do it anyway (of course fathers are welcomed at my parenting classes/I always include the father when I visit), or men are too dangerous or difficult to include (he works during the day and we are not paid to visit in the evening/he's a horrible man, always swears at me and I'm quite scared of him). See Box 5.2 for a case example.

Box 5. 2 Case example

A health visitor was involved with a family where one of the children was failing to thrive. The child was so weak and had been refusing food for so long that he was being fed via a naso-gastric tube. Every time that the health visitor attended this family home, the father sat silently in a chair, just watching the health visitor and the mother and the child. He never wore a shirt and he never spoke. The health visitor was distraught. The child remained very ill and the health visitor found the father's attitude intimidating. One day the social worker visited, arriving at a mealtime. The mother had gone out, and the father was tube-feeding the child. It seemed that the father was the one who did everything for the child, but in front of the (female) health visitor he could not show that side of himself. Did the health visitor's attitude towards him accentuate the 'macho' image he tried to portray when she was there? Why had the health visitor missed the central role that this father took in the child care arrangements of this family?

Professional values

It is becoming clear then that nurses and social workers have underlying ideological values that overlap, albeit their expression may be different. Interestingly for this debate, it has been argued that with recognition of the complexity of nursing, there are two emergent metaphors: individualism and 'the community as caring'. 'The community as caring metaphor is a view of health care as the promotion, maintenance and restoration of client well-being in a co-operative community' (Wurzbach 1999, p.97).

Although Wurzbach acknowledges the complexity of such metaphors, she suggests that nurses can use them to evaluate their practice, as they provide values to aim for and to defend. So for the purposes of this book, this metaphor could be rephrased as 'a view of health care that promotes, maintains and restores father well-being in a co-operative community'. However, such a rephrasing tends to point to underlying values and these can be difficult to identify unless stated specifically.

Social work is explicit in stating its professional values and in training students have to demonstrate and provide evidence for the core values associated with social work. These are centralised on anti-discriminatory practice. Education training is similar, with explicit values which are imbibed within the profession and in which trainee teachers are required to show competency. Some of the values that are shared between education and social work include:

- Value the individual – promote equality of opportunity and fairness and adopt anti-discrimination in practice.

- Be fair and consistent.

- Promote rights of children and adults.

- Demonstrate sound judgement in decision-making.

- Evaluate and justify own practice.

If social workers do not engage with men in child care and protection, this can be challenged because it is contrary to the stated values of the profession. Nursing, midwifery and health visiting, though, do not produce stated values. Hamilton and Keyser (1992) suggest that the essential values of nursing include altruism, concern for the welfare of others, equality and fairness, but such values do not appear in any assessment strategy. There are of course core philosophical bases and there is a fundamental assumption that these incorporate values, but it is almost impossible to find a list of core values that student nurses must demonstrate in their practice. These are seen as inherent within the practice competencies of the profession (UKCC 1992b). This may lead us to assume that nurses can therefore pick and choose a little, within a framework of 'caring', what values they might hold. Of course an external imposition of certain values is not necessarily evidence of the internalisation of these and it can be constraining as well, as we argue in Chapter 4. Nonetheless, it is far more difficult to challenge a value if it is not overt, or if the fundamental philosophical basis is interpreted widely.

Key Issues from Theory

1. Two of the most dominant concepts in nursing are caring and reflective practice.

2. Nurses may use the concept of patient-centredness both to reinforce their arguments and to hide behind.

3. Some understanding of human values is essential for both health and social care practitioners.

4. An emphasis on caring for one family member may screen out another.

5. Politicised labels can create a barrier to effective practice.

6. If nursing is caring, it cannot marginalise a large population of those who help provide child care and protection.

7. Effective practice involves self-awareness and recognition of one's own value judgements.

8. Health and social care practitioners have underlying ideological values that overlap.

9. In training, social workers have stated values that must be demonstrated competently in practice.

10. In training, nurses do not have the same number of overt value lists that social workers have, although these values are seemingly subsumed within their competencies.

Practising within the Current Situation

So far in this chapter we have looked broadly at the ideological basis of nursing, focusing in particular on the concepts of caring and reflective practice. We now turn to how this might be played out in practice. Health visitors are the health care professionals most likely to have the opportunity to engage with men. Appendix III contains a simple check-list that can be used with fathers to assess their level of involvement in infant care.

Child surveillance is emphasised throughout health visitor training. Health visitors provide a universal service and have an access to families that no other professional has in the same way. Child protection is implicitly and explicitly central to their role and they increasingly identify and intervene with vulnerable families (D. M. Williams 1997). One study has shown that 97 per cent of health visitors have had direct involvement with at least one child protection referral (Gilardi 1991), so their uniqueness and their centrality within child care and protection cannot be overemphasised. However Butler (1996), a male lecturer in social work, argues that nurses are caring and thus it is not their job to be involved in child protection. We would argue the opposite: surely a caring ideology is exactly why health visitors are involved in child protection. It has been pointed out, though, that health visitors frequently mention child protection, yet make few attempts to define the process (Appleton 1994). The caring ideology (child protection) is emphasised without the reflection, even though the most important thing a public health nurse can do is to acknowledge any limitations (Hanafin 1998). So it appears that there is a discourse that advocates the value of engaging with men, but this amounts to little more than rhetoric if it is not translated consistently into practice.

In an analysis of health visiting practice as related to working with men, Chalmers (1992) devised two hypothetical continua – health visitors' conceptualisations of men, and interventions with men. Whilst this was a small, convenience sample and no quantitative data is offered as to how many fell into each category, the low conceptualisation/low intervention category reinforces the point made here. In this study not only were many health visitors having little to do with the father (despite opportunity), they had little conceptual idea of any possible role he might have.

Although health visitors have been identified as some of the key workers expected to include fathers as equal partners in raising their children, there is actually very little available information on how much time they spend interacting with fathers. In a study that examined fathers' views of health visitors, R. Williams and Robertson (1999) reported the following:

- Information on fathers was not routinely collected.

- Some men had never met the health visitor.

- Many felt ignored or dismissed by the health visitor.

- Overall, fathers felt marginalised.

- Health visitors anticipated lower levels of knowledge or ability from fathers.

Such views, concluded the authors, lead to fathers viewing the relationship between mothers and health visitors as a 'secret agent thing'. Box 5.3 sets out an attempt to look at the needs of fathers.

Box 5.3 A health promotion strategy for expectant fathers

As part of her degree, health visitor Barbara Wood initiated monthly local antenatal clinics to which both partners were invited, but which were aimed specifically at expectant fathers. She points out that this was essentially a theoretical exercise and was not put into practice in this form. Using an eclectic model, she developed a health promotion strategy to increase men's support for their breastfeeding partners. Topics included the benefits of breastfeeding, practical management and the importance of fathers' support. Based on this experience, Barbara provided us with an anecdotal account of some of her observations on the process of planning such a health promotion strategy:

- It is not unusual to find unemployed men who are always with the mother when seen by the health visitor, who have insight into the needs of children and who willingly take on children from the mother's previous relationships.
- More men now attend well baby clinics than they did 10 or 20 years ago.
- However, far too many men still leave the room or hide behind a newspaper when the health visitor arrives.
- Few expectant fathers come to antenatal classes.
- In positive parenting groups, the ratio of men to women attendees is in the order of 1:10.

Although this is only one account, it is probably not unusual. Wood poses the question:

Does the fact that health and social care is dominated by women confirm for fathers that this is not their area of interest?

Throughout the literature on parenting, what is usually meant by parenting is in fact mothering. Perhaps some practitioners do not consider the father to have a role in child care. In an attempt to find the extent to which health visitors engage with men, Chalmers (1992) gives an example of one health visitor who had worked with one abusive and neglectful family (with other professionals) for a number of years. This particular health visitor conceptualised the mother as the caretaker, and the father, in her view, was not considered important. This may be surprising to many health visitors, but the literature shows repeatedly that the reality of practice is that men in general, and fathers in particular, are not being engaged with meaningfully. Consequently, mothers remain the main focus of intervention.

Parenting classes are a prime example. 'It takes courage to be a health visitor. It takes more courage to run courses for parents about parent–child relationships' (Angeli 1997, p.338). But how often are parent classes in fact mother classes? There is certainly the intention that men are invited and welcomed to such classes, but in practice few attend. Such courses are increasingly popular, but may divert attention from social factors that affect family relationships (Gaze 1997). A similar pattern is seen in midwifery, where men are missing out on ante-natal classes (Combes and Schonveld 1992) and in support for their expectant father role (Lavender 1997). In the UK, health visitors often refer to 'my mums' when they talk of such classes. An article on facilitating parenting skills (Angeli et al. 1994) included some fathers, but the accompanying photograph showed only mothers and children. Throughout the literature that describes parenting classes, there is an underlying emphasis on mothers, even though attendance by fathers is increasing and parenting classes just for men are now growing (see Ryan and Little 2000 for a useful summary of some of this work). Uptake, though, remains low. The situation is changing, but in offering such classes it is crucial to be aware of the language used, the different employment patterns of mothers and fathers and the range of activities that are offered. Fathers need to be engaged with meaningfully: few will engage themselves in classes that appear to be aimed at women.

Opportunities from 'caring'

Van Hooft (1999) describes caring as a virtue, central to nursing practice and the basis of its 'moral practice'. He argues that 'the virtue of caring embraces all aspects of action, including the emotions, motivations, knowledge and ethical thinking that enter into it' (p.189). Although we might take issue with the notion of caring as a 'virtue', this is a useful framework to use in identifying the opportunities for practice that 'caring' might afford. Van Hooft describes caring as having eight features, and we have related these to engaging with fathers:

1. *The field of the virtue*: the range of environments, policies, personal and social issues that are linked with health care. In engaging with men in child care and protection, this means that we have to consider the role of men within the family, community and political environment. What are the personal issues that fathers bring to families? What are the social issues that an unemployed father may bring to that family for example? Effective dialogue may extend to helping him deal with his current joblessness – practically by giving advice on interview skills or where job clubs are held; psychologically by recognising his loss of self-esteem and purpose and teaching him coping mechanisms; socially by putting him in touch with a fathers' group, for example. It may be difficult to measure the impact of such interventions, but it is more likely to make a positive difference than a negative one.

2. *The target of the virtue*: the enhancement or preservation of health in individuals, families or communities. A broad concept of health that includes social and psychological well-being must include fathers in child care and protection. So far it seems that fathers are not the target of our practice by design. How many health visitors deliberately arrange their visits for when both parents are present? Does the organisation allow and even fund evening visits for example?

3. *The agent's understanding of the field*: the knowledge base of nurses, including competency in critical thinking. Reflective practice, properly structured, can help health care professionals acknowledge where engaging with men can have a positive impact. For example, does the child protection situation arise because the mother is overwhelmed? Can the father be encouraged to take on three small child care tasks a day that could make an enormous difference to the way the mother feels? Could this change the balance of the situation in a positive way?

4. *The agent's motivation*: the professional commitment of the nurse (van Hooft sidesteps the notions of 'kind of love' espoused by others), even where at an individual level there is no caring

motivation. It can be difficult to feel 'caring' for a father who has (for example) sexually abused a child. Embracing a wider concept of care will not automatically screen out such a man from any intervention that is best for the child.

5. *The agent acting on the basis of motivation:* where there is a distinction between 'caring' as a behaviour and 'caring' as a virtue. What we do is not necessarily what we are, and conflating the two can be a barrier to effective practice. Engaging with men is a behaviour that may be more caring for the child than not engaging with him.

6. *The beneficiaries of the virtue:* what are the benefits not only to the individual patient/client, but also to the wider family or community? Engaging with men in child care and protection may make a huge difference to the whole family. The implications may not be apparent, but for example, directing a heroin-addicted father to a drug rehabilitation unit may have many benefits, from reducing the risk of blood-borne infections to the rest of the family through the opportunity for needle exchange, to creating a safer community where he no longer needs to steal to support his habit.

7. *The agent feeling appropriate emotions:* van Hooft tends to agree that too much emphasis is placed on individual emotions involved in caring and that we can act from the virtue without any particular emotional state of concern. However, there must be a strong and effective commitment to the goal of health. Engaging with men in child care and protection is a professional requirement. It does not come on the basis of intuition or the mood of the professional on a particular day.

8. *Preparedness to reflect:* the requirement not only to keep up with relevant theoretical knowledge, but also to engage in a review of the moral qualities of professional actions. Reflective practice is an essential component of the caring ideology.

It is possible that a lack of clarity in defining who we are as nurses makes it less possible to work effectively. A role definition (which includes a clear understanding of what is meant by caring if that is the component we want to define ourselves by) that we are sure of will give confidence in clarifying the aims and objectives of engaging with men in a child care and protection context. Further, we need to be clear of what we mean by 'patient' or 'client' – is it only mothers and children in child care and protection, or is it equally fathers?

The word 'caring' may be an easier term for using with mothers and children rather than with fathers, and this may explain why we do not engage with men. Caring, however defined, has nurturing properties that socially and culturally are likely to be directed to the health and social care provision of mothers and children. We may need to challenge our understanding of this and recognise how such an ideology can impact on practice with fathers. It is always easier to care for people who want to be cared for and who respond to our actions (see 'the unpopular patient' literature and debates refered to earlier in the chapter, especially Johnson and Webb (1995)). Whether or not we choose to accept caring as an integral part of nursing, or whether we prefer a less evangelical thrust to the profession, it cannot be denied that there are elements that ring true in our service provision. Within the limits of the caveats that we stated at the beginning of the book, then fulfilling the challenge of care must include fathers: it concerns responding to their needs and requires time spent engaging with them.

Opportunities from reflective practice

Health visiting practice has been likened to intuition by means of motivation, sensitivity, emotion and speed of thought (Goding 1997). Intuitive practice involves the ability to see the whole problem, rather than concentrating on individual parts, which is also useful as a basis for choosing from a number of action plans. There needs to be balance between analytical reasoning and intuitive knowledge, with neither being emphasised at the expense of the other (Goding 1997). In a critical examination of 22 local authority social workers who were undertaking child protection investigations, Bell (1999) highlights the conflicts that can arise given the sometimes contradictory nature of the legal base of interventions and decision-making processes. Bell calls for a clarification of such processes as crucial if we are to engage fully with all family members. Many people have contact with health visitors, as opposed to the 'policing' nature of social work, but for health visitors there is no current clear legal framework to guide practice, placing them in an even more untenable position than social workers.

It is central to this debate that there is no clarity, for example, about how to respond to biological fathers who do not have legal responsibilities or to men who may be married to the mothers, but who are not the biological fathers. It is possible that this allows practitioners some leeway in choosing whether to 'confer' fatherhood to a particular male or not (Daniel and Taylor 1999). They may choose to exclude men who seem dangerous or unreliable, but they may include fathers who demonstrate a commitment to the well-being of children. It is clear that a consistent approach is lacking. Reflecting on both personal and professional practice may be one answer to this dichotomy.

Just as a sociological analysis is essential, it has been suggested that nursing theory must consider the socio-political context of the work and take account of changes in political ideology (Caldwell 1997). The social work child care curriculum has attempted to do just that and contemporary social work has an explicit value base of anti-oppressive practice. For practice with parents the focus is on recognition of the inequalities that abound in society on the basis of gender-reflective practice. The guidance for child care and protection is informed mainly by feminist theory which has challenged a number of assumptions about parenting (see Chapter 4), for example that women are biologically prepared for mothering and that the nuclear family is essential for adequate child rearing (Thompson 1997). Social work professionals, therefore, have made a start in theorising about gendered assumptions in practice with parents; has the health care profession? There is more work to be done on the role of fathers and the aims of engagement with fathers, and there are a number of questions that we need to reflect on, such as:

- To what extent are gendered assumptions made about parenting roles in health visiting child care practice?
- What potential is there for health visiting to develop ideas of anti-discriminatory practice in work with both mothers and fathers?
- As providers of a universal service, is there a role for health visitors in empowering both men and women as parents?
- Is it easier to 'care' for mothers than it is fathers?
- Do health care professionals engage with men by chance or by design? (Taylor and Daniel 2000)

Opportunities from a value base

In practice there is an argument for both engaging with men in child care and protection (this is the caring thing to do), and equally avoiding or marginalising men, because this too could be seen as the caring thing to do. It is essential to recognise both the personal value base we work from and the social construction of our professional values.

Social workers need to consider how they articulate anti-discriminatory practice. It may be that they are too forgiving and may consequently ignore the impact of their behaviour on other people. There is a need to monitor our feelings, as it is legitimate to feel anger or hatred, but unethical to allow such hidden feelings to impinge on our relationships with clients. Nurses need to be more careful with some of their phraseology: 'my mums' for example is very patronising and is recognised as such by clients. Men may feel excluded just by the terminology. It is too easy to forget that our own values do impact very strongly on clients and are an enormous barrier to effective practice.

Key Messages for Practice

1. Child care and protection is implicitly and explicitly central to the health visitor's role.

2. The role of health visitors in child protection needs clarification.

3. Current practice of health care professionals engaging with men operates more by chance than design.

4. There is a need to distinguish 'parenting' classes from 'mothering' classes.

5. There is a need to separate care as a behaviour from care as a virtue or care as a feeling.

6. Engaging with men in child care and protection may have a positive effect on children, families and communities.

7. Effective practice entails reflective practice.

8. Such reflection must include questioning the gendered assumptions that encroach upon practice with parents.

9. Personal and professional jargon can inhibit practitioner–client relationships.

10. Personal and professional values need to be recognised and understood – they impact on clients.

Try it for Size

In a small group generate a list of commonly heard phrases or concepts that are used within your profession. Now individually give each of these a 'cringe factor' (1 = does not make you cringe at all, 5 = makes you cringe dreadfully). For example, what may make some people cringe is health visitors, especially women, who refer to their clients as 'my mums' and social workers, especially men, who describe themselves as liberal feminists, and they would score these with a 5. Compare the ratings you have made and discuss the following:

- Are the phrases and terms we use reflected in our practice?

- If so, how?

- If not, how can you be sure?

- If we are trying to engage purposefully with men in child care and protection, are our underlying values, possibly portrayed through our expressions, a barrier or a help?

Chapter 6

Fathers as Risks

Introduction

In this chapter we cover the issue that is at the heart of child care and protection practice: engaging with fathers who pose risks to their children. This is the most difficult and complex subject about which to develop practice guidance. Facing up to, and grappling with, the many potential ways in which men may pose risks to their children requires a pessimistic approach; it means considering the worst possibilities and contemplating the disturbing fact that fathers can inflict direct or indirect harm on their children. It is perhaps because of the disturbing nature of the issue that current practice so often skirts around the problem and concentrates on mothers instead. For example, it is very difficult to apply the nursing concept of caring when encountering men who sexually abuse their children. But putting our heads in the sand with regard to such men does not make them disappear. We argue that ignoring or minimising the potential risks that men pose is negligent and dangerous and that therefore, the riskiness of men has to be appraised.

However, we also move into what is perhaps an even more complicated territory: that of men who may pose a risk to their child, but may simultaneously have something to offer them. Some might argue that fathers must forfeit their right to a relationship with their children if they pose any kind of risk to them. This might indeed be the simplest response, but it is a response that misses out the child's perspective. The strength and complexity of children's attachments to significant adults cannot be underestimated. Such complexity can be most starkly manifested in cases where the father has sexually abused his child. We are aware that this is a highly sensitive and emotive area, and we do not believe that we have all the answers. What we do assert, though, is that all intervention must be built around a careful assessment about what is in the child's best interests. The key message is that each individual case has to be considered in great detail and with consultation and supervision.

In the first part of this chapter we will consider the evidence about the different ways that men can be risks to children, focusing on a range of abuse and neglect situations. In the second part we return to each of these situations and make suggestions for practice.

Risk Due to Child Abuse

On the basis of current research we know that men (but not necessarily biological fathers) commit a vast majority of the sexual abuse against children and about half of the physical abuse (Creighton 1992). In examining the perpetrators identified in the studies summarised in *Messages from Research*, Ryan and Little (2000) give figures for fathers ranging from 36 per cent to 55 per cent. The profile of perpetrators is different for different types of abuse, both in gender distribution and in characteristics of the abuser. Figure 6.1 shows the Scottish breakdown of perpetrators for different types of abuse.

Physical Abuse

Surprisingly there is very little research that separates out the characteristics of fathers and mothers who physically abuse. Most of the literature refers to abusive 'families' or 'parents'. In an examination of 76 studies Martin (1983) found only two that dealt exclusively with males. Thus, the research information about physical abuse is impoverished because the specific role of fathers is not recognised and there is an overemphasis on the role of the mother (Muller and Diamond 1999).

In a detailed comparison study of the longer term effects of physical abuse on 170 children Gibbons *et al.* (1995) found abused children to be more likely to exhibit behaviour problems at home and school, to have more friendship problems, and to score lower on some cognitive tests. They conclude that physical abuse in itself seems not to be associated with poor outcomes, but rather the context of 'a harshly punitive, less reliable and less warmly involved style of parenting' within which it occurs.

Abuser over 16	% Physical injury	% Sexual abuse	% Failure to thrive	% Emotional abuse	% Physical neglect	TOTAL	%
Birth father	43.4	34.2	20.0	33.3	18.7	371	36.0
Birth mother	32.2	3.7	40.0	48.8	77.4	346	33.6
Male sibling	1.7	6.3	0.0	0.0	0.6	26	2.5
Female sibling	0.2	0.7	0.0	0.8	0.0	4	0.4
Stepfather	6.9	8.6	20.0	9.8	0.6	70	6.8
Stepmother	0.2	0.0	0.0	0.0	0.0	1	0.1
Male cohabitee	8.6	7.4	0.0	0.8	0.0	62	6.0
Female cohabitee	0.0	0.0	0.0	0.0	1.3	2	0.2
Male relative	2.3	14.9	0.0	1.6	0.0	53	5.1
Female relative	0.8	0.0	0.0	0.8	0.6	5	0.5
Male foster carer	0.6	0.4	0.0	2.4	0.0	7	0.7
Female foster carer	0.2	0.0	0.0	0.8	0.0	2	0.2
Male other	2.1	23.4	0.0	0.8	0.6	76	7.4
Female other	0.2	0.4	20.0	0.0	0.0	3	0.3
Male residential care staff	0.4	0.0	0.0	0.0	0.0	2	0.2
Female residential care staff	0.2	0.0	0.0	0.0	0.0	1	0.1
TOTAL	479	269	5	123	155	1031	

Figure 6.1 Scottish figures showing the relationship to the child of suspected perpetrators of abuse, by main category of abuse (excluding Strathclyde and Tayside). This table originally appeared in the Scottish Office Statistical Bulletin Child Protection Management Information 1994–95, ISBN 07480 5672 6, published October 1996.

The research about the impact of physical abuse upon children does not tend to differentiate between the effects of abuse by the mother, father or stepfather. This is strange because, for example, it could be expected that to be subjected to a constant stream of small smacks all day from your mother might have a different impact than to be given a severe beating from your father once a year.

Profile of perpetrators of physical abuse

The combined figures for physical abuse suggest that both mothers and fathers are equally likely to physically abuse children. Physical abuse is mainly perpetrated within the context of the parental relationship, as a form of discipline for example, or as a result of family tensions (Claussen and Crittenden 1991, p.13). As such, therefore, it is necessary to look at the context of care. It is women who are mainly responsible for the care of children, therefore they inflict less physical abuse in proportion to the amount of time that the children spend in their presence (Ryan and Little 2000).

When the figures are examined in detail the emergent picture is very complicated, and in some ways contradictory. Compared with mothers, fathers, and especially stepfathers may be more likely to be responsible for the more serious abuse and death. But, although we have argued throughout the book that fathers and father-figures should be given equal consideration, when it comes to physical abuse it seems that there are differences between the risks that biological fathers pose and those that stepfathers pose. There also seem to be differences on the basis of severity of abuse.

A study of 32 cases of infanticide (Brewster et al. 1998) showed the perpetrator to be the biological father in 77 per cent of the cases. However, this sample may not be representative of the whole population as it was based on the US army and the group contained a large number of biological parent couples. Other studies suggest that children are far more likely to be killed by a stepfather than by a biological father or mother. For example, Kotch (1998) cites a study suggesting that stepfathers pose a 100 times greater risk to children under two than biological fathers (Daly and Wilson 1988).

Moving from infanticide to injury, in a study of high-risk children recruited at birth in North Carolina, Kotch (1998) found:

the presence of a non-biological father-figure in the home increases the risk of maltreatment more than two times above that for families with both biological parents in the home. The risk of maltreatment given the presence of the mother's partner (non-biological father-figure) in the home is twice that of single female-headed families (p.4).

In their study in the UK, Gibbons *et al.* (1995) found the perpetrator of physical abuse to be the female caregiver in 40 per cent of cases, the male caregiver in 43 per cent, and both together in 11 per cent. When looking in more detail at the biological relationship of the male perpetrator they found, like Kotch, that stepfathers were a greater risk, being responsible in 50 per cent of cases, while the biological father was responsible in 37 per cent of cases. But, in contradiction to the study by Kotch, they found males and females to be equally likely to inflict severe injury when acting separately, and when acting together likely to inflict the most serious injury.

There are some indications that physical abuse from one parent is correlated with physical abuse from the other (Muller and Diamond 1999), which highlights again the issue of the parenting atmosphere. As Gibbons *et al.* (1995) found, children who had been subjected to abuse tended to live in families where there was more violence and inconsistent discipline and where they felt they could not rely on their parents.

Research into the characteristics of parents who abuse their children has not systematically separated males and females. Gibbons *et al.* looked at main caregivers and found them to have more emotional distress, poorer health and more money problems than non-abusers. In a major review of the characteristics of perpetrators of abuse (Milner and Dopke 1997) the discourse switches between the use of 'mothers' and 'parents', and the dearth of research upon fathers is mentioned. In summary, mothers/parents were found to:

- be more likely to have low self-esteem and negative views of their children

- attribute more blame and hostile intent to children, to hold inappropriate expectations of their behaviour, and exhibit lower empathy for their children

- experience higher levels of stress, emotional problems and feelings of social isolation.

A Scottish study of 43 cases of physical abuse found neither parent to be particularly hostile to their children; instead they found a pattern of children with extreme behaviour problems in conjunction with an atmosphere of lax parental discipline (Pitcairn *et al.* 1993).

Practice

The treatment of men and of women who physically abuse children is different. Farmer and Owen (1995) found that when the perpetrator was a man there was more likelihood of him being removed from the home, but that if it was a woman, the child was more likely to be removed. Also, in 77 per cent of cases where the perpetrator was the mother, the child's name was placed on the child protection register, as opposed to 48 per cent of cases where the father was the perpetrator. When the father was the perpetrator intervention focused on persuading the mother to separate from him, and if this did not occur, to offer emotional support to the mother and to concentrate on the mother and child care issues. There was very little intervention aimed specifically at modifying abusive behaviour with either mothers or fathers.

> It is an interesting and disturbing paradox that in child protection work there is so much focus on controlling and regulating the actions of mothers, given that the child protection system was set up in the wake of public anxiety about child deaths, most of which were inflicted by men (Farmer and Owen 1998, p.562).

Neglect

Overwhelmingly the figures for perpetration of neglect sum up the situation described throughout this book: that mothers are considered to be primarily responsible for the nurturing of their children (Swift 1990; Turney 2000). Daniel (1999) has described the scant attention that the neglect literature pays to fathers of children who are neglected. Essentially, fathers are not even considered to be perpetrators of neglect. They are described as having a 'tangential' relationship with the family (Crittenden 1996). What research there is suggests that the mothers appear to get little support from the fathers of their children (Coohey

1995). From a study of mothers' perceptions of their male partners Lacharite, Ethier and Couture (1996) found that 'men in neglectful families are perceived by the mothers as being less adequate marital partners, less supportive and more violent.' But they also found that they were 'perceived by the mothers as being equally adequate as a paternal figure as men in non-maltreating families'. This suggests the potential for men to be involved positively in parenting, even if they are not involved in a relationship with the mother.

Again, current child care practice concentrates upon mothers. From a detailed study of neglect case files Swift (1995) found that caring for children was clearly viewed as the role of the mother. Whilst mothering deficiencies were noted in detail, any child care action by a father, however minimal, tended to be written in case files as positive, whereas partial or total absence was unnoted.

Children who are neglected are at high risk of very poor long-term outcomes (Stevenson 1998). At the moment the role of the father in neglecting children is not delineated, but from the point of view of their children, fathers of neglected children are failing them just as much, if not more, than the mothers who are struggling to care for them under difficult circumstances.

Sexual Abuse

The incidence and prevalence figures of child sexual abuse vary tremendously because of different definitions and different methodology. A UK survey found 59 per cent of girls and 27 per cent of boys to have experienced some form of child sexual abuse before the age of 18 (Kelly, Regan and Burton 1991). There are 1.1 million projected offenders in the UK who could commit an average of 380 crimes in their lifetime (Calder 1999). Child sexual abuse of both boys and girls is therefore a widespread problem that can have devastating effects on the lives of children and their non-abusing parents.

More information is being accumulated about the potential for women to sexually abuse children, but all the current evidence shows men to be responsible for the overwhelming majority of child sexual abuse (Finkelhor 1984). Many of these men are fathers or father-figures, if not to the children they are sexually abusing, then to other children. As Figure 6.1 shows, in Scotland the figures for sexual abuse perpetrators for 1994–95 indicate 95 per cent to be male and 72 per cent of them to be related to or living in same household as the child, with many of the rest known to the child (Social Work Services Inspectorate 1997). One study showed the abuser to be the natural father in 31 per cent of cases, stepfather in 21 per cent and the mother's cohabitee in 11 per cent (Waterhouse and Carnie 1992). Sharland *et al.* (1995) found that fathers were suspected of responsibility in 28 per cent of cases, father-figures in 16 per cent and known but unrelated male adults in 32 per cent.

The characteristics of sexual abuse perpetrators are, in some ways, different from the characteristics of perpetrators of other forms of abuse. Of course, many sexual abusers may also carry out physical abuse, sometimes as part of the enforcement of sexual activities, but the seductive behaviour and degree of planning that is characteristic of many sexual abusers points to the addictive nature of sexual abuse (Calder 1999; Frosh 1995).

For the purposes of this book it is important to consider whether men who abuse children in their own families have different characteristics from men who abuse unrelated children. Citing a range of research (Abel and Rouleau 1990; Barker and Morgan 1993; Waterhouse, Dobash, and Carnie 1994; Williams and Finkelhor 1991) the Social Work Services Inspectorate in Scotland provide the following summary (1997):

Familial child sex abusers

- …live in the home of the victim at the time of the offence

- …are more likely to offend against female children

- …tend to have fewer victims (but may commit more offences) than non-familial child sex abusers

- …do not show deviant sexual arousal to child stimuli

- …appear passive, dependent and isolated individuals, with no masculine identification.

Non-familial child sex abusers…were more likely to have grown up in disrupted families in which they experienced significant violence from their parents and experienced periods of separation from their parents or to have grown up in an institutional context. They were also more likely to:

- have experienced sexual abuse as a child themselves
- have lived alone at the time of the offence
- have previous criminal records
- have used physical force in the offence
- be socially inadequate
- have been sexually attracted to young children from an early age
- commit acts of sexual violence against children while under the influence of alcohol or through loss of control in the course of sexual offending. (pp.63–4).

Such distinctions have to be treated with caution; for example, Abel *et al.* (1988) found that 49 per cent of the men referred to their treatment clinic for sexual abusers were abusing children both within and outside their family.

This would suggest that in any assessment of a child's situation an explicit consideration of the male figure is essential. However, it seems that this is not routine practice. In a study to identify recurrent social work errors in child protection public inquiries in Britain, Munro (1998) discovered that social workers often overlooked the mother's male partner when assessing risk and family functioning.

From the child's point of view, being sexually abused by a father or father-figure is very likely to have specifically complex implications. Within the context of a parental relationship there is far more potential for the abuser to use psychological coercion, to exploit that relationship and betray the child's trust (Faller 1990). It is also likely that the child will be subjected to abuse over a long period of time. Box 6.1 describes in more detail how perpetrators sexualise their relationship with their victim, and the ambivalent feelings that children often express about their abusers.

Risk due to Domestic Violence

As with sexual abuse, men commit the overwhelming majority of domestic violence. Fathers who are violent to women pose both direct and indirect risks to their children.

Box 6.1 Perpetrators of child sexual abuse

Berliner and Conte (1990) interviewed children who had been sexually abused. Abusers included fathers, mothers' boyfriends, neighbours and babysitters. Conte, Wolf and Smith (1989) interviewed sexual abuse perpetrators in a treatment programme. The number of victims admitted to was between 1 and 40, with an average of 7.3 each. The youngest was 18 months. More victims were females, some were related to the perpetrator, and nearly all were known to him.

The offenders claimed that they could write a manual of how to sexually abuse children and could provide a range of ways to befriend a needy child, and to gradually desensitise or frighten him or her. The behaviour described by both children and offenders often incorporated a level of threat, aggression and coercion. Sometimes the threats were psychological and manipulated the children's feelings about the offender and about other members of the family.

Many of the children described ambivalent feelings about the offender; 'over half said they loved him, needed or depended on him'. For example: 'At that time I really needed love, and he did love me and told me this. He made me feel really important.'

The key message from the two studies for practice for treatment and prevention is the recognition of three processes:

- the sexualisation of a relationship by gradual escalation
- the justification of contact by the offender in a variety of ways, under the guise of sex education for example
- the ability of offenders to ensure the child's co-operation by exploiting vulnerability, and a child's normal wish to feel loved.

Extent of domestic violence

We can never be sure of the extent of domestic violence because it is so frequently kept a secret. It is known to be a likely feature in a third of divorces (Hester and Radford 1996) and 45 per cent of female murders. Although violence often occurs in secret and practitioners will not be aware of it, there are particular times when it is more likely and where practitioners could potentially play a role. During pregnancy and just after childbirth are particularly vulnerable times for the onset of violence against women (Mezey and Bewley 1997). Another dangerous time for women is during and after separation or divorce, especially during child contact arrangements (Hester and Radford 1996). Often practitioners assume that separation will solve the problem of domestic violence, and may urge women to leave violent partners. However, men will often pursue women who have left and subject them to further violence, sometimes also physically abusing the children.

In a comprehensive review of the literature Hester, Pearson and Harwin (2000) summarise the various ways in which children may be affected in:

- that the domestic violence perpetrator may also be directly – physically and/or sexually – abusive to the child

- that witnessing violence to their mothers may have an abusive and detrimental impact on the children concerned and

- that the perpetrators may abuse the child as part of their violence against women. (p.30).

Impact upon children

Seeing, hearing and living with violence against their mother by their father increases the chances of negative outcomes in children. Of 108 women who had experienced domestic violence (with 246 children between them), 91 per cent said their children were affected negatively (Abrahams 1994). All 100 participants in a study of black women's experiences of domestic violence felt their children had been badly affected (Mama 1996). It has long been known that living in an environment of parental strife is bad for children (Rutter and Rutter 1993). The constant threat of violence can create as damaging an atmosphere for children as actual violence, as can the attendant fall-out of:

- the need for secrecy or dissembling about their mother's injuries

- embarrassment, including anxiety about taking friends home

- missing school as a result of home disruption

- needing to move home

- possibly living in a refuge

- feeling the need to protect the mother

- feeling to blame, for example if a discipline issue sparks the incident

- not having a caring, non-violent father.

Witnessing violence can result in pre-school children having physical symptoms of anxiety; primary age children showing behavioural and emotional problems; and adolescents turning to drugs, early marriage, pregnancy, running away or crime (Hester *et al.* 2000).

Links with child abuse

There is an association between assault of the mother and sexual, physical and emotional abuse of children. Hester and Pearson (1998) carried out a detailed study of the profile of 111 cases dealt with by the NSPCC. Of the cases, 77 per cent centred on child sexual abuse, and the father (or father-figure) was identified as the perpetrator of that sexual abuse in 53 per cent. In over half of the child sexual abuse cases domestic violence was also an issue. In the cases where the father was the perpetrator, domestic violence was an issue in 69 per cent. In other words, sexual abuse against the child by the biological father and violence against the mother were likely to coexist.

Farmer and Owen (1995) studied 44 child protection cases in detail. In 40 per cent of the child sexual abuse cases and 59 per cent of the physical abuse, neglect and emotional abuse cases there was also a history of domestic violence. Further, these were the cases where the children had the worst outcomes and yet the issue appeared to be largely ignored by the practitioners.

Ironically, it is in the arena of child contact after divorce that it has been suggested that the rights of fathers are given too much priority and that the potential risks to children are minimised. Research pointed to the dangers of the family mediation approach when domestic violence is an issue and indicated that violent fathers were using contact arrangements to harass or harm women and children (Hester and Radford 1996). Following this, national guidelines have been produced in England that warn against joint mediation meetings in divorce cases where domestic violence is known or suspected to be an issue (Home Office 1994). Subsequent research into the practice of family court welfare officers and voluntary sector mediators (Hester and Radford 1996) found improved practice in that mothers and fathers were being seen separately, but found a lack of systematic screening as to whether domestic violence might be an issue.

Practice issues

Women who are experiencing domestic violence often do seek professional help; for example, a survey of 109 women in refuges showed that 11.5 per cent had contacted social services after the first attack, 40 per cent after the worst and 60 per cent after the last (Dobash and Dobash 1985). Unfortunately they receive a patchy service. For women from ethnic minorities there are added problems, particularly when practitioners feel paralysed by anxieties about condemning 'cultural' norms (Mama 1996; Mullender 1996).

Fathers who are committing domestic violence rarely contact social services, but they do come into contact with other services. Many approach their GPs, usually presenting with drug or alcohol problems or with depression (Hearn 1998). It is extremely rare for GPs to probe further into suggestions of violence, and then to follow up with referrals to the health visitor or to social services.

In the past the professional response was geared towards keeping the family together, but this has shifted towards an expectation that women will leave violent partners. Mullender (1996) suggests that this approach is also problematic as it puts all the pressure upon the woman to make changes and it fails to recognise that violence will often continue, or even escalate during and after separation.

What all practitioners singularly fail to do is engage directly with the fathers who are causing the problem in the first place. Stanley (1997) highlights the extent to which men as risks to their female partners (and by inference to their children) are overlooked and refers to the 'invisible men' who pervade the child protection system. The potential for men to intimidate female social workers is seen as contributing to their not being engaged with in the process of child protection (Munro 1998).

It has been pointed out that women pose a greater risk to social workers than men (O'Hagan and Dillenberger 1995, p.40); however, there is often little choice about engaging with mothers, who, as the statistics suggest, are most likely to hold primary responsibility for child care. Ironically, therefore, the very 'dangerousness' of men may contribute to their not being assessed appropriately (O'Hagan and Dillenberger 1995, p.32).

Violent men

Hearn (1998) interviewed 60 men in England who had committed violence against known women and concluded that 'violence…is a powerful way of demonstrating that someone is a man.' He found that the men were at pains to describe themselves as not typically violent men; instead they constructed the violence as a response to the 'real problem' of drink, stress and so on. The men gave little attention to the effects on the woman and there was very little recognition of the possible effect on children. They had taken for granted assumptions about relationships with women and used lots of justification for their violence. Although the men were abusing their power, many of them did not feel powerful, but instead felt caught by addiction to drink and drugs and often felt depressed.

Mullender (1996) considers the range of explanations that have been put forward for male violence which include:

- individual pathology or mental illness
- loss of control
- transgenerational transmission
- drink
- social and material stress
- provocation by the victim
- cultural influences.

None of these explanations fully accounts for the gender distribution of aggressors and victims, and Mullender suggests that an explanation has to be located within a recognition that there is something wrong:

> with the institution of intimate relationships between men and women …and the way it is mediated in society. Men are encouraged to be dominant and controlling and the logical extension of this is abuse. (p.49)

However, a monolithic explanation on this basis does not explain why some men are not violent, and here we would suggest that for an individual man to become violent there will be an interaction between the enabling social environment and specific factors such as the experience of childhood violence.

Key Issues from Theory

1. It is essential that all practitioners assess the potential risks that any man associated with the child might pose.

2. The figures for physical abuse suggest mothers and fathers to be equally likely to be responsible, but the fact that children spend far less time in the sole care of fathers indicates that they in fact pose a greater risk.

3. Current practice does not tend to focus directly on male violence against children; instead it concentrates on mothers' parenting skills and ability to protect.

4. Fathers are virtually invisible in research and practice literature about neglect.

5. Social workers and health visitors may aspire to involve fathers, but covertly and overtly their actions and language imply that caring is the job of mothers.

6. The overwhelming majority of child sexual abuse is perpetrated by men, many of whom are fathers to their victims and/or to other children.

7. Sexual abuse of a child by the father entails a betrayal of trust and violation of the parental relationship.

8. When planning intervention following child sexual abuse practitioners must assess carefully what is best for the child in the short and long term.

9. Domestic violence has indirect and direct negative effects upon children and is highly associated with child abuse.

10. Separation or divorce from a violent man does not necessarily ensure the safety of the woman or children.

Intervention in the Context of Child Abuse

Physical abuse

Health visitors offer family support, but they also have a vital monitoring and surveillance role, even if that does not always feel comfortable.

They are in a position to pick up on all forms of abuse, and vigilance is needed in:

- observation of behaviour
- physical examination
- asking the right questions
- knowing about the level of parental supervision
- listening if a parent is trying to express concerns.

Those formulating the immediate protection plan should consider whether there is a gender bias, for example whether the decision to remove the child is based upon the perpetrator being the mother. Planning follow-up intervention following parental physical abuse should be tailored according to whether the perpetrator is:

- the mother
- the father
- both parents
- unknown.

If the father is the perpetrator the mother may benefit from support, but the father must also be engaged with directly, especially, but not exclusively, if he lives with the children. Explicit engagement with the father retains a focus on him as responsible for the abuse rather than on mothers to protect. If the father is not the perpetrator he may be a valuable source of support for the mother and child.

Physical abuse mainly occurs within the context of child care, and many parents will benefit from advice and guidance, which should not be confined to the mother. Both parents can be asked about their experiences of discipline and the influence that this has had on their parenting behaviour. It should be recognised that men, in particular, may have been subjected to physical abuse as children. Studies of intervention after physical abuse suggest that casework does show some success in reducing physical abuse (Gibbons *et al.* 1995). Azar (1997) alerts us to the fact that reducing overt abusive behaviour is not sufficient; in addition there should be attention to the underlying parenting environment. A cognitive-behavioural approach that looks at restructuring thoughts and attributions about the child is advocated.

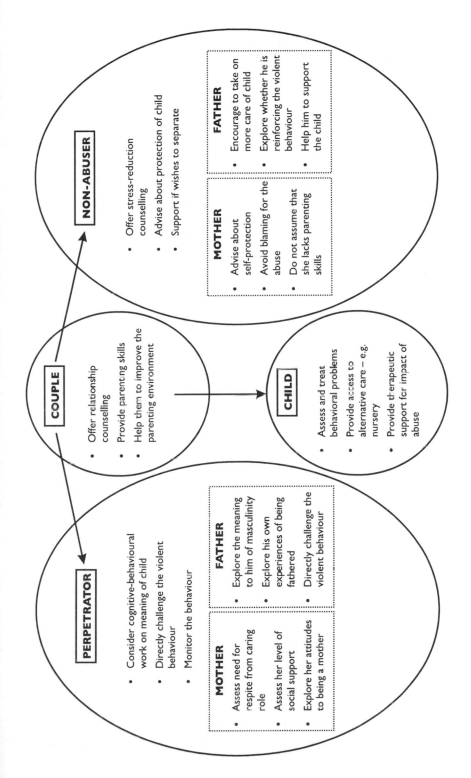

COUPLE

- Offer relationship counselling
- Provide parenting skills
- Help them to improve the parenting environment

NON-ABUSER

- Offer stress-reduction counselling
- Advise about protection of child
- Support if wishes to separate

FATHER

- Encourage to take on more care of child
- Explore whether he is reinforcing the violent behaviour
- Help him to support the child

MOTHER

- Advise about self-protection
- Avoid blaming for the abuse
- Do not assume that she lacks parenting skills

CHILD

- Assess and treat behavioral problems
- Provide access to alternative care – e.g. nursery
- Provide therapeutic support for impact of abuse

PERPETRATOR

- Consider cognitive-behavioural work on meaning of child
- Directly challenge the violent behaviour
- Monitor the behaviour

FATHER

- Explore the meaning to him of masculinity
- Explore his own experiences of being fathered
- Directly challenge the violent behaviour

MOTHER

- Assess need for respite from caring role
- Assess her level of social support
- Explore her attitudes to being a mother

Figure 6.2 Suggestions for practice with men, women and children, guided by whether the mother or father is the perpetrator.

It is necessary to pay attention to the quality of the parenting environment: something for which all adults in the household are responsible. Exclusive work with the mother can potentially be undermined by the mutual reinforcement of an atmosphere of violent discipline within the couple relationship. Such an atmosphere may compound and be compounded by children's excessive behavioural problems. In these instances work with all members of the family is indicated. Parents may need joint counselling about their relationship and, specific advice on parenting skills, and children may require behaviour modification.

Finally, methods should match assessed need. An example of a possible matrix of intervention is shown in Figure 6.2.

Neglect

It seems unfair that the parent who is left alone struggling with the care of children under difficult material, financial and emotional conditions difficulties be held solely responsible for the neglect of the child. When neglected children are living with a lone mother, or a mother and step-parent, then rigorous attention should be paid to finding the father and carrying out a comprehensive assessment of what he may have to offer. If the child's name is to be placed on the child protection register, then consideration should also be given to naming both parents as perpetrators, rather than only the mother. Both parents should be invited to case conferences and any other proceedings.

Similarly, if the child is living with two parents there should be assessment of both parents, not just the mother. The aspiration may be to involve the father in partnership by sharing the child care tasks. Here the aim would be to establish 'shared parenting'. Alternatively, if the child's mother is unable to 'mother' him or her in the traditional fashion of mothers, then the engagement of the father may incorporate an aspiration that he take on the care of the child and become a father who 'mothers'. The fact that such a role is very unusual for men with female partners in this society must be taken into account when engaging on such terms. Men may not need encouragement to take on more child care responsibility, but they may well need pragmatic advice about it. Some men may feel uncomfortable about asking for advice and workers need to be sensitive to this issue. Although men typically receive more practical support when they take on the 'alternative mother' role, it is nonetheless fraught with potential difficulties, as described in Chapter 2.

Sexual abuse

Social workers and health visitors play a key role in the ongoing monitoring of safety of the child who has been sexually abused. Practice has to be based upon the knowledge that sexual abuse perpetrators can be manipulative, charming, convincing and can elicit sympathy. It is essential to check who male figures in the household are, particularly for health visitors who may not have met the alleged perpetrator of abuse.

One of the most challenging aspects of work with sexual abusers occurs when there is sufficient evidence to conclude that a child has been sexually abused, but insufficient evidence to charge or convict a perpetrator. Child protection legislation allows for the separation of the child from the suspected perpetrator (by removal of either child or father) under such circumstances, but the scope for constructive work with the father is minimal when there is denial of culpability (Bentovim, Elton and Tranter 1987). In these situations the concentration of effort has to be upon the child and non-abusing parent and ongoing monitoring for signs of further abuse.

Treatment of convicted sexual offenders is a specialised area and must be carried out by well-trained workers with support (see e.g. Calder 1999).

INTERDISCIPLINARY ISSUES

Calder (1999) stresses that all work with the offender has to be child-centred, that is, with the well-being of the specific child and other children as the underpinning principle. The first and most important issue is that of communication between all the professionals involved. McEwan and Sullivan (1996) suggest that all professionals involved need an integrated approach that takes account of the extent to which the whole family system may have been 'groomed' by the perpetrator. As a result families may minimise the ongoing danger, make excuses for the perpetrator, wish to retain familiar patterns and be blamed by the perpetrator. A common philosophy is required that incorporates the following principles:

- Responsibility for abuse 'lies exclusively with the offender', and may cause, but is not caused by family dysfunction. The victim must remain the primary focus, but not be blamed for the abuse.

- Detailed assessment of the needs of all the family members, including siblings and non-abusing parents must be carried out before intervention.

- Family reconstruction cannot be the aim of assessment, although it may emerge as a goal of intervention. If the precedent is set before the full assessment, for example by implementing supervised contact immediately, then intervention may be skewed towards this end.

- Sex offenders cannot be 'cured' and do not always offend against the same victim group. They may abuse outside the family or commit rape against adult women.

CONTACT BETWEEN THE FATHER WHO HAS SEXUALLY ABUSED AND THE CHILD VICTIM

As described in Box 6.1, children who have been abused by their father are likely to have very ambivalent feelings about him. Other people in the system, including the family and professionals involved will have strong feelings about what is best for the child. The child may say that they want to see their father, the father may say he wants to see the child, courts may want to preserve a familial bond, practitioners may want contact to cease.

When considering the issue of contact between the child and father (and possible reunification of the family) it is first important to appreciate the extent to which familial sexual abuse is likely to have been an ongoing process, perhaps over many years, involving psychological manipulation of not only the child, but possibly other family members as well. There may be an assumption that supervised contact will address the dual needs for contact and protection; however, the potential for ongoing psychological damage and manipulation remains and can be exacerbated during supervised contact visits. For example, the father may try to gain the child's sympathy for his plight or he may subtly reinforce the idea that the victim was to blame for the abuse. Contact should therefore be suspended in the first instance to allow time for a detailed assessment of all the complex aspects of the situation (Berliner 2000; Calder 1999; Saunders and Meinig 2000). Berliner points out that the way that the perpetrator behaves during this period can provide useful prognostic information. If the father is obstructive, insists on seeing the child for his own needs and so on, then the chance of developing constructive therapeutic intervention is reduced. This period gives the father an opportunity to demonstrate what he is willing to do to ameliorate the damage he has caused. Separation may last from one to two years, particularly if lengthy court proceedings are involved.

Based upon clinical experience Berliner (2000) suggests that when the perpetrator is the biological father the child will want to resolve the nature of the biological relationship because it is, by definition, enduring. When the perpetrator is the stepfather he may or may not have an important family connection to the child, but in many cases he will be the father of half-siblings, thus ensuring some ongoing connection. Berliner describes sometimes having to help children to decide what they can live with, rather than what they would ideally like to happen. From the beginning, therefore, there needs to be an assessment of what the relationship means to the child.

Saunders and Meinig (2000) provide a very helpful conceptualisation of the coexistence of two relationships, that of father and child and that of perpetrator and victim. They state that the 'presence of the offender–victim relationship does not eliminate the psychological reality of the parent–child relationship for the child, nor *vice versa*'. The underpinning principle of their work is family resolution. Resolution does *not* imply reunification; rather it describes an arrangement that takes account of both aspects of the relationship and is tailored to the individual needs and wishes of the child. Such an arrangement will fall on a continuum from face to face contact, to contact by letter, telephone or video to no contact at all.

The child protection system is preoccupied with short-term goals of protection, but also needs to consider the effects in five, ten or fifteen years' time. 'It is likely that in most cases of parent–child sexual abuse, families will persist in one form or another long after the professionals have exited their lives.' (Saunders and Meinig)

First there has to be an assessment of the nature of the relationship between the child and father and whether there are any aspects worth salvaging. The resolution plan should only build in contact if there is a meaningful emotional attachment, the child can be kept safe and the child wants contact. The history of manipulation by the offender of the whole family system needs to be assessed. For example, many perpetrators prepare for disclosure by consistently presenting the victim as troublesome, or a liar. The cognitive distortions that the child undergoes in order to survive emotionally need to be recognised and 'unlearned'. The non-offending parent is also likely to have been manipulated. All members of the family must accept that the offender was responsible; for example, many perpetrators will blame alcohol, an excuse that is often easier for the rest of the family to accept than that the father calculatingly set up circumstances to allow him to sexually abuse his child.

Those working with the offender need to co-ordinate with those working with the child and family. All professionals and non-abusing parents and relatives should avoid telling the child how they 'should' think about the offender. They should neither be required to forgive, nor to hate their father. Children need time to assess the relationship with the abuser and to try to tease out which aspects can be attributed to the parent–child relationship and which to the offender–victim relationship. They also need time to develop appropriate personal independence and the consistent support of the non-offending.

This conceptualisation may be a useful model for practitioners, who often need to connect with the man on different levels, and it might be helpful to separate the aspects of the working relationship that are specific to the man as offender and those that are specific to the man as father. Health visitors may be in the position of monitoring the health and safety of younger siblings or stepsiblings of the victim. They may need to relate to the man as the biological father in relation to his younger children whilst being mindful of the risk he poses as an offender against an older child and potential offender against a younger child.

FAMILY RECONSTITUTION

Family reconstitution may be the resolution plan, but not necessarily. It is only likely to be possible if the offender accepts responsibility, the child is not blamed, there is no collusion, the non-offending parent supports the child and the child is confident (Bentovim, Elton and

Tranter 1987). Calder (1999) summarises the factors that are essential for safe family reconstitution:

1. That the parents:

   - Have accepted responsibility for the abuse.
   - Are working for and achieving changes.
   - Have demonstrated commitment to rehabilitation.
   - Are open and honest with professionals.
   - Have willingness and capacity to ask for help if problems occur.
   - Have realistic expectations of the child and understand and accept the problems that remain.

2. Relationships within the family are stable and supportive.

3. External stressors are manageable.

4. There is an agreed child protection plan, which is SMART (specific, measurable, appropriate, realistic, and time-limited).

5. Which is consistent with the child's needs and wishes and feelings. (p.167)

Intervention in the Context of Domestic Violence

Identifying instances of domestic violence

One of the main blocks to effective practice with regard to domestic violence is that it is so often unrecognised. Therefore, the first practice message is that practitioners must be aware of the prevalence of violence in the home, its damaging impact upon children and the association with child abuse. Agencies need to build screening for domestic violence into their routine assessment procedures. The NSPCC, for example, developed a project in which a domestic violence framework was built into assessment procedures (Hester and Pearson 1998). Women and men need to be asked separately about the relationship. Secrecy, fear and shame must be recognised as powerful influences upon the willingness of women and children to describe their experiences. Careful examination of case records may well reveal a history of concerns about violence. Hester *et al.* (2000) provide a set of questions that can open up the issue, which include:

- How are arguments settled?
- What happens when you argue/disagree?
- Do you ever feel/have you ever felt frightened of your partner?
- Has your partner ever physically hurt you? How, what happened?

As one of the few professional groups with routine access to women in their own home, health visitors have an especially unique potential role in the identification of domestic violence, especially as abuse often starts or gets worse during pregnancy (Mullender 1996). A study of health visitors' experience in two NHS trusts suggested that health visitors need to be questioning and proactive in order to uncover abuse, although some expressed fear for their own safety (Frost 1999).

Other health agencies are another part of the pattern of contact of men with agencies. Men may approach their GP or other health-related agencies about depression, drugs or alcohol. Practitioners in these agencies should also be alert to indications that these men are resorting to violence in the home, and should liaise with the health visitor with regard to the children's safety. The police also have a vital role to play and in some areas they will now routinely alert the social services if they are called to a domestic violence incident in a household where children live.

Practice with domestic violence

Once domestic violence has been identified, a network of practitioners is usually involved from Woman's Aid, probation services, children and families teams, specialised therapeutic agencies and so on. The best known British multi-agency arrangement is the Leeds Inter-Agency Forum which manages the Leeds Inter-Agency Forum Project (Women and Violence). It has links with 60 agencies and carries out developments in many areas of work with women, men and children (Mullender 1996).

It is often assumed that the problem has ended with separation, but, in fact, this can be one of the most dangerous times, for both women and children. It is generally agreed that it is not appropriate to carry out family or couple work whilst violence is still occurring (Mullender 1996). This should only occur when:

1. The offender has accepted full responsibility for his violent behaviour and has made concerted efforts to change that behaviour.

2. The victim is clearly able to protect herself, measured by her understanding and willingness to assume responsibility for her protection.

3. The potential for further abuse is minimal (there is never a guarantee).

4. The degree of intimidation and fear felt by the victim is significantly reduced, so as not to interfere with open discussion of marital issues. Make sure she does not think the issues she raises during the session will be used as an excuse by her husband to assault her after the session.

5. The goals of the couple are mutually agreed upon and couple work is entered into freely by both partners. Make sure he has not instructed her to remain silent on contentious issues. (Sinclair 1985, p.82)

It should not be assumed that contact with the father is necessarily appropriate. The safety of the mother and the child may be compromised. For example, sometimes contact orders entail passing on the address of a refuge (Mullender 1996). Men may use children to get to the mother. The children themselves may be subjected to physical, sexual or emotional abuse.

However, neither should it be assumed that contact should necessarily cease, at least over the long term. Each individual case has to be assessed in detail. Women who have been subjected to domestic violence often feel it important for the children to know their fathers and indeed will sometimes place themselves at risk in order to facilitate contact (Hester and Radford 1996). The challenge for a practitioner is finding ways to facilitate contact that is safe for all concerned and that is genuinely for the benefit of the children, not for the adults involved. Contact centres can be used, as can other forms of contact by phone or letter and so on. Again, the key issue has to be what is assessed to be in the child's best interest, not what meets the ideological criteria of any of the practitioners or family members involved.

All child care practitioners must beware of conscious or unconscious avoidance of violent men (O'Hagan and Dillenberger 1995). It is easy to become deflected to issues of the mother's co-operation, whereas the focus must be kept firmly on the fact that the problem originates in the man's violence (Mullender 1996). The careful use of language would mean avoiding discussion of dangerous, or violent 'families', rather describing the behaviour of each parent towards each other and to the children. If the bulk of the intervention is to be with the mother, there should, nonetheless, be explicit acknowledgement of the impact of the father's violence. As Farmer and Owen describe, practitioners tend to slip into a focus on 'mothering' skills and on stress support (1998). Although this may be what the mother needs, it should be clearly delineated as a separate strand of intervention, complementary to, rather than replacing, attention to the issue of domestic violence.

The man, as a father, may still have something to offer his children, and may still be entitled to information about their well-being. Such information exchange may need to be managed via a third party, for example a family member, probation officer or staff at a voluntary agency.

Practitioners will need information about what resources are available to support violent men who want to change. There are a number of court-mandated programmes to counter male violence, and it is evident that some men do manage to make use of therapeutic support and choose to change their behaviour (see Box 6.2).

Box 6.2 Working with violent men

Specific programmes aimed at changing men's violent behaviour were first developed in the USA and Canada, with the most well known being the Domestic Abuse Prevention Project in Duluth, Minnesota (Pence 1988). This and other similar programmes are run on pro-feminist principles and, using cognitive-behavioural methods, are built upon violent men fully accepting personal responsibility for their behaviour. Similar programmes in Britain have been evaluated and shown to have some success in reducing violent behaviour (Dobash et al. 1996). Eight stages of change have been identified in men reducing their violent behaviour (Dobash et al. 1996):

- recognising that change is possible
- having the motivation to change
- seeing that the benefits of change outweigh the costs
- shifting to see oneself as a subject in control of events, not the object of actions by others
- moving from external constraints to internal controls
- changing their language about violence to a more reflective, responsible discourse
- learning new attitudes and behaviours by talking and listening
- benefiting from specific aspects of programmes including:
  - discussion focusing on minimisation and denial
  - discussion to identify 'triggers' to violence
  - video work to show well-known scenes
- learning to take 'time outs' to prevent violence.

The women reported that after attending the programmes men were more likely to:

- see their point of view
- be aware of their feelings
- respect them
- be more sympathetic
- be less self-centred
- be less likely to restrict their life
- take responsibility for violence.

There were three 'stories of change':

- men who cannot or will not change despite the intervention
- men who engage in limited change maintained by the external controls of legal or threatened legal sanctions
- men who change their violent behaviour and attitudes and become regulators of their own behaviour – these were most likely to be successful.

Practitioners may encounter men whose behaviour is of concern, to themselves, others or both. They may, for example, self-refer to a GP. Sometimes their wish to change is triggered by a recognition of the impact of their behaviour upon their children. Practitioners in this field have observed that there is a real lack of resources for men who have never been convicted of a violent crime and who therefore are not required to attend treatment programmes. Also, in times of limited resources, tensions can arise between those who wish to provide services for the female victims of violence and those who wish to offer services for violent men. Therefore, there is an identified need for group and individual programmes based upon voluntary referral but it is essential for anyone aiming to start a programme for violent or potentially violent men to consult in detail with local support services for women. Box 6.3 gives an example of one such group for men who already want to change their behaviour.

Box 6.3 Violence Intervention Programme

A voluntary project in Edinburgh (Spring 2000) is aimed at men who are worried about their tendency to violence. The fundamental principle is that violence can be controlled if the man takes responsibility for it. Violence is seen as something that men are brought up to find acceptable and even to admire. The aim is to help men to explore the reasons why they use violence and help them to take control of their own behaviour. Female partners are advised that the men's attendance at such a group does not guarantee their safety and that they are not expected to support him or continue in a risky partnership. Men are not naturally violent. Violence is not something that just happens. It is a result of a decision made by the man, in the hope of achieving something. It is one of many ways of trying to control women. He can change the decision. The following is an extract from the leaflet:

Have you ever

1.   hit, slapped, intimidated or threatened your partner?

2.   trashed your flat?

Do you

1. have a problem with violence?

2. have a hard time controlling your temper?

3. feel like physically harming your partner, yourself or anyone else?

4. try to get your own way by using force, threats, abuse, shouting at or ignoring your partner?

Do you want to do something about it?

Most either self-refer or are referred via a mental health worker or their GP. Many say that they have come because they do not want their children to end up like them. The men are met on an individual basis on a number of occasions before they come to the group. For many men the usual way of coping with difficulty is to work it out alone, therefore they may find the concept of a group alien at first.

Early on in the group work there is the opportunity to explore relationships with their children. Mike Spring observes that, in exploring the difficulties they have with their children, men often uncover areas of their own distress. Many describe childhood experiences of humiliation and seem to have been taking out that humiliation on others ever since. They do not want their children to see their aggression, do not want them to end up like themselves, and hate themselves. They know there is no excuse.

For many the problem is not so much the stopping of violence as coping with the changes that stopping reveals, for example difficulties in communication. Being unable to communicate makes some men feel stupid, so they lash out instead. For many men the way of avoiding violence is to go off alone, but this is difficult for their partner who is then perceived to be 'winding him up' if she tries to follow.

The group has worked for some men. As Mike Spring points out, the best people to evaluate such groups are the men's partners and it is their opinion that is sought.

Clearly a group such as this is attended by men who are already motivated to change; men who do not accept that their violence is a problem are not likely to consider attending such a group and will need a different approach. Nevertheless, the fact that many do self-refer suggests that there is a demand for initiatives of this type.

Contact: Violence Intervention Programme, c/o EVOC, 14 Ashley Place Edinburgh.

Obviously great care has to be taken in setting up such a programme to avoid the dangers of unconscious collusion or reinforcement of violence. Anger-management programmes alone are not sufficient, as there is a need specifically to address the gendered nature of domestic violence. Programmes for violent men should address violence at all levels; they should address the socio-cultural support for male aggression, and the way in which family structures can reinforce power imbalances. Such programmes will also need to allow individual men the opportunity to explore their personal pathway to violence. Standard social work skills may not be sufficient as they tend to be based upon anger-management techniques; instead there needs to be a clear understanding of the controlled use of violence by men in many domestic situations (Hester *et al.* 2000).

Key Messages for Practice

1. When carrying out an assessment the question must be asked with regard to any adult associated with the child: 'Does this person pose any risk to the child?'

2. When carrying out an investigation and assessment into the physical abuse of a child, practitioners need to consider the caregiving context; that is, asking who mainly looks after the child, how much time each parent spends with the child and so on.

3. If the father has perpetrated physical abuse then there must be a direct focus upon this. If it is decided that intervention will focus on the mother, then the reason for this must be made explicit and written into assessment documentation.

4. More information is required about the role of the father in cases of child neglect, and consideration should be given to registering him also as perpetrator.

5. Working to engage fathers when children are neglected requires more than a rhetoric of involvement. Fathers need to be drawn into discussions, meetings, clinic visits and so on. Overall the aim should be to give the message that their presence is expected, rather than a pleasant surprise.

6. The level of secrecy around sexual abuse should never be underestimated; all professionals need to be open to considering the unthinkable.

7. Exploring the father–child relationship separately from the offender–victim relationship may assist assessment when a child has been sexually abused by their father.

8. Domestic violence has indirect and direct negative effects upon children and is highly associated with child abuse.

9. Health visitors are in a unique position to pick up signs of domestic violence and its impact upon children.

10. The issue of ongoing contact between a violent father and child should be assessed according to the child's best interests.

Try it for Size

- Go through each child care and protection situation on your case load.

- For each case make a list of every man, whether related or not, whom the child has contact with.

- Look at your list and ask yourself whether you have assessed fully the potential risk that each of these men could pose.

- Are there men on the list whom you have never met or whom no other professional involved with the case has met?

- Have you encountered men in any of the households whom you have not been introduced to and whom you have not enquired about?

- Devise a systematic approach to help you with the assessment of the potential risks that men can pose to both women and children.

Chapter 7

Fathers as Assets

Introduction

It makes sense to draw on all possible resources when trying to improve the situation of vulnerable children and there is no doubt that fathers can in many cases be a resource that is missed. To return to some of the ideological frameworks held by health and social care practitioners, the notions of caring, reflective practice and anti-discriminatory practice all have relevance. If we do want to base practice on these ideologies, then a discourse of caring or a discourse of anti-discriminatory practice would both support and be supported by a framework that aims to enhance the material and psychosocial resources available to children. Rather than concentrating only on mothers and children, practitioners should be aware of the resources that can be offered by fathers.

Within child care and protection it is easy for concerned professionals to ignore the potential ways in which men may be an asset to their children. But if we ignore men as potential assets in child care and protection, the consequences can be damaging to the very children we are committed to protecting. Most men, whatever their background or behaviour, have the potential to offer something positive to children as partner to the mother, 'alternative mother', luxury or as a unique role model. By failing to engage explicitly with fathers then, we not only reduce our available resources for helping vulnerable children, we also diminish our ability to act effectively (O'Hagan and Dillenberger 1995). In this chapter we look at some of the theoretical issues surrounding men's contribution to parenting. We consider the beneficial impacts of fathering, in particular highlighting the research on development and interpersonal growth. We then discuss how practitioners can work with both mothers and fathers in 'harnessing' the assets that fathers bring to the parenting relationship.

First, we must emphasise that the well-being of the child or children in any situation is paramount, closely followed by the safety of the mother and of practitioners. If assessing the potential assets of men compromises this stance then it is clearly misguided. There are times when it is right to exclude fathers, and experienced practitioners will recognise that. What is needed is a balance (and we realise that this is like walking a tightrope) between what is best for the child and what is best for the father. We suggest that all men can bring potential assets to child care, but that it will not always be right to harness that potential. However, we cannot automatically neglect to assess this potential. If we do, then we could rightly be accused of causing more damage to the very children we are committed to protecting.

Present Fathers

There are mixed messages from the research, but overall men seem to influence child development in a way that should not be overlooked. Hawkins *et al.* (1993) suggest a number of ways in which fathers can be seen as assets by being the developmental force in their children's lives. If a father's ideal is to be involved in his children's lives, he may engage in behaviours that help him to realise this ideal. Men's involvement in child care can be a potent developmental force in helping children achieve psychosocial health in midlife, suggesting they have something unique to offer children (Snarey 1993).

Clare (2000) suggests that fathers who treat their daughters with love and respect will raise girls who (rightly) expect this from all men. Equally if men teach their sons to be caring and fair they will grow up to regard women positively. However, it is sometimes pointed out that men often leave being involved with their children until it is too late. More does not necessarily mean better, and it is acknowledged that increased participation can bring conflict and disruption (Parke and Tinsley 1981). There is also some, albeit contentious, evidence that fathers are more important than mothers in the sex-role development of children (Parke and Tinsley 1981).

Lamb's (1981) review of studies on delinquent boys demonstrated an association with fathers who are asocial or hostile. By the same token, the presence of an involved father has been found to be associated with a reduced likelihood of becoming involved in delinquent activities (Garbarino 1999).

Perhaps the clearest evidence emerges from the area of education. So, for example, there is evidence that the presence of a positive relationship with the father is associated with more positive attitudes to school, especially for boys (Katz 1999). Similarly, fathers' provision of warmth and control relates significantly to the academic achievement of children (Coley 1998). Lamb (1981b) also points out the influence that has been shown by involved fathers on child social competence, psychological adjustment and academic performance.

Researchers conclude that whilst fathers do have an impact on child development, its specific effect is probably limited and there is not a straightforward relationship between children's experiences and their future development (Burghes, Clarke and Cronin 1997).

It is easy to become lost in a labyrinth of views about whether children do in fact *need* fathers. A review of the literature suggests that there is simply insufficient evidence to draw a firm conclusion. There is research to suggest that father absence can be associated with negative outcomes for children; there is also research to suggest that children can thrive and succeed without father involvement. This whole debate is, in fact, still riddled with the lack of methodological rigour that was highlighted some years ago (Lamb 1981b). Indeed, as long as men and women are treated differently, it is hard to tell what difference men make (Oakley and Rigby 1998). Some firmly emphasise the social and moral deterioration in society attributable to fatherlessness (Daker 1999; Dennis and Erdos 1993; Haskey *et al.* 1998). Their clear message is that children suffer from such arrangements. However, many children reared by lone mothers thrive and we do not advocate a simple message that 'families need fathers'. As Lamb concludes:

> While there is evidence that fathers do have significant effect – both positive and negative – on their children's development, none of the evidence…suggests that increased paternal involvement *necessarily* has beneficial consequences for children. Instead, it seems that paternal involvement can have positive consequences when it is the arrangement of choice for the family concerned. (Lamb, Pleck and Levine 1986, p.142)

One pathway out of the maze is to see the father as one of the potential resources for a child. The fewer resources that the child has to call upon, the more risk he or she has of a poorer outcome in the face of adversity (Daniel, Wassell and Gilligan 1999). We are not advocating that the father must be present, but neither do we suggest that he should not be. In reality, parenting is a difficult job: if two people can make it easier and help each other, then that sounds like a good idea. The presence of an involved, non-abusive father, perhaps as a partner to the mother, therefore, can be a protective factor for a child. When the father is absent the risks may come not so much from his individual absence as from the fact that it leaves the mother and child with fewer buffering material and emotional resources. This may not be a problem when other resources are available, but may be when they are not.

The parameters of what constitutes a 'good enough' parent may be different for fathers and mothers and this might go some way towards explaining why the research is so confused about fathers' contributions. The only absolutely unique aspect of a father is his maleness. Hence the only unique aspect that a father can offer is to be a good 'male role model'. But there is a lack of common consensus about what a 'good male' should be. Perhaps we should be looking to both mothers and fathers to act as good 'human role models'.

What should matter most in such controversies is the child's own view: what kind of relationship do children want with their fathers? Research on the views of children concludes that they do not hold stereotypical views of nuclear families and are aware of wide variations in family practices and structures (Morrow 1998). Children have an accepting, inclusive view of what is a family, and definitions do not centre on biological relatedness or the 'nuclear' norm. They are realistic, with love, care and mutual respect being seen as the key characteristics of families. In Milligan and Dowie's (1998) study, interviews with children showed that what children need from their fathers is:

- a role model
- quality time
- supportive behaviour
- expressions of love
- physical contact.

So, children themselves recognise the value of fathers, and lay emphasis upon their human, nurturing qualities. Indeed, these qualities are encapsulated in the potential roles described in Chapter 2. This must be the driving force in child care work.

Psychological Availability

To be an asset to the child the father does not necessarily need to be present in the household and in some cases, certainly should not be. One of the fundamental ways in which a father can enhance his child's development is by being psychologically available. Availability need not necessarily denote physical presence in the household in which the child lives. Most of the evidence points to the primacy of the quality of the relationship, not the physical living arrangements. Also, as Garbarino (1999) explains, the presence of a violent father can be as damaging as the absence of a 'good' father. Fatherhood debates tend to conflate physical and psychological presence (Burghes *et al.* 1997). There is an assumption that resident fathers are always present for their children, whereas absent fathers are neither physically nor emotionally available. Clearly this is a biased account, as fathers can be 'technically present but functionally absent' (LaRossa 1989). Some resident fathers provide little for their children, while many absent fathers maintain excellent relationships with their children.

Twenty-five per cent of children under 16 currently experience parental divorce, and the children who come to the attention of child care and protection professionals are even more likely to have experienced the divorce or separation of their parents. It is now recognised that divorce is only part of a process that has ongoing implications for children and their parents. It is also now recognised that the most damaging environment for children is one of parental conflict and poor communication. The children who cope best with divorce are the ones who can maintain a meaningful relationship with both parents, in a situation of minimal conflict and good communication between parents (Walker 1995). Where communication is maintained after separation, especially for teenagers, research has shown that this provides positive role models for both relationships and communication (Catan, Dennison and Coleman 1997).

In reviewing the literature on contact with fathers who no longer share the same household as their children, Burghes *et al.* (1997) conclude that there is limited information in the UK, with both ends of the spectrum represented in the literature. They point out, though, that fathers tend to maintain contact more with their sons than with their daughters, an issue warranting further investigation.

Socio-genealogical Connectedness

In a society that places great symbolic and emotional value upon the knowledge of genetic origins the father is an asset because he possesses half the child's genetic and genealogical heritage. Genetic information may be important for health reasons, but the lack of information about origins can have other effects. Many children are able to develop a robust sense of self without such knowledge, but for some children this gap is keenly felt, perhaps particularly for children of mixed-race heritage. A study of children in lone-parent families which looked at the importance of socio-genealogical connectedness for child well-being (Owusu-Bempah and Howitt 1997) showed that contact was not necessary for connectedness. However, it was seen as extremely important that children had information about their fathers, about their culture and heritage. Children from mixed-race marriages for example may have an absent black father and need to know about him (McAdoo 1986).

There is also increasing evidence that it is important for children to know about their biological heritage. In cases of assisted reproductive technology (ART) by donor insemination, many children still want to know about their heritage. Whilst the identity of donors remains secret by law, the long-term consequences of this 50 per cent contribution to a child's genetic and family history are unknown and the issue is beginning to raise a number of ethical and practical questions (McWhinnie 2000). Children want to know about their religious and cultural heritage. They also need to know about their genetic history (McWhinnie 2000).

Finally, in a society that does stigmatise lone mothers, it is likely that some of that stigma can impact upon children. To have nothing to offer to playground conversations about their father may be the situation that many children find themselves in, and each individual needs to find a way to account for their circumstances.

Socio-economic Factors

As was described in Chapter 2, in contemporary society the most commonly articulated role for the father is providing materially for the family, either solely, or in conjunction with the mother (Warin *et al.* 1999). Mothers, of course, also frequently provide economically for their children, but owing to the nature of employment patterns and inequities of pay it still tends to be the case that men's financial contribution to the support of children is higher. We do not advocate the maintenance of this status quo, but practitioners need to be realistic in working with the current situation.

Women and children appear to bear the brunt of social disadvantage. Seven out of ten children living with lone mothers receive less than 50 per cent of the national average wage and of 1.1 million families claiming income support, only 33 per cent contain a man (Graham 1993). A recent study of 1655 lone mothers in Northern Ireland reveals an even bleaker picture, with the mothers here being both single parents and benefit claimants for much longer than lone mothers in the rest of Great Britain (Evason, Robinson and Thompson 1999). And, regardless of social class, single parents have much reduced incomes. This trend has recently been termed as the feminisation and juvenilisation of poverty (Bianchi 1999), where poverty is concentrated in mother–child families. It is also known that children of single parents have a poorer morbidity than do those who have two parents (Thomson, Hanson and McLanahan 1994) and disrupted family life (whether through conflict, divorce or separation) can affect children badly (Rutter and Smith 1995). Further, children are disproportionately affected by economic disadvantage, because households without a main wage-earner tend to be households with a larger number of children (Ryan and Little 2000). In summary:

- In the UK, the proportion of people living in low-income households more than doubled between the late 1970s and the early 1990s.

- One in three children live in households that bring in less than half of the national average income (Department of Social Security 1999).

- Whatever measures of social disadvantage are used, poorer districts have higher mortality rates than more affluent areas (Reading 1993).

- More than 2000 UK child deaths per annum could be prevented if overall death rates were the same as for those in the top two social classes (Reading 1997).

- Higher income is protective and there remains an association between income inequality and mortality over and above anything that can be accounted for by statistical artefact (Wolfson *et al.* 1999).

So why mention socio-economic circumstances when discussing engaging with men in child care and protection? The reason is this: there is no stronger single factor common to child abuse or neglect than the relationship with poverty (N. Parton 1995; Pelton 1994). Parenting and disadvantage are clearly linked in complex and numerous ways and cannot be ignored (Baldwin and Spencer 1993). Maltreated children are still twice as likely to live in single-parent, female-headed households as non-maltreated children and they are four times as likely to receive state benefits (Wolfe 1991). Maltreated and neglected children are many times more likely to be in receipt of public assistance than are non-maltreated children (Baldwin and Spencer 1993; Creighton 1992; Wolfe 1991). In Glasgow for example, substantial correlations between unemployment and registrations for abuse have been documented (Gillham *et al.* 1998).

Of course this does not imply that parents with fewer economic, material or social resources are worse parents. Neither does it suggest that children living in family households containing a man, especially one who works, are automatically going to do well. It does show, though, that high income acts as a protective factor (Sedlak 1993). The links are complex, but economic hardship reduces effective parental support (Ho, Lempers and Clark-Lempers 1995). Parenting is demanding enough in the best of circumstances and financial deprivation exacerbates stresses and strains. This must be a consideration when discussing the resources that fathers can bring to a child care situation. Even if a father is not in a position to contribute to the emotional care of his child it may be possible to support him in his efforts to contribute financially.

Key Issues from Theory

1. Marginalising fathers focuses interventions on mothers and sacrifices the potential of fathers as both risks and assets. Ignoring a possible resource can be damaging to children.

2. The potential for fathers as assets is not restricted to their biological relationship with the child.

3. Although studies often lack the methodological rigour required for definite conclusions, there are important messages that can be learned from the research into the roles that fathers can play in their children's lives.

4. Regardless of gender, both parents can aspire to be good role models for their children.

5. The absence of an involved father can reduce the emotional and material resources available to the child, therefore increasing the risk of poor outcomes in the face of adversity.

6. Fathers' influence on children's development is complex and controversial. Overall, fathers seem to be important in helping children develop psychosocially and in their academic performance.

7. It is the quality of the relationship, whether present or absent, that is important to children. They want to be loved and valued.

8. A father can be psychologically available to his child, whether or not they live in the same household.

9. Fathers are important in providing children with a sense of their culture and history: with their geneaological connectedness.

10. Poverty and inequality are the most important determinants of health worldwide. Women and children bear the brunt of social and economic hardship.

Practice Aimed at Enhancing Assets

As professionals, we need to be clear what our own notions of fatherhood are so that we can recognise the potential in the fathers we work with, and then encourage it. As professionals, where do we stand on such issues as gay adoption, for example? Have we fully acknowledged the reparative care and new role models that foster fathers can bring? What are our considered views on fathers in families, and where is our cut-off point? Milner (1996) argues that the tendency of practitioners to pull mothers into formal systems and push fathers into the background reflects their different expectations of what it is that mothers and fathers do and what qualities they exhibit (see Chapter 2). In order to recognise men for the value they can bring in child protection cases, we need to be clear about our notions of fatherhood.

Innovations in practice such as case management and family-centred practice can go some way towards establishing a working relationship with fathers. There are examples of schemes where fathers are actively encouraged to be partners in parenting. In New Zealand, for example, the Commissioner for Children and the Save the Children Fund are working together on just such a project and there are similar ventures elsewhere (Grant 1998).

There are numerous opportunities for practitioners to consider the potential resources provided by fathers. Throughout the book we have highlighted some examples of how men can be engaged with purposefully. This section highlights a number of ideas as they relate specifically to the theoretical issues of how men can be seen as an asset within child care and protection. Box 7.1 gives a case example.

The parameters of what constitutes parenting behaviours are different for men and for women. Good enough parenting perfomed by a man may be different from good enough parenting performed by a woman. Fathers could make the difference between good enough and not quite good enough, but they may require help to fulfil this potential: help that practitioners need to first recognise the need for, and then

Box 7. I Case example

Jessica is the daughter of a Scottish mother and a Jamaican father. Alex, the father, was unaware of his daughter's presence until traced by Mike, Jessica's maternal uncle and godfather when Jessica's mother, Stacey, was involved in a road accident two years ago. Stacey has been left with serious residual neurological deficits and needs permanent nursing care in a young adults' neurological rehabilitation unit. Uncle Mike and his partner Tom have assumed full-time care of Jessica, who despite a traumatic childhood appears bright and well adjusted. However, there are many who are concerned that two gay men are raising Jessica, even though they have had a committed relationship for over ten years and take Jessica regularly to see her mother.

Stacey does not recognise Jessica, and Mike and Tom have recently agonised over their decision to maintain these visits, as Jessica increasingly seems to be distressed by them. Alex is keen to meet his daughter, but has shown no intention of wanting anything else. He is grateful, though, to Mike and Tom and occasionally sends money for his daughter. He has recently begun to send her postcards and she, in turn, is keen to know more about Jamaica. Mike and Stacey's parents (Jessica's grandparents) have been involved peripherally, but are in conflict with Mike over his 'lifestyle', as they call it.

Despite the unusualness of Jessica's situation, she is an articulate, active and happy child with good relationships with Mike and Tom and a developing one with her father. Do you think this is the best arrangement for her?

provide. When there are child protection concerns the issue of the father's involvement is equally as important as that of the mother's.

In considering fathers as assets there may be some situations where the father can take primary responsibility and provide what is traditionally associated with mothering, to become, in effect, an 'alternative mother'. For example, an infant may be failing to thrive and only the father may be able to establish an adequate feeding relationship that will reverse the adverse nutritional status of the child. Even when fathers do not participate in feeding, they can influence its success in indirect ways through their relationship with the mother (Parke 1981).

So health and social care professionals may need to think through the practical arrangements and help men to undertake them. We know that often men are not reluctant to take on larger roles in child care, but might need encouraging to do so and may need pragmatic advice. As we have already stated, this might mean rearranging the times of family visiting, or changing the focus from a mother-centric discussion to one that incorporates fathers equally.

One study (Edwards 1998) demonstrated that engaging with men was helpful to health and social care providers because men:

- are more likely to follow face-to-face instructions if given directly, rather than second-hand through the mother

- may reinforce messages that professionals give to mothers

- can provide women with extra support (e.g. as a substitute for professionals or wider family).

As we have emphasised throughout, the importance of fully including the roles of men in any assessment cannot be overstated. For instance, a man who is physically abusive to his child may also offer access to important extended family members. Grandparents, who may offer stability unknown anywhere else for the child, may be excluded unless this access is considered.

It is likely that mothers will appreciate the importance of such questions (Taylor and Daniel 2000). The relationship of trust between client and professional will be enhanced when the practitioner acknowledges the assets such a man may bring to the children. Consider, for example, a woman who has been afraid of divulging information concerning the domestic abuse that occurs in her household because she knows that her son adores his father and she does not want to destroy that relationship. If practitioners convey a message that acknowledges their recognition of both the need for her protection and the continued good relationship between father and son, the future for all three participants is likely to be more positive.

Other male figures involved with the family need to be considered in their own right. Male partners who are not biological fathers of the children referred should not be screened out. Such men may be temporary family members, but they may also have developed a crucial role. Whichever scenario applies, the presence of such a man will have an impact upon the children. If he is to become a long-term member of the family he may be a potential resource in the care or protection of the children. The facts of the situation cannot be established without asking explicitly.

Farmer and Owen (1998) starkly demonstrated some of these issues. In 60 per cent of the case conferences in their study, the issue of whether the mother could protect the child was considered, whereas the father as a protector of the child was considered in only 19 per cent of cases. One of the key messages these authors suggest is to assess for men's potential role as protector of children. The first part of this process is to ensure that the non-abusing father actually attends the case conference, something that is currently fairly uncommon. Rather than writing to parents jointly, it may be helpful to send an individual letter to each parent. The letter of invitation should state explicitly that the case conference will want to explore the role that each parent can play in the protection of the child. If the father is working and has to take unpaid leave, the local authority could consider reimbursing him. During the case conference every effort should be made to seek the views of each parent separately. Following the case conference the key worker should make every effort to keep contact with both parents rather than focusing all efforts on the mother. Box 7.2 describes a project that supports non-abusing fathers of children who have been sexually abused.

Box 7.2 NCH: the Kite Service

The Kite Service is a therapeutic service for children and families who have experienced the trauma of sexual abuse (Putz 2000). Those involved in the Service do not work with the alleged abusers, but recently have become more successful in engaging with male carers (non-abusive) in their work. These are fathers, male partners of the mothers, or foster fathers. Children need to be living in a stable environment with carers who understand the impact of abuse on them and who are able to be emotionally available to support the child. In order for carers to support the child, they too need support with their feelings in response to the sexual abuse and help in understanding the long-term impact on the child.

The aims of working with men are usually to provide help with one or several of the following:

1. their own issues and feelings re their own childhood abuse
2. their own issues and feelings re the abuse of the child
3. supporting the child (e.g. understanding behaviour)
4. the couple relationship – areas of difficulty or difference.

The Kite Service aims to involve men from the beginning by checking whether there is a male carer, by including him when writing to families, by inviting him to assessment meetings and involving him in all discussions. If workers have failed to engage with the male carer during assessment and initial stages, they will try to involve him later. It may also be that the female carer is single and now wants her new partner involved. The success of engaging with the male carer depends to some extent on the quality of the relationship of the couple, and the male carer's motivation – he does not always see the issue as a problem.

The Kite Service identifies some of the difficulties in engaging men, which broadly fall into two categories, those of gender socialisation issues and those of work issues:

- It is not usual for men to seek help from outside agencies.
- It is not usual for men to talk about their feelings.
- It is not usual for men to believe that talking and thinking about issues helps (i.e. put the past behind you).
- Men tend to have a mistrust or fear of being seen to be vulnerable.
- Men have expectations that the female carer is there for support, so there is no need to involve others.
- There may be working schedules and difficulties in asking for time off, or because of working away all week.

To overcome such difficulties, the Kite Service has found a number of ideas useful:

- Offer individual sessions to men.
- Clarify the purpose of the work so that men can identify the need for it.
- Work from the assumption that their contribution is useful.
- Show that the work will be at a pace the man feels comfortable with.
- Two workers work with the couple.

- Maintain the balance between vulnerability and safety.
- Accept men's show of masculinity and strength – only then will they reveal their sense of vulnerability.
- Use options of male workers if this seems useful.

Case example

Three children referred for therapy had all been sexually abused by an older child. During the assessment it became clear that both their mother and stepfather had also experienced sexual abuse in their own childhoods. Each member of the family was offered individual therapy with different workers. The stepfather attended regularly. Work with him focused on his experience of sexual abuse, his father's death and the children's behaviour. He was ambivalent about the process, struggling between the desire to suppress memories and a need to talk about them. His motivation for attending was 'second-hand', in that his partner had told him he should come and he wanted to be able to help his stepsons. These two factors helped to counteract his fears about the process and his doubts about its efficacy.

Contact: NCH, The Kite Children and Families Counselling Service, Kayll Road, Sunderland SR4 7TW. Tel: 0191 567 4801 Email: netk@mail.nch.org.uk.

Sometimes child protection workers are confronted with men who appear 'suddenly' in the household of an apparently insecure lone mother. They are right to be suspicious, given that there have been a number of known sexual abusers who make a habit of targeting such families. Such suspicions should not be ignored: they are yet another reason to assess explicitly the situation. The implicit messages need to be uncovered and explored openly with the family members in order to spell out the aims of engagement with fathers. Child protection should not just be the mother's responsibility. Of course, important managerial issues emerge: this is delicate and potentially dangerous work, where individual professionals need both supervision and protection. It also raises ethical issues concerning the core principles of confidentiality and accountability. Nonetheless, the aims of engagement with fathers must include an assessment of the potential assets he may bring. 'For many couples, then, the resolution to this…is to find ways to help men accept greater responsibility for nurturing children' (Hawkins *et al.* 1993, p.56).

It is possible that the father could provide cognitive stimulation for both mothers and children that they may sometimes be missing. However, fathers may need encouragement to recognise the value of the cognitive support they can provide and a small change of habit can be a huge asset in providing mental support to both the mother and the child. One study (Levy-Shiff, Sharir and Mogilner 1989) has shown that on initial discharge from hospital after birth, fathers consistently surpass mothers in playing with and stimulating the child. Whilst this could be explained by the fact that most post-natal mothers experience extreme fatigue, it is still beneficial to the child. It is important to consider what it is that fathers and children do together (Burghes *et al.* 1997). Play is crucial for child development and social adjustment and so a father who contributes little else but daily football is still very important. Both mothers and fathers though may need help in recognising the importance of play to a child's development. They may need help with ideas, with access to community activities, or even with resources.

Another potential asset that fathers may bring is in the authority and control they can show to the children. It has been demonstrated that inductive discipline is most associated with conscience development (Schaffer 1996), so in a traditional model of fatherhood, if fathers are seen as the 'disciplinarians', the strengths of this can be also emphasised. Again, men may need help with this. If parenting classes, for example, address issues such as dealing with challenging behaviour, then such classes need to be held at a time convenient to men, and they need to be advertised and organised in a way that does not make fathers feel excluded. Following a traditional partnership model, some men may feel that the unique role they have as fathers is in being the main disciplinarian. This can be emphasised, although they may need help in recognising what are appropriate boundaries and controls.

If practitioners want to increase the likelihood of having a significant positive impact upon the outcomes for children they should pay particular attention to their educational needs. Children who already experience adversity at home are likely to be doubly disadvantaged if their educational opportunities also suffer. By the same token, academic success and/or a positive school experience can help to mitigate some of the negative impact of abuse or neglect (Rutter 1991).

Successful educational experiences are fostered by a good home-school alliance. Fathers can make a real difference to children's attitude to schooling if they demonstrate to children that they are interested in their education. This applies whether fathers are resident or non-resident and is one of the ways that a father can offer something unique to his children.

Practitioners first need to recognise this fact, then help fathers to recognise the important role that they can play, and then support fathers in finding ways actively to encourage and support their children's education. Men whose own experience of schooling was unhappy or traumatic, or who lack confidence in their own academic abilities may feel daunted by the task. However, with imagination, practitioners and parents should be able to find ways of linking the child's natural enthusiasm for an activity with habits of more formal learning, for example:

- setting aside a regular time for the father and child to read together

- arranging for the father to visit the school on a regular basis to talk to the teacher and see the child's work

- encouraging the father to enrol in adult education classes

- building on a joint interest, for example in a sport, to encourage basic skills – for example mathematics for scoring and writing for contacting fan clubs

- encouraging the father to take the child to places such as museums, libraries, galleries, city farms, castles and so on

- encouraging fathers to help out in local schools in the way that mothers are currently encouraged to.

In a study of parental involvement in schools, teachers said that they did not see much of fathers because they were working (Le Couteur, Clough and Johnson 2000). However, in fact, the rates of employment for both fathers and mothers were very similar. Teachers felt that they had invited both parents to school events, but fathers did not feel involved. The study suggested more direct and specific approaches should be made to fathers. Parents suggested that fathers should be targeted on a skills basis, for example by being invited in to help with maths and IT. They also suggested that specific times and places should be offered for meetings with fathers.

Of course, as discussed in Chapter 4, professionals face a dilemma when trying to target fathers. By approaching them through 'masculine' activities such as asking them to help with renovations, run sports days, help with computing and so on, they risk stereotyping fathers. A way to move beyond this might be for schools to invite both mothers and fathers to take part in a much broader range of activities that do not pigeonhole parents according to gender.

It has been demonstrated that when nurturing a child, caring behaviour is more important than gender (Geiger 1996). And, as we have seen, it is the nurturing quality of parents that children value. Mothers of vulnerable children are often highly stressed and their coping strategies are severely reduced. A father (or father-figure) who helps to reduce this stress and increase coping strategies is an asset to the child. Some men may provide high levels of social support, some none at all, and Oakley and Rigby (1998) emphasise that women have to support men too, often to their own disadvantage. However, as well as providing emotional support to both mothers and children (which may need to be acknowledged even in the worst cases seen in child protection), practitioners should recognise the emotional state of men and how to direct this as an asset. If the traditional 'breadwinner' role has been eroded because of continuous redundancies, male self-esteem is likely to be affected. This may need addressing to turn it into an asset: the situation could be reframed as a positive one that gives men more time with the family, for example. The paternal asset of imbuing the mother with confidence in her parenting ability may also be an exemplar in this category. Even where mothers are highly intelligent, they may receive little stimulus from being continuously with children or only talking about children. A father may be able to provide practical support by staying in regularly whilst the mother takes the opportunity to undertake an activity that provides adult company, such as tennis lessons or evening classes. It is also easy to fall into patterns of non-communication at home, slumping in front of the television or going out for 'a quick pint'.

We might want to consider the kinds of support we offer to men. Milner (1996) has abstracted issues about fathers from case conferences, and found that a few men receive services, which tend to be addiction counselling, detoxification, grief counselling and family therapy. Mothers however are offered more practical assistance, such as furniture, clothing, cash, debt counselling, holidays and domiciliary care.

Fathers may provide children with access to a range of activities that support their development. This may be through a religious or ethnic organisation that provides identity and support to a child (McAdoo 1986) by offering positive ethical values and orientation (McAdoo and McAdoo 1989). Even where a man is described as having no role with the children, he will have some sort of influence by virtue of his presence. It must be recognised that the presence of the father represents a distinct social context for the child (Kromelow, Harding and Touris 1990). It is up to us as practising health and social care professionals to recognise and encourage the assets that fathers can bring to a parenting relationship.

Again we emphasise that when discussing fathers, we do not restrict ourselves only to men with a biological relationship with the child. Foster fathers, often undervalued, have also been shown to be important because they:

- are good companions to the children

- provide an adult role model

- can help young girls to recover from the trauma of sexual abuse

- can provide emotional meaning to their foster children

- can be mentors in social development. (Gilligan 1998)

As Gilligan argues though, the response to the fact that a few foster fathers have been abusive has tended to be over-restrictive to the majority, with the added danger of then losing sight of the unique qualities they can bring. Similar contributions have been outlined for men working in children's centres (see Box 7.3).

Fathers can also be important assets to children with disabilities. Chudleigh (1999) runs a support group in Australia for fathers of children with disabilities. He finds that it tends to be mothers who suggest that men attend the group. However, once they start attending the group the men are incredibly supportive to each other. For example, at the very first meeting of the group one man became tearful when

Box 7.3 Men in children's centres

Jim Liddle is involved in an informal support network for men that work in children's centres in the Lothian area of Scotland. The following are some comments made from this group:

1. Good male role models are desperately needed in order to contradict macho male myths.

2. Deep levels of security can be formed and the healing of previous hurts take place by children getting close to men who reveal their thoughtful and gentle side.

3. Women appreciate the co-partnership of men in care.

4. It helps women to trust men again.

5. Men value the space of relating to other men.

Contact: Jim Liddle, Parkway Children's Centre, 8 Muirhouse Parkway, Edinburgh EH4 5EU. Tel: 0131 332 1949.

talking of the diagnosis of his son's deafness. Another man put his arm around his shoulder to comfort him while the other men listened respectfully to his account. Chudleigh has never observed any member of the group putting down another man for crying. The main function of the group is to bring fathers together because of the isolation they feel.

When children have a disability the need for two parents may be even greater. Even the physical care of some children may need two people. Fathers of children with special needs may feel a keen sense of financial responsibility because of the extra costs entailed. If this is the case they are likely not to be available when practitioners visit, and yet they should be involved in discussions about support and resources. An investigation into health care delivery for fathers of children with special needs argues that there are many steps professionals can take to engage men in becoming supportive figures in the lives of their children (May 1996). See Box 7.4 for further details.

Box 7.4 Fathers: the forgotten parents

May (1996) has been investigating the health care delivery for African-American men in Seattle. In his capacity as Project Director for the National Fathers' Network, May has been interviewing men in order to produce a videotape that highlights particular challenges black fathers have in caring for children. Concentrating on fathering for children with special needs, May nonetheless offers some pointers for professionals that may translate to other situations as well. In this attempt to specify ways in which professionals can engage with men, the positive results of engaging with fathers are emphasised:

- enhanced family communication
- less family fatigue and depression
- more sharing of parental responsibilities
- more acceptance of new children.

The main argument given in this paper is that professionals are gatekeepers of the issue of whether men will be full participants in child health care or not. Although some of these points probably fit an American context more than they do a British one, May suggests that there are numerous ways for professionals to engage men, summarised thus:

- Have an attitude and willingness to engage with them.
- Provide places for men to learn.
- Ensure flexible schedules.
- Promote fathers' strengths, not deficits.
- Provide opportunities for men to hug their children.
- Encourage men to talk about their own fathers.
- Provide places for them to grieve their losses.
- Promote their talking with other men.
- Insist corporate America be father and family friendly.

Recognising and Encouraging Psychological Availability

Men may not always realise how important they can be. Adolescent fathers, for example, have been shown to have more unrealistic expectations of their children's developmental capabilities than adolescent mothers (Dallas, Wilson and Salgado 2000). Teenage fathers have often been targeted as a 'high risk' group of parents, but there is encouraging research that demonstrates that such young men want to be involved, particularly as good role models. Parenting classes that were driven by their needs, not those of the teenage mothers, have been evaluated very positively (Dallas, Wilson and Salgado 2000). Although more research is needed, it is clear that emphasising the unique contribution of these young fathers is more useful than writing them off as potentially 'poor' parents. In the USA, a publicly and privately funded organisation has developed a large-scale programme of support for fathers (J. M. Johnson 1998). In ten cities three-year demonstration programmes have been established where job-support agencies and community-based organisations work in partnership to provide support and services to young and impoverished fathers. A detailed group work programme has been developed called the Fatherhood Development Curriculum, consisting of 25 discussion sessions. These sessions are organised around five themes:

1. personal development

2. life skills

3. responsible fatherhood

4. relationships

5. health and sexuality.

The organisation also provides training in its curriculum in Britain.

If fathers are physically absent, they should not automatically be screened out of the picture. Many of the children involved in child care and protection proceedings are living in households where the mother is the lone parent. This should not necessarily be taken to mean that the father does not have a meaningful relationship with the child. How often is there an explicit engagement with the father himself in this situation? First it is essential to establish whether there is any reason to believe that the father may pose a risk to the child or mother. The reason for father absence may well be that the mother has intentionally put a safe distance between them. Of course the mother's views are important: it would be quite wrong to suggest that a man who is absent because of his violence should even be told where the family lives. If this is the case, then child and mother safety must be the guiding principle that influences any further plans. However, the majority of absent fathers do not fall into such a category.

Rather than focusing on the negative aspects of father absence, it is more fruitful to consider ways in which separated or divorced parents can develop a successful model of co-parenting, where non-custodial fathers share responsibility for child rearing (Kissman 1997). Fathers may be extremely important in children's lives, yet not have either the financial or emotional resources to draw upon in maintaining that relationship. Are such instances even considered? Are there any practical ways that he can feel more involved? For example, could the mother be encouraged to send copies of the child's school report to him? In turn, is there anything that he can offer that can encourage the child's academic performance?

Although a father may have a poor relationship with the child's mother, he may have an individual and highly satisfactory relationship with the child. In one study fathers were quite open about expressing strong love for their children (Barclay and Lupton 1999). Absent fathers are not exempt from the benefits fathers can bring to a child's life, as has been shown by the example of men in prison. Even when a father is imprisoned, he can still provide access to wider family, such as grandparents or other male figures. It is too easy to miss the contribution that this can provide to a child's overall well-being. Even though the roles of incarcerated men are restricted, it is a mistake to suggest that they do not have any possible useful role (Hairston 1998). A third of the men in prison in England and Wales have dependent children and this is painful and detrimental to the children and the fathers (Katz 1999). Security measures make it difficult to increase contact, but innovative work has been undertaken in at least one prison, where male prisoners are encouraged to read bedtime stories on tape which are then sent to the children (see Box 7.5).

Box 7.5 Stories from 'ma cell'

This is an extract from an article written about work carried out with young men in prison (Tripney 2000).

> 'Who's doing the time here, me or my children?' It was inmates' comments like this in Polmont Young Offenders Institution (YOI) that made a colleague and me think of starting a 'parenting group'.

We were surprised to find that almost 15 per cent of Polmont's population, which normally runs at between 450 and 500 young offenders, were fathers. These figures may well fall short of the truth, not least because many offenders might not even know or want to admit they are fathers.

Effective fathers

We decided that our main objective should be to devise and encourage good communication between offenders and their families: a skill that is sadly lacking among many of our young offenders. Our next objective is to instil in the young men a sense of their responsibilities as fathers.

Polmont's Positive Parenting scheme began by targeting those offenders who were most likely to benefit from it; namely fathers who had maintained contact both with their children and with partners who were the mothers of those children. Our programme runs for 42 hours over 6 weeks and involves working with young offenders in small groups of 6. This includes a 2-hour bonding visit with partners and their children.

How the programme works

The introductory sessions outline the aims and objectives of the course and lay down the group rules. Each member of the group describes their family of origin, which gives them and us the opportunity to examine the variations that exist in family life. We discuss with the fathers the aspects of their children that they miss the most. We also discuss their responsibilities as fathers, which they frankly accept they could well do without. In this way, we identity just what being a father entails. This helps the group to bond quickly and lets members know that they are not alone in their thoughts and feelings. Two sessions are subsequently spent discussing the pros and cons of verbal and non-verbal forms of communication. Fathers are taught how to communicate with children using open questions rather than those that elicit only 'yes' and 'no' answers. These sessions stress the importance of maintaining good communications in the family unit and the value of maintaining a positive family contact.

Following these discussions, we had originally intended to record fathers reading bedtime stories on audiotape. However, because video-recording facilities were available, we decided to film them reading the stories. This approach was a great success because the children were able to see their fathers as well as hear them. Partners also gained from this approach insofar as they too could sit and view the recording with their children. It was decided to call this part of the programme *Stories from ma cell*. The play on the words 'ma cell' (short for 'myself') pleased the fathers greatly.

We collected a range of children's books for the storytelling and it was not long before two particular editions became firm favourites. One was a pop-up book about animals and the other was about farmyard tales. This had the added attraction of a small yellow duck hiding in each of its pages. All group members took part in the reading sessions and their value became patently obvious to all concerned.

Respect and trust

We continued the video sessions by recording the families during the bonding visit, enabling the child to see Mum, Dad and themselves as a complete unit. This was also a great success. Each family had the opportunity to meet and play in a 'normal' way. For example, one father took the opportunity to push his baby son in his buggy around the visit area. While this may seem of little importance, it transpired that this was the first time he had ever done this.

The feedback from the pilot scheme, including self-reports from the men themselves, was very positive. One father wrote as follows: '*The group is the best thing that has happened to me as a prisoner... We were given the respect and trust to sit at a visit and play with kids... I enjoyed doing what a father and should be doing.*' In similar vein a partner wrote: '*The group gave us the chance to be together as a family...*'

Although sessions on first aid, health and safety, relationships and responsibilities were included, the storytelling and videoing aspects were by far the most popular. Media interest has taken us completely by surprise, with coverage in the national press, television and radio. One shot shown on TV, of a child watching the video of her father reading the story and shouting out with great excitement, '*That's my Daddy*', made our hard work truly worthwhile.

The journal *Relational Justice Bulletin* is published by the Relationships Foundation, which can be contacted at: 3 Hooper Street, Cambridge CB1 2NZ. Tel: 01223 566333 Fax: 01223 566359 Email: r.f@clara.net. Enquiries to Dr Jonathan Burnside.

Billy Tripney can be contacted at: Polmont Young Offenders Institute, Scotland. Tel: 01324 711558.

If the child does not have any contact with a father there can be an assessment of the extent to which this may pose or exacerbate risks to the child's development by:

- contributing to adversity in the family circumstances
- upsetting or distressing the child
- reducing the financial and material conditions.

If the child has known the father who is now absent he or she may experience and express a whole range of emotional responses including:

- hurt
- guilt
- grief
- sadness
- betrayal
- curiosity
- anxiety
- anger.

Feelings of loss and hurt can contribute to a difficult relationship with the parent who is present: the mother. The mother may bear the brunt of the child's distress and may be the target of anger. Such problems may suggest the need for focused intervention about loss. Jewett's book on helping children with loss and separation provides a wealth of practical suggestions for direct work with the child and for support of the resident parent (1984). The possibility of facilitating a link with the father, perhaps via his family, can be explored, for example by providing financial support for visits.

Enhancing Socio-geneaological Connectedness

If the child has never known the father and has no information about him, he or she cannot have an emotional sense of loss that is specific to an individual, but may feel a sense of disconnectedness. Children often want to know about their past. Knowing who they are and where they come from can give children a sense of belonging, even if they do not want anything else from the father. There may be physical and genetic characteristics that the child wants to know about, even if the father is absent. Adopted children brought up in white middle-class establishments may be keen to know of their Bosnian heritage, for example. Practitioners not only should be aware of the importance of genealogical connectedness, but may find innovative ways in which fathers can contribute to this need, even whilst keeping them away from the child physically. In this situation there may be scope for gathering information about the father to share with the child. As Owusu-Bempah (1997) found in his study:

> regardless of the reasons for parental 'loss' and the families' material circumstances, children who possessed adequate and favourable information about the absent parent fared better on measures of behaviour, academic achievement, and emotional well-being than those who either had no information or had inadequate or damaging information about the absent parent. (p.202)

Schnitzer (1993) describes how many families where the father is absent manage to convey a 'lively father-presence' through the use of shared stories about the absent father.

Finally, all children need a 'coherent story' (Dowling 1993) that enables them to account for their circumstances. Mothers of children whose fathers are absent may need support in helping their children to develop such a coherent and meaningful account that incorporates information about the absent father and why he is absent. They may also require support in offering their children support in developing a 'public account' of why their father is absent.

Taking Account of Socio-Economic Factors

There is a difficult line to tread between not describing single-mother households as deficient, and recognising the potential importance of fathers to children. Whilst we resist any political agenda of single-mother 'bashing', it is quite clear that women and children in single-parent households face material disadvantage more extremely than two-parent families, even though one of the parents may not have a biological relationship with the child. As mothers and children bear the brunt of socio-economic disadvantage, the resources that a father brings may in some cases be purely financial. We do not want to suggest that men are only important because of the relief they bring to socio-economic circumstances; however, when considering men as assets, this aspect cannot be ignored. Although they may not be the financial providers themselves, their presence may allow the mother to work, may save on child care and transport arrangements, and provide a level of social support that helps alleviate some of the disadvantages that accompany material hardship. Men may provide a defence against the deficits of gendered disadvantage (Oakley and Rigby 1998). Of course it is not necessarily men who have to provide this, as other family members or same-sex partnerships may fulfil a similar function, but here we want to concentrate on the role of men as assets in such situations.

If we acknowledge that there is a role for men (whether present or absent) in reducing the exigencies of socio-economic disadvantage, what are the practice issues? If a father is absent, perhaps because he has been violent to the mother, the mother needs absolute assurance that her safety and the safety of the children is not compromised. This should be handled carefully, but professionals need to ensure that mothers know their rights and can claim child maintenance for example, whilst at the same time remaining out of the reach of such men. Fathers who are unemployed or disabled may need guidance not only in seeking their allowable benefits, but in finding appropriate work. Non-resident fathers are more likely to be unemployed or in low-income jobs than other men of the same age, they may not live in accommodation suitable for children and geographical distance can be problematic. They may have another family, which can make arrangements more complicated, and their relationship with their previous partner (and the mother of their children) may be very acrimonious.

These issues are recognised as a crucial component in a young fathers' programme in Arizona. Here young, poor fathers are encouraged to understand and undertake the financial, emotional and legal responsibilities of fatherhood (Valois 2000). Valois explains that such USA models have implications for the UK, where we still need to recognise all the things that impact on a father's financial contribution to child care. It has been shown that adolescent fathers remain involved with their children and take their financial responsibilities seriously, but practitioners may need to help them pursue educational or vocational qualifications in order to give them a realistic opportunity of doing so (Elster and Lamb 1986).

It is easy to direct the response to such a bleak scenario to the wider social policy level, where strategies to reduce child neglect must address centrally the key issue of poverty (Dubowitz *et al.* 1993). Within the context of our argument though, such issues have an individual dimension and must be taken seriously when assessing the impact of fathers as assets in child care and protection. The impact of father presence is especially important in light of the high rate of poverty among children raised by single mothers (Kissman 1997).

Income is a protective factor and this needs to be acknowledged, even if it is the only asset that an abusing father, for example, may bring. Practitioners and mothers will be familiar with the difficult questions that such a man raises. Is it better to be poor and safe, or to have a reasonable income but live with the fear of further abuse? Given what we know about the impact of poverty on all aspects of children's lives, there are sometimes uncomfortable compromises to be made. Our overall approach is concerned with raising the margin of material and social resources available for children and their families. The benefits of helping a father to contribute to this should not be understated.

Key Messages for Practice

1. Practitioners must avoid stereotyping men or seeing them in a one-dimensional way. Anti-discriminatory practice involves assessing the potential assets that any fathers may offer to their children.

2. Grandfathers, uncles, older brothers, foster fathers may all be important to children. When undertaking an assessment of the child's attachments there should be active consideration (preferably through observation) of the type of relationship the child has with all male figures.

3. Practical considerations can make it difficult to engage with men. In particular, the time of visits may not coincide with men being at home. If this is the case then health and social care professionals need to raise this issue at an organisational

level and request consideration of 'out of hours' visits because fathers can make a difference to their children's lives.

4. Fathers may play unique roles, such as playmate or disciplinarian, which can be encouraged; however, practitioners should be open to seeing the ways in which both parents can be positive role models.

5. Men may be very willing to take on more child care responsibility, but they may need pragmatic advice that they are uneasy about requesting. Practitioners need to be sensitive to this issue.

6. Helping fathers to take an active interest in their children's education can have a significant impact upon the likelihood of positive outcomes.

7. Fathers may not realise the value of cognitive, emotional and social support – both to the mother and to the child. This needs to be explained and encouraged.

8. Where a father is absent, attention should still be given to the possible resource he provides for children. Whilst having regard for safety, intervention can aim to increase the psychological availability of the father. Even if he never sees the child he may need help to fulfil some kind of role as a father.

9. Children can be helped to develop a 'coherent story' about their origins if they are provided with information about their paternal heritage.

10. Single-parent families are generally more socio-economically disadvantaged than others. Most fathers do want to support their children financially and may need help and advice about how to do this.

Try it for Size

Step one

Make a list of the qualities you would expect a 'good' father (or father-figure) to possess. As a guideline, aim for at least ten essential qualities and at least ten desirable qualities.

Step two

Now think of one worst-case scenario where a father behaves in a manner that has put his child at risk (e.g. sexual abuse).

Step three

Return to your list.

- Which of these qualities are compromised by the father's actions?

- Which qualities remain intact?

- Which could be maintained or repaired if the abusive action stopped?

- Do your answers change according to the action you chose? Are the same qualities compromised?

- As a practitioner working with this family, devise an action plan for enhancing the assets that this man can bring to the family.

Chapter 8

Framework for Practice

In this final chapter we will return to some of the issues that have been discussed in detail in previous chapters and draw them together as a series of questions child care and protection practitioners can ask themselves when planning intervention.

We cannot provide all the questions that might be asked, or all the answers to these questions, nor do we deny that the questions themselves can raise contentious issues. But, as has been highlighted throughout the book, the failure even to recognise that questions need to be asked leads to impoverished practice with fathers.

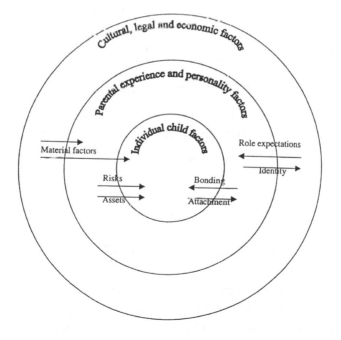

Figure 8.1 A diagram to show the importance of taking an ecological approach when assessing the needs of children and their parents.

These questions follow the structure of the book and are based upon an ecological approach, whereby assessment is made at the level of the child, at the level of the parent and extended family and at the level of the wider society, and also examines the interplay between them (Bronfennbrenner 1989). Figure 8.1 shows one way of mapping these different levels and some of the many interconnections.

What are the cultural, legal and economic circumstances? (Chapter 1)

Before practitioners engage meaningfully with service users and clients they must have the opportunity to reflect upon their own values about children, parenting and gender roles. Such reflection has to be informed by knowledge about prevailing social attitudes and opinions and about the current realities of family life and ethnic variations. During the course of writing this book, our own values have been challenged and we approach the end of the book with fewer certainties than we began with. Similarly, social workers and health visitors must question their own certainties. Such questions can include:

- Do I carry a white, Euro-centric, nuclear family template that acts as a norm against which I assess all families?
- Do I believe that families need fathers?
- Do I have deep-seated suspicions about men?
- Do I equate commitment with marriage?

The context of parenting interweaves biological and social strands. If we ask whether biological connections are important, we have to reply 'yes and no'. Certainly the biological connectedness that children and fathers have is a fact and to ignore that basic fact is to ignore a significant aspect of the child's life. At the same time, social connections can be equally or more salient. As suggested in Chapter 1, it may be helpful to decouple consideration of the parent–child relationship from consideration of the parent–parent relationship. This decoupling is illustrated in Figure 8.2.

An assessment has to start by establishing who has social connections with the child and who has biological connections to the child. The biological father and social father may be the same man or may be embodied in different men. Each aspect is important and the distinctions are far too often blurred and unclear in assessment documents.

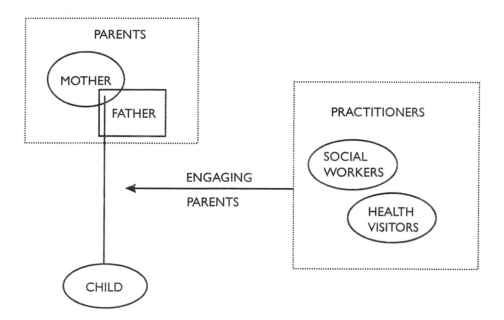

Figure 8.2(a) When parents are together, practitioners tend to take a unified approach to the assessment of parenting.

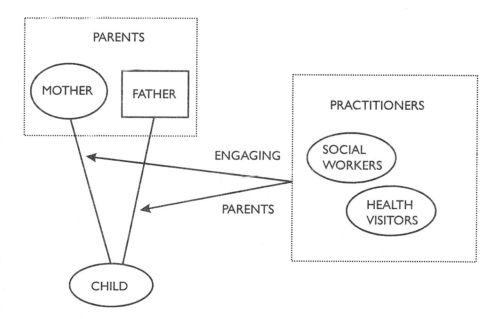

(b) An alternative model would encourage practitioners to assess each parent's relationship with the child separately, whether the parents are together or not.

Parents, especially fathers not married to their children's mothers, are often unaware of the complexity of the situation with regard to fathers' parental responsibilities and rights. Practitioners themselves need to be clear about the legal position and as part of their assessment must clarify:

- who is biologically related to the child
- who has legal responsibilities and rights and by what route
- what the parents' own understanding is about their legal position.

We know that poverty is one of the most damaging environmental factors to impinge on children. We also know that the most commonly articulated aspect of fatherhood is still economic provision. This makes it doubly important that assessment involves detailed analysis of the economic and material circumstances of the child. Such assessment should be specific about who:

- earns money
- is the recipient of any benefits, or may be entitled to benefits
- has debts
- is the named tenant of rented accommodation
- would describe themselves as a breadwinner
- is actually the breadwinner
- spends the money, and on what.

The assessment must also be clear about what is the precise impact upon the child. There are many people living in poverty who by a range of strategies manage to buffer their children from some of the worst effects. On the other hand, there are parents whose own lives are so shattered by poverty and the associated risks of alcohol or substance abuse, debt, mental health problems and so on, that their ability to parent is undermined.

What are the role options? (Chapter 2)

Practitioners need to be clear about what roles they envisage fathers playing in their children's lives. These can include the ones we have suggested:

- partnership (either traditional or non-traditional) with the mother
- alternative mother
- a luxury
- a unique role (for example: male role model).

Other role options might also be considered. This equates to the question: what is the aim of trying to engage with fathers? Unless practitioners are clear about the aim of intervention their practice is likely to be confusing.

It is very easy for practitioners and fathers to talk at cross-purposes. The health visitor might suggest to the parents that the father take a more active part in the care of his child. The worker could be envisaging the father becoming involved in the discipline of the child, the father might think he is being asked to play more with the child, the mother might imagine the father bathing the child and cleaning up the bathroom afterwards.

What it is crucial is to explore with any man who is significant to the child is:

- what role he is playing
- how his role may be widened
- what the man's view of his role is
- what the rest of the family view his role to be
- what support may be needed.

We are quite clear that practice must be informed and guided by theory. Indeed, there is a need for more detailed, theoretical analysis of individual, family and social forces upon gender identity, roles and expectations and their implications for child care and protection practice. Without theoretical guidance it is easy for practice to be based upon stereotypical views about male and female roles and for unwarranted assumptions to be made about children's needs. Drawing on theory we can ask a series of questions, all springing from an assessment of the needs of the child.

What does this child need? (Chapter 3)

Attachment theory can provide a helpful basis on which to assess the child's needs. Attachment theory has been criticised for its overemphasis upon the mother–child relationship. However, rather than rejecting attachment theory as helpful for guiding practice with fathers, we suggest that the principles can be useful. In fact, the incorporation of an analysis of attachment to fathers enriches and enhances attachment theory. As has been asserted, children flourish when they have a network of supportive attachments which meet a range of different and overlapping needs (M. Lewis 1994). Therefore, practitioners should always start from an assessment of the child and look at the range of developmental domains. Social workers, for example are advised to look at:

- physical development
- intellectual development
- psychological development
- emotional development
- spiritual development
- sexual development
- social development. (CCETSW 1991)

When assessing current attachments, practitioners need to take great care not to make assumptions. For example, a study of paediatric consultations carried out in American and Scottish hospitals showed that when doctors spoke to mothers they assumed that they were competent. This was not the case when they spoke to fathers:

Doctor	What was the weight at birth then?
Father	Seven and a half pounds.
Doctor	Gosh, you've got a good memory! I expect mothers but not fathers to remember. It's seven and a half pounds, you think?

...fathers (who rarely came but were encouraged to do so) could get lavish praise, but with mothers this was unnecessary. Mothers' competence was just not an issue, it was simply taken for granted. Moreover, overt praise might even be a sign that a character was seriously in doubt. (Note the way the doctor ends his response to the father with 'you think' – a qualification never made for mothers.) (Strong 1988, p.242)

When we have an assessment of the child's needs we can move on to look at how these needs can be met.

Who can best meet this child's needs? (Chapter 4)

The child development evidence suggests that both genders can be equally effective carers. When the roles are 'reversed' there is ample evidence to suggest that the man can be a primary attachment figure. So, in answer to the question about who can meet the child's needs we can, in theory, reply: the father. In reality, though, this is too simplistic a response. The clearest message from the model of anti-discriminatory practice, drawn from feminist theory and theories of oppression, is that gender roles are socially constructed, assigned and reinforced.

Theories of oppression warn us, therefore, that we cannot work in an anti-sexist way without taking account of structural forces. The failure to examine these forces and how they impact upon the individual explains why simple exhortations to men to be more involved have minimal effect and, of course, why simple exhortations to practitioners to engage with fathers have minimal effect. Structural forces affect us all, and it is not easy for an individual to adopt gender role behaviour usually associated with the opposite sex. Two pieces of information can suggest the different levels of assessment that the practitioner has to take into account:

1. With adequate motivation and supportive circumstances men can be effective primary caregivers.

2. Such a role runs counter to social expectations and is therefore not supported by social institutions and structures.

We are not advocating simple 'role reversal' (unless this suits a couple). Instead, we would suggest that non-sexist practice implies promoting the range of caring activities in both, based upon individual preference, comfort, practicalities and so on.

This leads us to another tricky issue in anti-sexist practice. If we are trying to engage with fathers should we simply extend our traditional practice to include men or do we need a different kind of practice? Should we widen the net or do we need a different kind of net?

So are there ways in which by our very attempts to involve fathers we fall into the trap of gender stereotyping? It has been suggested, for example, that the political agenda behind encouraging more father involvement is one of 'shoring up traditional male authority in the family' (Ruxton 1992). This agenda has been linked with the impetus for crime reduction, based upon a view that father absence is associated with boys, in particular, exhibiting delinquent behaviour (Featherstone 2000). Apart from representing a simplistic analysis of the causes of crime, this agenda is also clearly based upon the gender stereotype: man as disciplinarian. It is based upon an assumption of difference, that men offer a different kind of care and need to be engaged with differently.

Take, for example, communication. There is a history of research into the different communication styles of men and women which boils down to the simple assertion that men are less willing, and/or able, to use the language of feelings. In his study of the views of young men in Belfast, for example, Harland (1997) found them to use humour and banter when discussing feelings: "'I wouldn't want to show feelings in front of people – none of my mates do. We just have a good laugh together – I've never done that – no way!'" (p.54). Harland suggests, 'male gender roles force boys to reject as feminine a wide range of characteristics that are simply human, such as the experience and expression of their emotions and feelings' (p.83).

Most social workers and health visitors are women, and, it can be argued, are trained in 'feminised' communications skills, built on the language of feelings. They will ask: 'What do you feel about this?' They may reward and be rewarded by responses in the same language. Men, it is argued, prefer a language of facts and would prefer the question: 'What is your opinion about this?' (Henry 1999).

The following example illustrates this problem.

A young boy is placed in residential accommodation. His father presents as threatening and aggressive. In review meetings he shouts angrily, making a series of statements, some of which are prefaced by,

'I know I'm out of order but...' He says, 'I was in residential care, the things that happened to me you wouldn't want to hear about, I never got any therapy!'

The social worker responds by nodding sympathetically, saying, 'I take on board what you feel.' The father becomes even more angry, aggressive and disruptive. His contact with his son is terminated on the basis that he poses a threat. He is not provided with information about his son's whereabouts or progress.

Whilst appreciating the concern of workers about his aggression, the decision to terminate his contract appears punitive, based on the assumption that he is a dangerous man. There is a subsequent change of social worker. The new worker engages the father in a language of facts – the father is provided with information about his son, his son's care and whereabouts. In this way the father's anxiety is acknowledged in a different way. Eventually, he is able to enter into a more therapeutic relationship with the worker and begins to explore his own dreadful experiences of residential care.

On an individual level, men who work in child care describe themselves as victims of gender stereotyping:

Almost all the male workers interviewed related how they had often, in the course of their social work careers, been pushed into acting as 'controllers' – a role which was both difficult and uncomfortable. Whilst this was regarded as more common in residential settings with difficult adolescents, it was still felt to be an issue in other areas of social work: 'It's something that I'm well aware of from residential work. The strong man will be used to control difficult children and that's all about power and threat and intimidation. I'm very aware of not wanting to do that' (project leader, Swindon). (Ruxton 1992, p.27)

Do these kinds of distinctions help us to develop guidance for practice or just confuse matters? Well, as we now know, research into sex differences tends to show a huge overlap in the attributes shown by each gender (Golombok and Fivush 1994). Many of the perceived differences are as much a result of stereotyping and assumptions as biological differences. Rather than advocating the adoption of a 'Male Dictionary' we would suggest that practitioners need to widen their repertoire for all service users and clients. Why assume that a woman will prefer to talk about her feelings? Perhaps she would welcome a task-oriented discussion. Communication skills lie at the heart of all helping professions, but communication depends on:

- listening
- gauging responses
- checking that you have been understood
- trying different ways of saying the same thing
- paying as much attention to non-verbal as verbal cues
- not imposing your interpretation of events
- not making assumptions about another's point of view.

Finally, there is some evidence to suggest that it is possible to have the best of both worlds. Research into the way that family centres in England and Wales involved fathers defined three broad orientations: 'gender-blind', 'gender-differentiated' and 'agnostic' (Ghate, Shaw and Hazel 2000a). One of the conclusions is highly illuminating:

> *Gender-blind* and *gender-differentiated* centres took opposite approaches to working with men. Gender-blind approaches stressed the similarity of need between mothers and fathers, and described their service as open to all on an equal opportunities basis. At these centres fathers were expected to join in with the same activities as mothers. By contrast, a gender-differentiated approach emphasised the different and sometimes conflicting needs of men and women. They tended to offer at least some sex-segregated activities, including men's groups. The study found that both these approaches were more successful in actually engaging fathers with family centre work than were *agnostic* centres which had not formulated any identifiable strategy towards working with men. Having some identifiable strategy for working with fathers mattered much more than what that strategy was (Ghate, Shaw and Hazel 2000b, p.2).

So, when examining who best can meet the needs of children, practitioners must have an appreciation of

- theories of oppression
- sexism and the implication for gender roles
- the range of the family structures and ways in which power relations can operate

- the impact of personal values

- how individuals can challenge stereotypes in the way that they choose to live their lives.

Crucially, it is important to discuss the issues with the people it is hoped will be involved in the care of the child. So, when carrying out home assessments for fostering, what questions are asked of the male about how he sees his role? Can we be sure that he does not try to present himself as an 'ideal father' in the traditional sense, believing that this is what is expected, when his actual inclination is to take a more nurturing role?

So, children's needs can be met by mothers and fathers who show parenting behaviours on a dimension that can be shifted according to personal inclination, ability, resources, social support and social expectations. The division of labour between mother and father does not need to equal a division of the child's needs.

How can they be supported to meet this child's needs? (Chapter 5)

In their role of supporting mothers to help them meet their children's needs, health visitors extend care to them. When health visitors talk of caring for parents and children, can they envisage this notion including fathers? We will consider this question with regard to men who exhibit violence and aggression, precisely because it is particularly challenging to extend care to the abusive man.

There are a range of explanations as to why male violence is so prevalent in comparison with female violence. Explanations fall on a dimension between the purely biological and the purely social. In this book we are concerned with men as fathers and we would argue, as we would for all parenting issues, that an interactional perspective is most helpful. In other words, it is necessary to look at the interplay of individual, familial and social factors and their impact upon parenting. It is also important to listen to individual accounts.

We have been struck by the recurrence of the theme of victimisation in conversations with practitioners working with men (Henry 1999; McFaddyen 1999; Spring 2000). When men are given the opportunity to reflect upon their current problems they often begin to describe difficult childhood experiences, especially of brutality. They recall instances of violence from their fathers or stepfathers and intimidation in the classroom and playground. The anecdotal evidence suggests that many of the men encountered in child care and protection practice have unhappy memories of their childhoods. Indeed, many of these men will have been brutalised in childhood. As a result of his study of the extreme situation, namely boys who have been convicted of murder, Garbarino talks of boys and young men growing up in a 'toxic environment' (1999).

Should aggressive or violent men be offered the opportunity to explore the impact of their childhoods upon their fathering? This is an area fraught with problems. Whenever the past is used as an *explanation* for behaviour there is the potential danger that it becomes used as an *excuse* for unacceptable behaviour. This is then a short step away from asserting that violence is beyond the individual's control. And yet we know that men often use violence and aggression in a controlled and controlling way. There is a danger that if practitioners engage with the *victim* within the man they lose their focus upon the *responsibility* of the man for his behaviour (Henry 1999). It is also possible to lose sight of the extent to which male violence is reinforced or condoned by society. This is the area that has perhaps caused the most tension between feminists supporting women and male practitioners supporting men.

However, intervention with women routinely takes account of the impact of childhood experiences upon current functioning. Practitioners are expected to consider the potential impact of abuse, neglect, sex-role expectations, violence and oppression upon ability to parent. Opportunities to reflect upon the past in formal or informal counselling are common. At the same time, child-protection practitioners maintain a balanced view of the chain that leads from adverse childhood experiences to impairment of current functioning to children being inadequately parented. Indeed, social workers and health visitors constantly attend to the balance between mothers' needs for support and children's needs for protection. Anti-discriminatory practice would suggest that we afford the same opportunity to fathers. Research based on attachment theory shows that if mothers are offered the opportunity to reflect upon adverse childhood experiences and to develop a coherent account for events, then they are more likely to have children who are securely attached to them. The messages from this work can be taken and applied to work with fathers so that they are offered similar opportunities. Box 8.1 describes one attempt to address a range of fathers' needs.

Box 8.1 Fathers and family centres: a practice example

'I feel like a pioneer' (father attending group work).

Many family centres are beginning to develop work with fathers. One of these is Bo'ness Family Centre in Scotland (McFaddyen 1999).

For every application to the centre there is a home visit with the aim of meeting both the mother and father. Men are asked generational questions to find out about their fathers and grandfathers and how they have influenced them. They are asked to identify 'heroes' and 'villains' in their lives. If it is only the mother who is seen, questions are asked about the level of involvement of the father and his perceived role with the children.

Some of the men are hard to track down but the male worker finds that with persistence he can often establish contact with the fathers, some of whom will go on to attend a group. McFaddyen believes that it is important to show the men respect, to introduce himself, shake them by the hand and invite them to come to the centre. Even if they do not attend the group, contact is maintained wherever possible, even if it is just to stop for a chat in the street.

Group work

The group is not run as an educational parenting skills group, but the discussion is always brought back to the children. Each session has a theme and is built around active listening about each others' experiences. For example, in pairs each one takes a turn as the listener, sometimes using a 'fishbowl' technique where the rest of the group observes. The aim is to provide a space in which the men feel able to show their vulnerabilities and where the fact of their gender does not obscure them as a person. In McFaddyen's experience, many of the men have been traumatised by their childhood experiences, with the result that they are inhibited from opening up. The aspiration is that they will learn to listen more actively to their children and that they will be better equipped to inhibit the repetition of the unhelpful patterns of father–child interaction that they experienced.

One-to-one work

A need was identified for the support for men who are worried about their violent tendencies. In common with many areas, there is a lack of local support for such men to change because the majority of programmes are aimed at men who have been convicted of violence. Individual psychotherapy with violent men is held at a local health centre, not in the family centre.

In one case the child was attending the centre and the mother was working with staff on parenting issues. However, the father (who was separated from the mother) frequently harassed her at home by breaking windows, etc. She was very frightened by his behaviour. She was asked to pass on the message that the male social worker at the centre would be willing to meet with him. The next day he was on the doorstep and began one-to-one counselling during which he revealed his child-hood experiences of severe trauma. It was his acceptance of the need for his children to be protected from what he went through that helped him to change his behaviour and cease his violence towards the mother of his child.

Contact: John McFaddyen, Bo'ness Family Centre (Central Regional Council/Barnado's), Duchess Nina House, Cadzow Crescent, Bo'ness. Tel: 01506 823 116.

It must be emphasised that any such work with men:

- does not imply excusing abusive behaviour

- does not preclude parallel work focusing on responsibility and self-control

- must be underpinned by the same kind of balancing of adult and child needs as currently occurs in work with mothers.

Has a full risk assessment been carried out with regard to all men involved in the care of this child? (Chapter 6)

As has been emphasised throughout, the failure to carry out a full risk assessment of all male figures associated with children has contributed to dangers being overlooked. Once actual and potential risk is identified, the emphasis must be upon protecting the child and placing the responsibility firmly with the abuser. As is currently the practice with mothers, there should be an assessment of the father's willingness and ability to change his behaviour. If he is willing to change then he must be offered appropriate and well-structured support to change. Some men who currently pose a risk to women and children may not be willing to change, and intervention then has to focus on supporting the mother and child and providing adequate resources for them to function independently of the father.

Although many aggressive and abusive men may not be willing to change, practitioners can influence future male behaviour. There are things that practitioners can do to contribute to the prevention of future male violence and aggression, by addressing the fact that the roots of male violence and aggression often lie in the socialisation of boys.

Despite huge social changes in the adult roles of men and women, it is still the case that sex-role stereotyping occurs. Toyshops still label sections as 'boys' toys' and 'girls' toys'. The girls' sections are still over-whelmingly pink, fluffy and domestic. The boys' sections are predomi-nantly associated with construction, space or war. One simple example sums it up: in a large home shopping catalogue the same basic child's bike is featured twice. One is painted in camouflage colours, has a walkie-talkie on the front and a boy in soldier fatigues riding it; the other is pink, with flower stickers, has a shopping basket on the front and a girl in a pink dress riding it. Does this matter? We would argue that such sex-role stereotyping limits the choices of expression for both boys and girls. Research into what makes children resilient in the face of adversity shows non-typical sex-role expectations to be associated with greater resilience. If we want children to become emotionally healthy adults we need to encourage girls to be autonomous and independent and boys to increase their abilities in the expression of emotions, social perception and nurturing (Werner 1990).

What is particularly relevant for the issue of aggressive men is that the pressure upon young boys to be 'masculine' is extreme and is often particularly exerted by fathers (Golombok and Fivush 1994). In some families boys are punished for signs of 'feminine' behaviour, and boys tend to be socialised to be over-independent and to minimise the need for close ties (Unger and Crawford 1992). The threat of being called a 'sissy' is a powerful control upon boys' behaviour, and this is in a modern society where physical strength and power is unnecessary for survival. In some situations these forces can be seen as abusive. At the same time, boys learn that aggression is an acceptable way to get what you want. Violence, bullying and aggressive behaviour is rewarded and often condoned.

Practitioners encounter young children all the time. They need to ask themselves what they can do to encourage boys and girls to find victimisation unacceptable. They need to consider the role they can play in teaching young boys alternative modes of expression. So, in residential units, nurseries, children's centres, family centres, foster homes and parenting classes they can ask what messages are conveyed about gender roles:

- Are phrases like 'he's got to toughen up...' going unchallenged?
- Are boys finding that aggressive behaviour leads to the rewards of more adult attention, or getting what they want?
- Is sexist behaviour tolerated in group care settings?
- Are male staff put in the position of being 'enforcers', thus providing role models of male power?
- Do the posters and books in nurseries encourage gender stereotyping?
- Are boys encouraged, or taught how to express feelings and emotions?

Has a full assessment been carried out as to what positive assets all men involved in the care of this child might offer? (Chapter 7)

This is a time when families are reconstituting and developing, a time of great demographic change and a time when women's roles are changing. It is difficult to pin down family life or identify who plays which role in such families. Social workers and health visitors encounter every type of family set-up, representing all the different arrangements possible. In this context the most clear-cut and unchanging structure is that of the mother–child dyad. Perhaps it is not surprising that within the welter of confusing family groupings, the archetypal image of mother and child is habitually revisited. Despite the changes, this image remains prevalent and resonant.

Social workers and health visitors practise within the constraints of social structures and it is evident that the structural forces upon men and women as parents are very powerful. The social rhetoric of new fatherhood has a limited expression in reality. Similarly, the practice rhetoric of working with parents is still largely expressed in intervention with mothers. For example, in the field of child sexual abuse there has been attention to the role of the non-abusing mother, but little is known about non-abusing fathers, as Box 8.2 describes.

Box 8.2 What about the dads? Children and Families Counselling Project, Glasgow

This was an NCH Action for Children Project, later joined by Children 1st, set up to provide a counselling service for children and their families whose lives had been affected by child sexual abuse (Hawthorn 1999). The 'findings' make no claim to be scientific in terms of numbers or methods, but the issues arising have influenced practice. Very little has been written about the effects of child sexual abuse on non-abusing fathers. Although the project attracted low numbers of men, when the men were brought together for an initial session, they were very clear about their agenda:

feelings about what had happened

to know about abuse

to know about people who do it

to know about 'what to look for'

what it does to a family.

The issues arising for fathers were grouped broadly into six areas:

1. Trust: they did not know whom to trust, they felt they could not trust their own judgement, partners had stopped trusting them with the children and there was a loss of trust in family and friends because of their denial or disbelief of the abuse.

2. Stigma: they felt they had been 'taken for a mug' and that the community felt they had failed to protect their own children.

3. Powerlessness: the men felt powerless to stop the abuse, they saw professionals as powerless, and they had a sense that the

system was suspicious that they may have known or even colluded with the abuse.

4. Gender and sexuality: their was a feeling of failure in their perception of role of the father (as protector), homophobia and fear for their children's sexuality, issues of being excluded further from their roles as fathers.

5. Intense feelings of anger: often unresolved and exacerbated by alcohol, such feelings could result in violence, projecting anger onto others, anger at the disbelief and denial of others, all of which led to isolation.

6. Intense feelings of grief and loss: this impacted on their intimate relationships with their partner, on their relationship with the child and on their relationship with the extended family.

Contact: Moyra Hawthorn, NCH, Family Support Falkirk, Camelon, Falkirk FK1 4QW. Tel: 01324 633772 or 0141 9503683.

A model for assessment of men in child care work has to be built upon a foundation of knowledge about the range of ways in which the role of father can be manifested. The aims of intervention with individual men as fathers have to be explicit and agreed. And, as has been pointed out (Lamb, Pleck and Levine 1986), the greater involvement of a father is only of benefit to the individuals involved if they also hold this as a value.

An important step here is to avoid falling into the trap of equating physical absence with psychological absence. It is easy to overlook the role that a father may play, or may potentially play, in his children's lives when he does not live in the household with them. We hope that this book has provided enough examples of the ways in which men can be assets to their children to stimulate creativity in this area. Such creativity can embrace both 'traditional' aspects of fatherhood, such as sport and play, and 'non-traditional' aspects such as nurturing. If children reside with their mother after separation or divorce then there is a strong likelihood of them losing contact with their father. Box 8.3 describes how contact centres can be used to help maintain or re-establish a father–child relationship.

Box 8.3 Contact with fathers at Child Contact Centres

On some occasions it may be necessary to arrange for children to meet with their fathers on neutral territory. Child Contact Centres provide a child-friendly environment to facilitate contact in such circumstances. For example, the Medway Child Contact Centre in England receives voluntary referrals from families; referrals from court welfare officers following divorce and child care proceedings; and referrals from social workers wanting to facilitate contact with children accommodated away from home (Gordon 1999). The centre does not provide supervised access, but can accommodate the court welfare officer or social worker if supervised access is required. Space and toys for children are provided as well as volunteers to facilitate play and activities between the father and child. This is seen as essential in some cases because to put a father and child together for two hours and expect them to interact can be unnatural and counterproductive.

As a result of witnessing a range of contact situations the director has a number of observations:

- Some children appear to be influenced by a mother's anger and disappointment with the adult relationship and are therefore initially reluctant to see their father. Once contact begins they often change their minds and develop an independent relationship with their father.

- Many of the fathers are very keen to see their children and show commitment to the contact visits.

- Sometimes the neutrality of the space enables the parents to communicate better and to move to more amicable terms. Sometimes a mother will return early and join the father and child in play.

- In many cases the contact centre is only used to establish an initial contact arrangement and the families are then able to make their own private arrangements.

- Children respond very well in the centre; they enjoy the toys and activities and the organised games.

- Some of the children are very boisterous and 'hyperactive' and require the help of volunteers to settle.

> - If the child is distressed by contact then the centre staff will recommend that it discontinue. For example, one little girl was required by court order to see her father, but cried through all sessions. The contact order was subsequently rescinded by the court as a result of this direct evidence that contact was not in the child's best interests.
> - The staff try to keep an open mind and to avoid becoming drawn into 'taking sides' with either parent.
> - Each family situation has to be treated as unique, without making assumptions about what is best for a child.
>
> Contact: Arnold Gordon, Medway Child Contact Centre. Tel: 01634 310028.

Initiatives and projects aimed at involving fathers in their children's lives are mushrooming. They may have different philosophies and different roots, but their development is a result of the recognition that for too long fathers have been overlooked. The roles that fathers already play are often not appreciated and the potential for those roles to be widened and enhanced is ignored or not supported. We have emphasised throughout this book that the needs of the child must be at the centre when planning intervention. Children's needs are complex and varied. Children also have much to offer those who care for them and can express clear views about what they want. Therefore, our simple final recommendation is that practitioners be guided by the needs and rights of children to safe, fulfilling and rewarding relationships with the adults involved in their lives, whatever their gender.

Exploring and Dividing Roles: An Exercise to Use with Couples

Stage One

Each parent individually lists all the tasks associated with parenting.

Stage Two

Make one big joint list from the two individual lists. It might be useful to compare them as well at this point. Do domestic chores feature on either list, for example?

Stage Three

Give each parent a copy of the list. Ask them to label each task with the initial of the person who mostly undertakes this task, or indicate if they think this is shared.

Stage Four

Do they agree? Are they both happy with the way the list is divided? Is there room for renegotiation of some of the tasks?

The following table is an example of a completed exercise (not all tasks are shown) for the parents of a 12-year-old girl:

The final task list	Mother responses	Father responses	Renegotiated	Comments
Shopping	Mother	Both	Both	Discussion, as father thought this was already shared
Cooking	Both	Both	Both	No change
Bedtime story	Both	Father	Father	Child growing out of this habit

Ensuring washed	Mother	Both	Both	Discussion, as father thought this was already shared
Ensuring dressed appropriately	Mother	Both	Both	Discussion, as father thought this was already shared
Taking to school	Mother	Mother	Both	Have agreed to share this a little more
Picking up from school	Mother	Mother	Both	Have agreed to share this a little more
General discipline	Mother	Father	Both	Large discussion required
Playing	Both	Father	Both	On discussion, mother spends little time in play
Getting up in the night	Mother	Both	Both	Rarely required now
Getting her up in the morning	Mother	Mother	Both	Have agreed to share this a little more
Making sure she has turned the lights out	Mother	Mother	Mother	Does not mind the task
Arranging babysitters	Mother	Both	Mother	Does not mind the task
Going to school plays	Mother	Both	Both	Father will make more effort
Making sure homework is done	Mother	Both	Father	Will take on this role
Taking her shopping for school shoes	Mother	Mother	Mother	Both hate the task, but father refuses
Making sure school bag is ready	Mother	Mother	Mother	Both hate the task, but father refuses
Giving pocket money	Father	Father	Father	Does not mind the task
Ironing	Mother	Mother	Mother	Both hate the task, but father refuses
Washing	Mother	Mother	Mother	Does not mind the task
Cleaning the toilet	Mother	Mother	Mother	Does not mind the task
Etc...				
Overall comments	Some useful discussions and a number of arguments. Both parents found this eye-opening: in their perceptions of what they did; what they were prepared to do; and what they did not mind doing. The mother felt she was having to do the 'nagging' tasks. Both were surprised that they seemed to fall into a reasonably traditional gender division of labour.			

APPENDIX II

Fathering Roles: a Case Example

Lesley and Chris have two adopted children, Sam aged five and Kim aged eight. These are happy children, who have adapted well to their new family and devoted parents. Lesley, a nurse, is the primary caretaker of the children, undertaking occasional agency work to supplement the family income. Chris, a surgeon, tends to work irregular hours, but makes sure of quality time with the children every day. This includes football (Sam's favourite) and horse riding (Kim's favourite). Following some painful decisions in their lives, Lesley and Chris agreed to a trial separation six months ago. They decided that the children should live with their mother, but regular contact has been maintained. Kim's teacher has now contacted social services. She is concerned by changes in Kim's behaviour. At the same time, both parents have individually contacted you with the same concerns.

1. What advice do you give Chris?

2. What advice do you give Lesley?

3. What advice do you give the teacher?

4. Who is the mother of these children?

5. Does your advice change depending on whether Lesley or Chris is the mother?

6. Did you make assumptions about gender based on occupation?

7. Are the children sons or daughters or one of each?

8. Have you made any assumptions and if so, based on what?

This case study can be used in training in different ways. For example, divide the group in two and with one group describe Lesley as the mother and Chris as the father, with the other group reverse this. Ask the students to come up with suggestions for practice and then compare the responses of the two groups.

Fathers and Infants:
The Father's Role in Infant Care

[This form to be completed by the Caregiver/Father]

Child's name: . . . . Child's age: . . . .

Caregiver's/Father's name:. . . . . Date: . . . .

Tick one box in each section for the answer which resembles your infant care routine most closely.

How often do you feed your child solids?
Shared with partner in time available . . . . ☐
More than once a week . . . . ☐
Once a week. . . . . ☐
Less than once a week. . . . . ☐

How often do you prepare your child's food?
At least four meals per week . . . . ☐
1–3 meals per week . . . . ☐
Less than once a week. . . . . ☐
Never . . . . ☐

Do you put your child to bed?
More than your partner . . . . ☐
Shared with your partner (50–50) . . . . ☐
1–3 times per week . . . . ☐
Once a week or less . . . . ☐

Is your morning role with the child:
regular caretaking (shared with your partner) . . . . ☐
occasional caretaking/regular play . . . . ☐
occasional (not regular) . . . . ☐
non-existent . . . . ☐

How often do you change your child's nappies?
At least once daily . . . . ☐
Less than once daily . . . . ☐
Less than once a week. . . . . ☐
Never . . . . ☐

How often do you take care of your child on your own?
Four or more times per week. . . . . ☐
1–3 times per week . . . . ☐
Less than once a week. . . . . ☐
Less than once a month . . . . ☐

Reproduced with permission of the author, Martin Herbert (1980).

References

Abel, G., Becker, J., Cunnigham-Rathner, J., Mittleman, M. and Rouleau, J. (1988) 'Multiple paraphiliac diagnoses among sex offenders.' *Bulletin of the American Academy of Psychiatry and the Law 16*, 153–168.

Abel, G.C. and Rouleau, J.L. (1990) 'The nature and extent of sexual assault.' In W.L. Marshall D.R. Laws and H.E. Barbaree (eds.) *Handbook of Sexual Assault.* New York: Plenum.

Abrahams, C. (1994) *The Hidden Victims – Children and Domestic Violence.* London: NCH Action for Children.

Ainsworth, M.D.S., Blehar, M., Walters, E. and Walls, S. (1978) *Patterns of Attachment.* Hillsdale, NJ: Erlbaum.

Alanen, L. (1994) 'Gender and generation: feminism and the "child question".' In J. Qvortrup, M. Bardy, G. Sgritta and H. Wintersberger (eds.) *Childhoo d Matters: Social Theory, Practice and Politics.* Aldershot: Avebury.

Angeli, N. (1997) 'STEPs for positive parenting.' *Health Visitor 70*, 9, 336–338.

Angeli, N., Christy, J., Howe, J. and Wolff, B. (1994) 'Facilitating parenting skills in vulnerable families.' *Health Visitor 67*, 4, 130–132.

Appleton, J.V. (1994) 'The role of the health visitor in identifying and working with vulnerable families in relation to child protection: a review of the literature.' *Journal of Advanced Nursing 20*, 167–175.

Atkins, S. and Murphy, K. (1995) 'Reflective practice.' *Nursing Standard 9*, 45, 31–35.

Azar, S.T. (1997) 'A cognitive behavioural approach to understanding and treating parents who physically abuse their children.' In D.A. Wolfe, R.J. McMahon and R.D. Peters (eds.) *Child Abuse: New Directions in Prevention and Treatment Across the Lifespan.* Thousand Oaks, Calif., London and New Delhi: Sage Publications.

Bailey, J. (1995) 'Reflective practice. Implementing theory.' *Nursing Standard 9*, 46, 29–31.

Bainham, A. (1989) 'When is a parent not a parent? Reflections on the unmarried father and his child in English law.' *International Journal of Law and the Family 3*, 208–239.

Baldwin, N. and Spencer, N. (1993) 'Deprivation and child abuse – implications for strategic planning in children's services.' *Children and Society 4*, 4, 357–375.

Barclay, L. and Lupton, D. (1999) 'The experiences of new fatherhood: a socio-cultural analysis.' *Journal of Advanced Nursing 29*, 4, 1013–1020.

Barker, R. (1994) *Lone Fathers and Masculinities.* Avebury.

Barker, M. and Morgan, R. (1993) *Sex Offenders: A Framework for the Evaluation of Community-Based Treatment.* London: Home Office.

Barker, P.J., Reynolds, W. and Ward, T. (1995) 'The proper focus of nursing: a critique of the "caring" ideology.' *International Journal of Nursing Studies 32*, 4, 386–397.

Bartholomew, K. and Horowitz, L.M. (1991) 'Attachment styles among young adults: a test of a four-category model.' *Journal of Personality and Social Psychology 61*, 226–244.

Beail, N. and McGuire, J. (1982) 'Fathers, the family and society: the tide of change.' In N. Beail and J. McGuire (eds.) *Fathers. Psychological Perspectives* (pp.234–246). London: Junction Books.

Beck, C.T. (1999) 'Quantitative measurement of caring.' *Journal of Advanced Nursing 30*, 1, 24–32.

Becker, P.T., Houser, B.J., Engelhardt, K.F. and Steinmann, M.J. (1993) 'Father and mother contributions to family functioning when the child has a mental delay.' *Early Development and Parenting 2*, 3, 145–155.

Bell, M. (1999) 'Working in partnership in child protection: the conflicts.' *British Journal of Social Work 29*, 437–455.

Bentovim, A., Elton, A. and Tranter, M. (1987) 'Prognosis for rehabilitation after abuse.' *Adoption and Fostering 11*, 1, 26–31.

Berliner, L. (2000) Personal communication.

Berliner, L. and Conte, J.R. (1990) 'The process of victimization: the victims' perspective.' *Child Abuse and Neglect 14*, 29–40.

Bianchi, S.M. (1999) 'Feminization and juvenilization of poverty: trends, relative risks, causes, and consequences.' *Annual Review of Sociology 25*, 307–333.

Binney, V., McKnight, I. and Broughton, S. (1994) 'Relationship play therapy for attachment disturbances in four to seven year old children.' In J. Richer (ed.) *The Clinical Application of Ethology and Attachment Theory.* The Association of Child Psychology and Psychiatry, Occasional Papers Series.

Boushel, M. and Farmer, E. (1996) 'Work with families where children are at risk: control and/or empowerment?' In P. Parsloe (ed.) *Pathways to Empowerment.* Birmingham: Venture Press.

Bowlby, J. (1951) *Maternal Care and Mental Health.* Geneva: World Health Organization.

Bowlby, J. (1969) *Attachment and Loss* (Vol. 1. *Attachment*). New York: Basic Books.

Bretherton, I. and Waters, E. (1985) 'Growing points of attachment theory and research.' *Monographs for the Society for Research in Child Development 50*, 209, 1–2.

Brewster, A.L., Nelson, J.P., Hymel, K.P., Colby, D.R., Lucas, D.R., McCanne, T.R. and Milner, J.S. (1998) 'Victim, perpetrator, family, and incident characteristics of 32 infant maltreatment deaths in the United States Air Force.' *Child Abuse and Neglect 22*, 2, 91–101.

Bronfennbrenner, U. (1989) 'Ecological systems theory.' *Annals of Child Development 6*, 187–249.

Brown, K.A. and Barbarin, O.A. (1996) 'Gender differences in parenting a child with cancer.' *Social Work in Health Care 22*, 4, 53–71.

Browne, J. (1995) 'Can social work empower?' In R. Hugman and D. Smith (eds.) *Ethical Issues in Social Work.* London and New York: Routledge.

Buchanan, A. and Ten Brinke, J. (1997) *What Happened When They Were Grown Up?* York: Joseph Rowntree Foundation.

Bullock, A. and Stallybrass, O. (1977) *Dictionary of Modern Thought.* London: Fontana.

Burgess, A. and Ruxton, S. (1996) *Men and their Children: Proposals for Public Policy.* London: IPPR.

Burghes, L., Clarke, L. and Cronin, N. (1997) *Fathers and Fatherhood in Britain, Occasional Paper 23.* London: Family Policy Studies Centre.

Butler, S. (1996) 'Child protection or professional self-preservation by the baby nurses? Public health nurses and child protection in Ireland.' *Social Science and Medicine 44*, 3, 303–314.

Calder, M. (1999) *Assessing Risk in Adult Males Who Sexually Abuse Children.* Lyme Regis: Russell House Publishing.

Caldwell, K. (1997) 'Ideological influences on curriculum development in nurse education.' *Nurse Education Today 17*, 2, 140–144.

Catan, L., Dennison, C. and Coleman, J. (1997) *Getting Through: Effective Communication in the Teenage Years.* London: Trust for the Study of Adolescence and the BT Forum.

CCETSW (1991) *The Teaching of Child Care in the Diploma in Social Work: Guidance Notes for Programme Planners.* London: CCETSW.

Chalmers, K.I. (1992) 'Working with men: an analysis of health visiting practice in families with young children.' *International Journal of Nursing Studies 29*, 1, 3–16.

Chudleigh, A. (1999) 'Fathers of children with special needs.' Paper presented at the Fathers Pride: Personal Issue – Political Agenda, Newcastle-upon-Tyne.

Clare, A. (2000) *On Men: Masculinity in Crisis.* London: Chatto and Windus.

Clarke, S. and Popay, J. (1998) '"I'm just a bloke who's had kids". Men and women on parenthood.' In J. Popay, J. Hearn and J. Edwards (eds.) *Men, Gender Divisions and Welfare* (pp.196–230) London: Routledge.

Claussen, A.H. and Crittenden, P.M. (1991) 'Physical and psychological maltreatment: relations among types of maltreatment.' *Child Abuse and Neglect 15*, 5–18.

Cohen, T.F. (1993) 'What do fathers provide? Reconsidering the economic and nurturant dimensions of fathers as parents.' In J.C. Hood (ed.) *Men, Work and Family* (pp.1–22). Newbury Park: Sage Publications.

Coley, R.L. (1998) 'Children's socialization experiences and functioning in single-mother households: the importance of fathers and other men.' *Child Development 69*, 1, 219–230.

Collins, N.L. and Read, S.J. (1994) 'Cognitive representations of attachment: the structure and function of working models.' In K. Bartholomew and D. Perlman (eds.) *Advances in Personal Relationships* (Vol. 5) London: Jessica Kingsley Publishers.

Combes, G. and Schonveld, A. (1992) *Life Will Never be the Same Again.* London: Health Education Authority.

Conte, J.R., Wolf, S. and Smith, T. (1989) 'What sexual offenders tell us about prevention strategies.' *Child Abuse and Neglect 13*, 293–301.

Coohey, C. (1995) 'Neglectful mothers, their mothers, and partners: the significance of mutual aid.' *Child Abuse and Neglect 19*, 8, 885–895.

Cox, M.J., Owen, M.T., Henderson, V.K. and Margand, N.A. (1992) 'Prediction of infant–father and infant–mother attachment.' *Developmental Psychology 28*, 3, 474–483.

Creighton, S. (1992) *Child Abuse Trends in England and Wales, 1988–1990: And an Overview from 1973 to 1990.* London: NSPCC.

Crittenden, P.M. (1996) 'Research on maltreating families: implications for intervention.' In J. Briere, L. Berliner, J.A. Bulkley, C. Jenny and T. Reid (eds.) *The APSAC Handbook on Child Maltreatment.* Newbury Park, London and New Delhi: Sage Publications.

Cronin, N. (1997) 'The law relating to fathers.' In L. Burghes, L. Clarke and N. Cronin (eds.) *Fathers and Fatherhood in Britain.* London: Family Policy Studies Centre.

Daily Telegraph (1998) 'Sharp rise in number of "absent" mothers.'

Daker, S. (1999) 'Burden of Boys.' *The Guardian*, 24 November, p.3.

Dallas, C., Wilson, T. and Salgado, V. (2000) 'Gender differences in teen parents' perceptions of parental responsibilities.' *Public Health Nursing 17*, 6, 423–433.

Daly, M. and Wilson, M. (1988) *Homicide.* New York: Aldine de Gruyter.

Daniel, B. (1999) 'A picture of powerlessness: an exploration of child neglect and ways in which social workers and parents can be empowered towards efficacy.' *International Journal of Child and Family Welfare 4*, 3, 209–220.

Daniel, B.M. and Taylor, J.S. (1999) 'The rhetoric versus the reality: a critical perspective on practice with fathers in child care and protection work.' *Child and Family Social Work 4*, 3, 209–220.

Daniel, B.M., Wassell, S. and Gilligan, R. (1999) *Child Development for Child Care and Protection Workers.* London: Jessica Kingsley Publishers.

Dempster, H. (1993) 'The aftermath of child sexual abuse: women's perspectives.' In L. Waterhouse (ed.) *Child Abuse and Child Abusers: Protection and Prevention.* London: Jessica Kingsley Publishers.

Dench, G. (1996) *The Place of Men in Changing Family Cultures.* London: Institute of Community Studies.

Dennis, N. and Erdos, G. (1993) *Families without Fatherhood* (2nd edn). London: IEA Health and Welfare Unit.

Department of Health (1995) *Child Protection: Messages from Research.* London: HMSO.

Department of Social Security (1999) *Opportunity for All: Tackling Poverty and Social Exclusion.* London: The Stationery Office.

Dobash, R.E., Dobash, R.P. and Cavanagh, K. (1985) 'The contact between battered women and social and medical agencies.' In J. Pahl (ed.) *Private Violence and Public Policy: The Needs of Battered Women and the Response of the Public Services.* London: Routledge and Kegan Paul.

Dobash, R., Dobash, R., Cavanagh, K. and Lewis, R. (1996) *Research Evaluation of Programmes for Violent Men.* Edinburgh: The Stationery Office.

Dowling, E. (1993) 'Are family therapists listening to the young? A psychological perspective.' *Journal of Family Therapy 15*, 403–411.

Dubois, B. and Krogsgrud Miley, K. (1999) *Social Work: An Empowering Profession.* Boston: Allyn and Bacon.

Dubowitz, H., Black, M., Starr, R.H. and Zuravin, S. (1993) 'A conceptual definition of child neglect.' *Criminal Justice and Behavior 20*, 1, 8–26.

Dubowitz, H., Zuckerman, D.M., Bithoney, W.G. and Newberger, E.H. (1989) 'Child abuse and failure to thrive: individual, familial, and environmental characteristics.' *Violence and Victims 4*, 3, 191–201.

Dunn, J. (1993) *Young Children's Close Relationships: Beyond Attachment.* Thousand Oaks, Calif., London and New Delhi: Sage Publications.

Edwards, J. (1995) '"Parenting skills": views of community health and social service providers about the needs of their "clients".' *Journal of Social Policy 24*, 2, 237–259.

Edwards, J. (1998) 'Screening out men: or "Has mum changed her washing powder recently?"' In J. Popay, J. Hearn and J. Edwards (eds.) *Men, Gender Divisions and Welfare.* London: Routledge.

Elster, A.B. and Lamb, M.E. (1986) *Adolescent Fatherhood.* Hillsdale, NJ: Lawrence Erlbaum Associates.

Evason, E., Robinson, G. and Thompson, K. (1999) *Mothers on Benefit – A Study of 1665 Lone Mothers in Northern Ireland.* Belfast: The Stationery Office.

Fahlberg, V.I. (1991) *A Child's Journey through Placement.* London: British Agencies for Adoption and Fostering.

Faller, K.C. (1990) *Understanding Sexual Maltreatment.* Newbury Park, Calif.: Sage Publications.

Farmer, E. and Owen, M. (1995) *Child Protection Practice: Private Risks and Public Remedies – Decision-Making, Intervention and Outcome in Child Protection Work.* London: HMSO.

Farmer, E. and Owen, M. (1998) 'Gender and the child protection process.' *British Journal of Social Work 28*, 545–564.

Featherstone, B. (1997) 'What has gender got to do with it? Exploring physically abusive behaviour towards children.' *British Journal of Social Work 27*, 419–433.

Featherstone, B. (1999) 'Taking mothering seriously: the implications for child protection.' *Child and Family Social Work 4*, 43–53.

Featherstone, B. (2000) 'Engaging with men as fathers: the implications for child protection practice'. Paper presented at the BASPCAN Fourth National Congress, York, 17–20 September.

Feeney, J. and Noller, P. (1996) *Adult Attachment.* Thousand Oaks, Calif.: Sage Publications.

Ferketich, S.L. and Mercer, R.T. (1995) 'Paternal–infant attachment of experienced and inexperienced fathers during infancy.' *Nursing Research 44*, 1, 31–37.

Ferri, E. and Smith, K. (1995) *Parenting in the 1990s.* London: Family Policy Studies Centre/Joseph Rowntree Foundation.

Finkelhor, D. (1984) *Child Sexual Abuse.* New York: Free Press.

Fox, N.A., Kimmerly, N.L. and Schafer, W.D. (1991) 'Attachment to mother/attachment to father: a meta-analysis.' *Child Development 62*, 210–225.

Fox Harding, L. (1996) *Family State and Social Policy.* Basingstoke: Macmillan Press Ltd.

Frosh, S. (1995) 'Characteristics of sexual abusers.' In K. Wilson and A. James (eds.) *The Child Protection Handbook.* London, Philadelphia, Toronto, Sydney, Tokyo: Ballière Tindall.

Frost, M. (1999) 'Health visitors' perceptions of domestic violence: the private nature of the problem.' *Journal of Advanced Nursing 30*, 3, 589–596.

Garbarino, J. (1999) *Lost Boys: Why Our Sons Turn Violent and How We Can Save Them.* New York: The Free Press.

Gardner, K. (1992) 'The historical conflict between caring and professionalization: a dilemma for nursing.' In D.A. Gaut (ed.) *The Presence of Caring in Nursing* (pp.241–255). New York: National League for Nursing Press.

Gastmans, C. (1999) 'Care as a moral attitude in nursing.' *Nursing Ethics 6*, 3, 214–223.

Gaze, H. (1997) 'All in the family.' *Health Visitor 70*, 9, 332–333.

Geiger, B. (1996) *Fathers as Primary Caregivers*. Westport, Conn.: Greenwood Press.

Ghate, D., Shaw, C. and Hazel, N. (2000a) *Fathers and Family Centres: Engaging Fathers in Preventive Services*. York: Joseph Rowntree Foundation.

Ghate, D., Shaw, C. and Hazel, N. (2000b) *How Family Centres are Working with Fathers*. York: Joseph Rowntree Foundation.

Gibbons, J., Gallagher, B., Bell, C. and Gordon, D. (1995) *Development after Physical Abuse in Early Childhood*. London: HMSO.

Gilardi, J. (1991) 'Child protection in a south London district.' *Health Visitor 64*, 7, 225–227.

Gilbert, T. (1998) 'Towards a politics of trust.' *Journal of Advanced Nursing 27*, 5, 1010–1016.

Gillham, B., Tanner, G., Cheyne, B., Freeman, I., Rooney, M. and Lambie, A. (1998) 'Unemployment rates, single parent density and indices of child poverty: their relationship to different categories of child abuse and neglect.' *Child Abuse and Neglect 22*, 2, 79–90.

Gilligan, R. (1997) 'Beyond permanence? The importance of resilience in child placement practice and planning.' *Adoption and Fostering 21*, 1, 12–20.

Gilligan, R. (1998) 'Men in foster care – A case of neglect?'

Glen, S. (1999) 'Educating for interprofessional collaboration: teaching about values.' *Nursing Ethics 6*, 3, 202–213.

Goding, L. (1997) 'Intuition and health visiting practice.' *British Journal of Community Health Nursing 2*, 4, 174–182.

Golombok, S. and Fivush, R. (1994) *Gender Development*. Cambridge, New York and Melbourne: Cambridge University Press.

Gordon, A. (1999) Personal communication. Medway Child Contact Centre.

Gough, D. (1993) *Child Abuse Interventions: A Review of the Research Literature*. London: HMSO.

Gough, D.A., Taylor, J. and Boddy, F.A. (1988) *Child Abuse Interventions: A Review of the Research Literature*. Glasgow: Social Paediatric and Obstetric Research Unit, University of Glasgow.

Goulet, C., Bell, L., St-Cyr Tribble, D., Paul, D. and Lang, A. (1998) 'A concept analysis of parent–infant attachment.' *Journal of Advanced Nursing 28*, 5, 1071–1081.

Graham, H. (1993) *Hardship and Health in Women's Lives*. New York: Harvester Wheatsheaf.

Grant, T. (1998) 'Fathers who care, partners in parenting project.' Paper presented at the Twelfth International Congress on Child Abuse and Neglect, Auckland, New Zealand, 6–9 September.

Greenburg, M. and Morris, N. (1974) 'Engrossment: the newborn's impact upon the father.' *American Journal Orthopsychiatry 44*, 520–531.

Greif, G.L. and Bailey, C. (1990) 'Where are the fathers in social work literature?' *Families in Society 71*, 2, 88–92.

Haas, L. (1993) 'Nurturing fathers and working mothers: changing gender roles in Sweden.' In J.C. Hood (ed.) *Men, Work, and Family*. Newbury Park: Sage Publications.

Hairston, C.F. (1998) 'The forgotten parent: understanding the forces that influence incarcerated fathers' relationships with their children.' *Child Welfare League of America 77*, 5, 617–639.

Hamilton, P.A. and Keyser, P.K. (1992) 'The relationship of ideology to developing community health nursing theory [corrected].' *Public Health Nursing 9*, 3, 142–148.

Hanafin, S. (1998) 'Deconstructing the role of the public health nurse in child protection.' *Journal of Advanced Nursing 28*, 1, 178–184.

Hansen, S.M.H. (1986) 'Parent–child relationships in single-father families.' In R.A. Lewis and R.E. Salt (eds.) *Men in Families* (pp.181–194). Newbury Park: Sage Publications.

Harland, K. (1997) *Young Men Talking: Voices from Belfast*. London: Youth Action and Working with Men.

Harrison, A.O. (1988) 'Attitudes toward procreation among black adults.' In H.P. McAdoo (ed.) *Black Families*. Newbury Park, London and New Delhi: Sage Publications.

Haskey, J., Kiernan, K., Morgan, P. and David, E. (1998) *The Fragmenting Family: Does it Matter?* (2nd edn). London: IEA Health and Welfare Unit.

Hawkins, A.J., Christiansen, S.L., Sargent, K.P. and Hill, E.J. (1993) 'Rethinking fathers' involvement in child care: a developmental perspective.' *Journal of Family Issues 14*, 4, 531–549.

Hawthorn, M. (1999) *What about the Dads?* London: NCH.

Hearn, J. (1998) *The Violences of Men.* London, Thousand Oaks, Calif. and New Delhi: Sage Publications Ltd.

Henry, M. (1999) Personal communication.

Herbert, M. (1980) *Child Care and the Family Resource Pack.* London: NFER-Nelson.

Hester, M. and Pearson, C. (1998) *From Periphery to Centre – Domestic Violence in Work with Abused Children.* Bristol: Policy Press.

Hester, M., Pearson, C. and Harwin, N. (2000) *Making an Impact: Children and Domestic Violence.* London: Jessica Kingsley Publishers.

Hester, M. and Radford, L. (1996) *Domestic Violence and Child Contact Arrangements in England and Denmark.* Bristol: The Policy Press.

HM Treasury (1999) *The Modernisation of Britain's Tax and Benefit System, No 4: Tackling Poverty and Extending Opportunity.* London: HM Treasury.

Ho, C.S., Lempers, J.D. and Clark-Lempers, D.S. (1995) 'Effects of economic hardship on adolescent self-esteem: a family mediation model.' *Adolescence 30*, 117, 217–131.

Home Office (1994) *National Standards for Probation Service Family Court Welfare Work.* London: Home Office.

Home Office (1998) *Boys, Young Men and Fathers: A Ministerial Seminar.* London: Home Office.

Howe, D. (1995) *Attachment Theory for Social Work Practice.* Basingstoke: Macmillan Press Ltd.

Jarvis, P. (1992) 'Reflective practice in nursing.' *Nurse Education Today 12*, 174–181.

Jewett, C. (1984) *Helping Children Cope with Separation and Loss.* London: BAAF.

Johnson, J.M. (1998) *Annual Report.* Washington: National Center for Strategic Nonprofit Planning and Community Leadership. www.npcl.org.

Johnson, M.M. (1988) *Strong Mothers, Weak Wives: The Search for Gender Equality.* Berkeley, Los Angeles: University of California Press.

Johnson, M. and Webb, C. (1995) 'Rediscovering unpopular patients: the concept of social judgement.' *Journal of Advanced Nursing 21*, 466–475.

Karl, J.C. (1992) 'Being there: who do you bring to practice?' In D.A. Gaut (ed.) *The Presence of Caring in Nursing* (pp.1–13). New York: National League for Nursing Press.

Katz, A. (1999) *Leading Lads.* Oxford: Oxford University, sponsored by Topman.

Keen, S. (1992) *Fire in the Belly. On Being a Man.* London: Judy Piatkus (Pub.) Ltd.

Kelly, L., Regan, L. and Burton, S. (1991) *An Exploratory Study of the Prevalence of Sexual Abuse in a Sample of 16–21 Year Olds.* London: Child Abuse Studies Unit.

Kirby, C. and Slevin, O. (1992) A new curriculum for care. In O. Slevin and M. Buckensham (eds) *Project 2000 – The Teachers Speak.* Edinburgh: Campion Press.

Kissman, K. (1997) 'Noncustodial fatherhood: research trends and issues.' *Journal of Divorce and Remarriage 28*, 1–2, 77–88.

Kotch, J. (1998) 'Is the mother's partner a risk factor for child maltreatment?' Paper presented at the Twelfth International Congress on Child Abuse and Neglect, Auckland, New Zealand, 6–9 September.

Kotelchuck, M. (1976) 'The infant's relationship to the father: experimental evidence.' In M.E. Lamb (ed.) *The Role of the Father in Child Development.* New York: Wiley.

Kromelow, S., Harding, C. and Touris, M. (1990) 'The role of the father in the development of stranger sociability during the second year.' *American Journal of Orthopsychiatry 60*, 521–530.

Lacharite, C., Ethier, L. and Couture, G. (1996) 'The influence of partners on parental stress of neglectful mothers.' *Child Abuse Review 5*, 1, 18–33.

Lamb, M.E. (1981a) 'The development of father–infant relationships.' In M.E. Lamb (ed.) *The Role of the Father in Child Development*. New York, Chichester, Brisbane, Toronto and Singapore: Wiley-Interscience.

Lamb, M.E. (1981b) 'Fathers and child development: an integrative overview.' In M.E. Lamb (ed.) *The Role of the Father in Child Development*. New York, Chichester, Brisbane, Toronto and Singapore: Wiley-Interscience.

Lamb, M.E., Pleck, J.H. and Levine, J.A. (1986) 'Effects of increased paternal involvement on children in two-parent families.' In R.A. Lewis and R.E. Salt (eds.) *Men in Families*. Newbury Park: Sage Publications.

LaRossa, R. (1989) 'Fatherhood and social change.' In M.S. Kimmel and M.A. Messner (eds.) *Men's Lives*. Boston: Allyn and Bacon.

Lavender, T. (1997) 'Family issues. Can midwives respond to the needs of fathers?' *British Journal of Midwifery 5*, 2, 92–96.

Le Couteur, A., Clough, J. and Johnson, R. (2000) 'Engaging Parents in a Primary School Setting.' Paper presented at the Fathers Pride: Personal Issue – Political Agenda, Newcastle-upon-Tyne.

Levine, J.A. (1993) 'Involving fathers in Head Start: a framework for public policy and program development.' *Families in Society 74*, 1, 4–21.

Levy-Shiff, R., Sharir, H. and Mogilner, M.B. (1989) 'Mother- and father-preterm infant relationship in the hospital preterm nursery.' *Child Development 60*, 93–102.

Lewenhak, S. (1992) *The Revaluation of Women's Work*. London: Earthscan Publications Ltd.

Lewis, C. (1986) 'The role of the father in the human family.' In W. Sluckin and M. Herbert (eds.) *Parental Behaviour* (pp.228–258) Oxford: Basil Blackwell.

Lewis, C. (2000) *A Man's Place in the Home: Fathers and Families in the UK*. York: Joseph Rowntree Foundation.

Lewis, M. (1994) 'Does attachment imply a relationship or multiple relationships?' *Psychological Inquiry 1*, 47–51.

Lord Chancellor's Department (1998) *Procedures for the Determination of Paternity and on the Law on Parental Responsibility for Unmarried Fathers* (A Lord Chancellor's Department Consultation Paper). London: Family Policy Division.

Lyons, J. (1999) 'Reflective education for professional practice: discovering knowledge from experience.' *Nurse Education Today 19*, 1, 29–34.

McAdoo, J.L. (1986) 'Black fathers' relationships with their preschool children and the children's development of ethnic identity.' In R.A. Lewis and R.E. Salt (eds.) *Men in Families*. Newbury Park: Sage Publications.

McAdoo, J.L. and McAdoo, J.B. (1989) 'The African-American father's roles within the family.' In M.S. Kimmel and M.A. Messner (eds.) *Men's Lives*. Boston: Allyn and Bacon.

McEwan, S. and Sullivan, J. (1996) 'Sex offender risk assessment.' In H. Kemshall and J. Pritchard (eds.) *Good Practice in Risk Assessment and Risk Management*. London: Jessica Kingsley Publishers.

McFaddyen (1999) Personal communication. Bo'ness Family Centre.

McGuire, J. (1982) 'Gender-specific differences in early childhood: the impact of the father.' In N. Beail and J. McGuire (eds.) *Fathers. Psychological Perspectives* (pp.95–125) London: Junction Books.

McKee, L. (1982) 'Fathers' participation in infant care: a critique.' In L. McKee and M. O'Brien (eds.) *The Father Figure* (pp.120–138). London: Tavistock.

McKeown, K., Ferguson, H. and Rooney, D. (1999) *Changing Fathers? Fatherhood and Family Life in Modern Ireland*. Wilton, Cork: The Collins Press.

MacLeod, M. and Saraga, E. (1988) 'Challenging orthodoxy: towards a feminist theory and practice.' *Feminist Review 28*.

McNay, M. (1992) 'Social work and power relations: towards a framework for an integrated practice.' In M. Langham and P. Day (eds.) *Women, Oppression and Social Work*. London: Routledge.

McWhinnie, A. (2000) 'Children from assisted conception: ethical and psychological issues.' *Human Fertility 3*, 13–19.

Mack, P. and Trew, K. (1991) 'Are fathers' views important?' *Health Visitor 64*, 8, 257–258.

Main, M. and Weston, D.R. (1981) 'The quality of the toddler's relationship to mother and to father: related to conflict behaviour and the readiness to establish new relationships.' *Child Development 52*, 932–994.

Main, M., Kaplan, N. and Cassidy, J. (1985) 'Security in infancy, childhood and adulthood.' In I. Bretherton and E. Walters (eds.) *Growing Points of Attachment Theory and Research: Monographs of the Society for Research in Child Development* (Vol. 50, 1–2, Serial No. 209).

Mama, A. (1996) *The Hidden Struggle: Statutory and Voluntary Sector Responses to Violence against Black Women in the Home.* London: Whiting and Birch.

Marsiglio, W. (1995) 'Fatherhood scholarship.' In W. Marsiglio (ed.) *Fatherhood: Contemporary Theory, Research and Social Policy* (pp.1–20) Thousand Oaks, Calif.: Sage.

Martin, J. (1983) 'Maternal and paternal abuse of children: theoretical and research perspectives.' In D. Finkelhor, R.J. Gelles, G.T. Hotaling and M.A. Straus (eds.) *The Dark Side of Families: Current Family Violence Research.* Beverley Hills: Sage Publications.

May, J. (1996) 'Fathers: the forgotten parent.' *Pediatric Nursing 22*, 3, 243–246, 271.

Mezey, G.C. and Bewley, S. (1997) 'Domestic violence and pregnancy.' *British Medical Journal 314*, 1295.

Millar, G. (2000) 'Working with Men: Paper on Developing New Ways of Working.' Perth and Kinross Council, Social Work Services: unpublished report.

Milligan, C. and Dowie, A. (1998) *What Do Children Need From Their Fathers?* Edinburgh: Centre for Theology and Public Issues.

Milner, J. (1996) 'Men's resistance to social workers.' In B. Fawcett, B. Featherstone, J. Hearn and C. Toft (eds.) *Violence and Gender Relations.* London: Sage Publications.

Milner, J.S. and Dopke, C. (1997) 'Child physical abuse: review of offender characteristics.' In D.A. Wolfe, R.J. McMahon and R.D. Peters (eds.) *Child Abuse: New Directions in Prevention and Treatment Across the Lifespan.* Thousand Oaks, Calif., London and New Delhi: Sage Publications.

MORI (1999) *Bringing up Children [online].* Access date: 11/9/1999: Available: http://www.mori.com/polls/1999/rd990322.htm.

Morrow, V. (1998) *Understanding Families: Children's Perspectives.* London: National Children's Bureau.

Morse, J., Bottoroff, J., Neander, W. and Solberg, S. (1991) 'Comparative analysis of conceptualizations and theories of caring.' *Image: Journal of Nursing Scholarship 23*, 2, 119–126.

Mullender, A. (1996) *Rethinking Domestic Violence: The Social Work and Probation Response.* London and New York: Routledge.

Muller, R.T. and Diamond, T. (1999) 'Father and mother physical abuse and child aggressive behaviour in two generations.' *Canadian Journal of Behavioural Science 31*, 4, 221–228.

Munro, E. (1998) 'Improving social workers' knowledge base in child protection work.' *British Journal of Social Work 28*, 1, 89–105.

NCH Action for Children. (1997) *Making a Difference: Working with Women and Children Experiencing Domestic Violence.* London: NCH Action for Children.

NOP Family (1998) *Attitudes to Parenting.* London: Prepared for Barnado's by NOP Family.

O'Brien, M. (1995) 'Fatherhood and family policies in Europe.' In L. Hantrais and M.-T. Letablier (eds.) *The Family in Social Policy and Family Policy.* Leicestershire: The Cross-National Research Group.

O'Hagan, K. and Dillenberger, K. (1995) *The Abuse of Women within Child Care Work.* Buckingham: OUP.

Oakley, A. and Rigby, A.S. (1998) 'Are men good for the welfare of women and children?' In J. Popay, J. Hearn and J. Edwards (eds.) *Men, Gender Divisions and Welfare* (pp.101–127) London: Routledge.

Olds, D., Eckenrode, J., Henderson, C.R., Kitzman, H., Powers, J., Cole, R., Sidora, K., Morris, P., Pettitt, L. and Luckey, D. (1997a) 'Long-term effects of home visitation on maternal life course and child abuse and neglect: 15-year follow-up of a randomized trial.' *Journal of the American Medical Association 278*, 8, 637–643.

Olds, D., Henderson, C.R. and Kitzman, H. (1997b) 'Does prenatal and infancy nurse home visitation have enduring effects on qualities of parental caregiving and child health at 25 to 50 months of life?' *Pediatrics 93*, 1, 89–98.

Ott, B.J. (1997) 'An absent father and his son: a case illustrating the importance of the father's role in the development of boys.' *Journal of Analytic Social Work 4*, 4, 37–51.

Owusu-Bempah, J. and Howitt, D. (1997) 'Socio-genealogical connectedness, attachment theory, and childcare practice.' *Child and Family Social Work 2*, 199–207.

Parke, R.D. (1981) *Fathering*. New York: Fontana.

Parke, R.D. and Tinsley, B.R. (1981) 'The father's role in infancy: determinants of involvement in caregiving and play.' In M.E. Lamb (ed.) *The Role of the Father in Child Development*. New York: Wiley-Interscience.

Parton, C. (1990) 'Women, gender oppression and child abuse.' In the Violence Against Children Study Group (ed.) *Taking Child Abuse Seriously*. London: Routledge.

Parton, N. (1995) 'Neglect as child protection: the political context and the practical outcomes.' *Children and Society 9*, 1, 67–89.

Pelton, L.H. (1994) 'The role of material factors in child abuse and neglect.' In G.B. Melton and F.D. Barry (eds.) *Protecting Children from Abuse and Neglect* (pp.131–181) New York: Guilford Press.

Pence, E. (1988) *Batterer's Programs: Shifting from Community Collusion to Community Confrontation*. Duluth: Duluth Domestic Violence Intervention Project.

Phillipson, J. (1992) *Practising Equality: Women, Men and Social Work*. London: CCETSW.

Pickford, R. (1999) *Fathers, Marriage and the Law*. London: Family Policy Studies Centre/Joseph Rowntree Foundation.

Pitcairn, T., Waterhouse, L., McGhee, J., Secker, J. and Sullivan, C. (1993) 'Evaluating parenting in child physical abuse.' In L. Waterhouse (ed.) *Child Abuse and Child Abusers. Protection and Prevention* (pp.73–90) New York: Jessica Kingsley Publishers.

Pullinger, J. and Summerfield, C. (eds.) (1998) *Social Focus on Women and Men*. London: The Stationery Office.

Putz, R. (2000) Personal communication. NCH.

Razack, N. (1999) 'Anti-discriminatory practice: pedagogical struggles and challenges.' *British Journal of Social Psychology 29*, 2, 231–250.

Reading, R. (1993) 'Geography as an indicator of social disadvantage.' In T. Waterston (ed.) *Perpsectives in Social Disadvantage and Child Health* (pp.27–30) Newcastle upon Tyne: Intercept Ltd.

Reading, R. (1997) 'Social disadvantage and infection in childhood.' *Sociology of Health and Illness 19*, 4, 395–414.

Richardson, A.J. (1998) *An Audit of Work with Fathers throughout the North East of England*. Newcastle: Children North East.

Rogers, J. (1994) 'Men as Users of Family Centres.' *Working with Men 3*, 12–13.

Rolfe, G. (1997) 'Beyond expertise: theory, practice and the reflexive practitioner.' *Journal of Clinical Nursing 6*, 2, 93–97.

Rowlingson, K. and McKay, S. (1998) *The Growth of Lone Parenthood*. London: Policy Studies Institute.

Rutter, M. (1981) *Maternal Deprivation Reassessed* (2nd edn). Harmondsworth: Penguin.

Rutter, M. (1991) 'Pathways from childhood to adult life: the role of schooling.' *Pastoral Care*, September, 3–10.

Rutter, M. and Rutter, M. (1993) *Developing Minds*. London: Penguin Books.

Rutter, M. and Smith, D. (1995) 'Introduction.' In M. Rutter and D. Smith (eds.) *Psychosocial Disorders in Young People* (pp.1–7) Chichester: John Wiley and Sons.

Ruxton, S. (1992) *'What's* He *Doing at the Family Centre?': The Dilemmas of Men Who Care for Children.* London: NCH.

Ryan, M. and Little, M. (2000) *Working with Fathers.* London: HMSO.

Sabatino, C.J. (1999) 'Reflections on the meaning of care.' *Nursing Ethics 6*, 5, 374–382.

Sadala, M.L.A. (1999) 'Taking care as a relationship: a phenomenological view.' *Journal of Advanced Nursing 30*, 4, 808–817.

Salmon, P. and Manyande, A. (1996) 'Good patients cope with their pain: postoperative analgesia and nurses' perceptions of their patients' pain.' *Pain 68*, 1, 63–68.

Saunders, B.E. and Meinig, M.B. (2000) 'Immediate issues affecting long term family resolution in cases of parent–child sexual abuse.' In R.M. Reece (ed.) *Treatment of Child Abuse: Common Ground for Mental Health, Medical and Legal Practitioners.* Baltimore: The John Hopkins University Press.

Scanzoni, J. (1978) *Sex Roles, Work, and Marital Conflict. A Study of Family Change.* Lexington, Ky.: D.C. Hetah and Company.

Schaffer, H.R. (1996) *Social Development.* Oxford: Blackwell Publishers Ltd.

Schaffer, H.R. and Emerson, P.E. (1964) 'The development of social attachments in infancy.' *Monographs of the Society for Research in Child Development 29*, 3, Whole No. 94.

Schnitzer, P.K. (1993) 'Tales of the absent father: applying the "story" metaphor in family therapy.' *Family Process 32*, 4, 441–458.

Schon, D. (1992) *The Reflective Practitioner* (2nd edn). San Francisco: Jossey Bass.

Sedlak, A. (1993) 'Risk Factors for Child Abuse and Neglect in the US.' Paper presented at the 4th European Conference on Child Abuse and Neglect: Acting upon European Strategies for Child Protection, Padua, Italy, March.

Segal, L. (1990) *Slow Motion. Changing Masculinities, Changing Men.* London: Virago Press.

Sharland, E., Seal, H., Croucher, M., Aldgate, J. and Jones, D. (1995) *Professional Intervention in Child Sexual Abuse.* London: HMSO.

Sinclair, D. (1985) *Understanding Wife Assault: A Training Manual for Counsellors and Advocates.* Toronto, Ontario: Ontario Government Bookstore.

Snarey, J. (1993) *How Fathers Care for the Next Generation: A Four Decade Study.* Cambridge, Mass. and London: Harvard University Press.

Social Work Services Inspectorate (1997) *A Commitment to Protect.* Edinburgh: The Scottish Office.

Speak, S., Cameron, S. and Gilroy, R. (1997) *Young single fathers: Participation in fatherhood – barriers and bridges.* London: Family Policy Studies Centre.

Spring, M. (2000) Personal communication.

Stanley, N. (1997) 'Domestic violence and child abuse: developing social work practice.' *Child and Family Social Work 2*, 135–145.

Stevenson, O. (1998) *Neglected Children: Issues and Dilemmas.* Oxford: Blackwell Science.

Stockwell, F. (1972 reprinted 1984) *The Unpopular Patient.* Beckenham, Kent: Croom Helm.

Strong, P.M. (1988) 'Minor courtesies and macro structures.' In P. Drew and T. Wootton (eds.) *Erving Goffman: Exploring Interaction Order.* London: Polity Press.

Swift, K.J. (1995) *Manufacturing 'Bad Mothers': A Critical Perspective on Child Neglect.* Canada: University of Toronto Press Inc.

Taylor, J.S. (1997) 'Nursing ideology: identification and legitimation.' *Journal of Advanced Nursing 25*, 442–446.

Taylor, J.S. (2000) 'A systematic review of the links between parenting, social factors and failure to thrive. Assessing heterogeneous evidence.' Unpublished PhD thesis, University of Dundee, Dundee.

Taylor, J. and Daniel, B. (2000) 'The rhetoric versus the reality in child care and protection: ideology and practice in working with fathers.' *Journal of Advanced Nursing 31*, 1, 12–19.

Thompson, N. (1997) *Anti-Discriminatory Practice* (2nd edn). Basingstoke: Macmillan.

Thomson, E., Hanson, T.L. and McLanahan, S.S. (1994) 'Family structure and child well-being: economic resources vs. parental behaviors.' *Social Forces 73*, 1, 221–242.

Trigiani, K. (1998) *Masculinity–Femininity: Society's Difference Dividend [online]*. Access date: 12/07/00. Available: http: //web2.airmail/ktrig/ out_of_cave/ essay.

Trinke, S.J. and Bartholomew, K. (1997) 'Hierarchies of attachment relationships in young adulthood.' *Journal of Social and Personal Relationships 14*, 5, 603–625.

Tripney, B. (2000) 'Stories from ma cell.' *Relational Justice Bulletin 7*, 5.

Trotter, J. (1997) 'The failure of social work researchers, teachers and practitioners to acknowledge or engage non-abusing fathers: a preliminary discussion.' *Social Work Education 16*, 2, 63–76.

Turney, D. (2000) 'The feminizing of neglect.' *Child and Family Social Work 5*, 1, 47–56.

UKCC (1992a) *Code of Professional Conduct*. London: UKCC.

UKCC (1992b) *The Scope of Professional Practice*. London: UKCC.

Unger, R. and Crawford, M.P.T.U.P. (1992) *Women and Gender: A Feminist Psychology*. Philadelphia: Temple University Press.

Valois, N. (2000) 'The state of the union.' *Community Care 24*, 2–8 March.

Van Hooft, S. (1999) 'Acting from the virtue of caring in nursing.' *Nursing Ethics 6*, 3, 189–201.

Van Manen, M. (1977) 'Linking ways of knowing with ways of being practical.' *Curriculum Inquiry 6*, 3, 205–228.

Walby, S. (1990) *Theorizing Patriarchy*. Malden, Mass.: Blackwell.

Walker, J. (1995) *The Cost of Communication Breakdown*. Newcastle upon Tyne: Relate Centre for Family Studies, University of Newcastle upon Tyne.

Warin, J., Solomon, Y., Lewis, C. and Langford, W. (1999) *Fathers, Work and Family Life*. London: Family Policy Studies Centre.

Waterhouse, L. and Carnie, J. (1992) 'Assessing child protection risk.' *British Journal of Social Work 22*, 47–60.

Waterhouse, L., Dobash, R. and Carnie, J. (1994) *Child Sexual Abusers*. Edinburgh: The Scottish Office Central Research Unit.

Werner, E. (1990) 'Protective factors and individual resilience.' In S. Meisels and J. Shonkoff (eds.) *Handbook of Early Childhood Intervention*. Cambridge: Cambridge University Press.

Whitfield, K. and Harwood, L. (1999) 'Parents' experience of child protection.' *Practice 11*, 2–5

Williams, D.M. (1997) 'Vulnerable families: a study of health visitors' prioritization of their work.' *Journal of Nursing Management 5*, 1, 19–24.

Williams, F. (1998) 'Troubled masculinities in social policy discourses: fatherhood.' In J. Popay, J. Hearn and J. Edwards (eds.) *Men, Gender Divisions and Welfare*. London: Routledge.

Williams, R. (1999) *Going the Distance: Fathers, Health and Health Visiting*. Reading: The University of Reading in association with The Queen's Nursing Insititute.

Williams, R. and Robertson, S. (1999) 'Fathers and health visitors: "it's a secret agent thing".' *Community Practitioner 72*, 3, 56–58.

Williams, L.M. and Finkelhor, D. (1991) 'Characteristics of incestuous fathers.' In W.L. Marshall, D. Laws and H.E. Barbaree (eds.) *Handbook of Sexual Assault*. New York: Plenum.

Wise, S. (1995) 'Feminist ethics in practice.' In R. Hugman and R. Smith (eds.) *Ethical Issues in Social Work*. London: Routledge.

Wolfe, D.A. (1991) *Preventing Physical and Emotional Abuse of Children*. New York: The Guilford Press.

Wolfson, M., Kaplan, G., Lynch, J., Ross, N. and Backlund, E. (1999) 'Relation between income inequality and mortality: empirical demonstration.' *British Medical Journal 319*, 953–957.

Woodward, V.M. (1998) 'Caring, patient autonomy and the stigma of paternalism.' *Journal of Advanced Nursing 28*, 5, 1046–1052.

Wurzbach, M.E. (1999) 'The moral metaphors of nursing.' *Journal of Advanced Nursing 30*, 1, 94–99.

Subject Index

absence
  and abused children 31
  psychological v. physical 13, 30, 228
abuse 24, 64–5, 121
  and discipline 122
  and family reconstitution 170–1
  and intervention 163–79, 165
  and mothers 23–4, 26
  and non-abusing fathers 227–8
  and parenting groups 28
  and poverty 187–8
  and violence 160
  see also physical abuse; sexual abuse
adoption 32, 206
'Adult Attachment Interview' 84, 93
alcohol 161, 162, 170, 172
alienation 131
anger 228
anti-discrimination 99–125, 126
  and fathers 180, 208
  and social workers 128, 131
anti-sexism 217, 218
assessment
  and abuse 178
  and gender assumptions 100
  and male figures 69, 225, 226–30
assisted reproductive technology (ART) 185
attachment
  and absent/harmful father 91
  of adults 79, 84–5
  classification of 73–4, 78, 79, 86
  and commitment 82–3
  components of 89–98
  from adult's perspective 80–3, 93–8
  from child's perspective 73–80, 89–90
  and history 81, 84, 86, 93, 98, 222–3
  and inner working model 76–7, 86, 95, 97
  and interaction 82
  and older children 92, 97
  patterns of 73–4, 78, 79, 86
  and primary caregiver 76, 77, 77
  and proximity 82, 83
  and quality time 81–2
  and reciprocity 82, 83

  and relationships 72–3, 78, 82
  secure versus insecure 74, 95–7
  and significant figures 71, 75, 149–50
attachment theory 10, 71–98, 80, 81, 216
  development of 71
  guide for practice 71, 87–98, 94
  limitations of 71
  and problems 71

biological heritage 185, 188, 205–6
black people 21, 47, 48, 159, 200
Bo'ness Family Centre 223–4
breadwinners see fathers as providers
breastfeeding 141
bullying 62

caretaking tasks 86, 89–90
  see also domestic tasks
caring 10, 127–8
  and beneficiaries 144, 147
  and fathers 126–48, 180
  features of 142–5
  and mothers 163
  and motivation 143–4
  in nursing 131–7, 138
    listed 132, 133
  and patient autonomy 134
  in practice 130–1
  and purposeful intervention 133
  as relationship 134–5
  and resource demands 133
  and trust 133–4
case management practice 189
child see children
child abuse see abuse; physical abuse; sexual
  abuse
child care 21–6, 112
  and abusive fathers 169
  and empowerent of women 106–8
  and health visitors 147
  provision of 102, 103, 108, 116, 124
  quality of 116
  reappraisal of 69
  responsibility for 15
  traditional model 22–3, 26
Child Contact Centres 228, 229–30
child development, and fathers 181
Child Protection: Messages from Research 14
child protection 21–6, 157

246

Name Index